D1524525

Land Reform and Social Change in Iran

Land Reform and Social Change in Iran

Afsaneh Najmabadi

University of Utah Press
Salt Lake City
1987

Library of Congress Cataloging-in-Publication Data
Najmabadi, Afsaneh, 1946–
  Land reform and social change in Iran.

  Bibliography: p.
  Includes index.
  1. Land reform — Iran. 2. Peasantry — Iran.
3. Iran — Rural conditions. 4. Agriculture — Economic
aspects — Iran. I. Title.
HD1333.I7N34   1987   333.3′1′55   87–31630
ISBN 0-87480-285-7

Contents

Tables and Figures

FIGURES

Acknowledgments

As with many such studies, this work originated as a doctoral dissertation. In the course of the many years that went into the production of the dissertation and its later conversion into a book manuscript, there are many people whose help in one form or another contributed to this work: Teodor Shanin, without whose insistence, patience, and support I would not have even started the dissertation; Hamza Alavi, without whose constructive criticism and supportive supervision I may not have completed it; my late father, Abbas Najmabadi, who guided me through the library and archives of the Ministry of Agriculture in Tehran; Dr. Ismail Ajami for making several unpublished reports on agricultural policy in Iran available to me; the staff of the Research Department at the John F. Kennedy Presidential Library, Boston, Massachusetts, and that of the Ford Foundation Archives, New York City, particularly Ann Newhall and Sharon Laist; Geoffrey Gardner, and Helen Snively, whose professional editing transformed a tedious thesis into a more readable work; and last but not least, Kanan Makiya, who read and re-read both the thesis and the later manuscript and made numerous suggestions throughout.

Land Reform and Social Change in Iran

1

Introduction: Why Land Reform?

On January 10, 1962, the Iranian cabinet passed certain amendments to an earlier land reform law. The cabinet was acting in lieu of the Iranian Senate and the Majlis, or parliament, both of which had been dissolved nine months before by the shah. Five days later the shah, working under special powers of decree, ratified the new land reform provisions.[1] The most important of these measures limited the holdings of any one landlord to the equivalent of a single village. Holdings in excess of this limit were to be sold to the government in return for annual payments spread over ten to fifteen years. In turn the government was to resell these holdings to peasants, who were required to pay for them in installments over a fifteen-year period.

The majority of the Iranian landed class greeted this new legislation, as well as the accompanying government propaganda campaign, with cynicism. Oppositional currents of the left and nationalist groups also took a deeply skeptical view. After all, for almost a decade there had been talk of land reform. More recently, in September 1959, the government had introduced a land reform bill which the landlord-dominated parliament had succeeded in rendering totally ineffective.[2]

To everyone's surprise, the government set about implementing the new legislation at full speed. Barely two months later, the shah personally handed the title deeds of land to the peasants of Maragheh, in the province of Azarbaijan. Over the next decade, two-thirds of the Iranian peasants became beneficiaries in one way or another of about half the total available agricultural land.[3]

The great majority of Iranian men of wealth soon adjusted to this changing reality. Government spending on development plans in the 1950s, focused primarily on infrastructural projects, had already prepared the ground for a vast growth of certain industries. The new push on land reform and the preferential terms for investment in industrial projects persuaded many landlords to switch from their old rentier sources of income to more profitable ones. Some even volunteered to sell their estates before being legally obligated to do so.

The second group of skeptics, composed of radical nationalists and socialist groups, was much slower in perceiving the significance of the changes. For years these groups continued to treat and denounce development plans in general and the land reform in particular as a political fraud designed to quiet mass discontent. This initial disbelief was partially a result of the previous record of the regime. The father of the shah, Reza Shah, had become the country's biggest landlord during the twenty years of his rule by confiscating more than two thousand villages and farms in the most fertile provinces, and politically the shah's regime drew its only social base of support from landlord conservatism.

The past record was only one reason for skepticism. What continued to fuel the opposition's initial rejection for more than a decade was its resistance to a situation in which the radicals were forced to hear their own program, or at least a program very similar to it, issuing from the enemy's mouth. Land reform had long been a central platform of radical nationalists, socialists, and Communists. Indeed, the land reform launched and implemented by the shah was far more radical than anything produced on paper by Mosaddeq's popular nationalist government during which two land reform decrees were issued. One of these decrees decreased the landlord's share of the crop by 20 percent, returning 10 percent to a village cooperative fund. The second Mosaddeq decree abolished all extra dues levied on peasants by landlords in the form of sheep, goats, lambs, butter, fuel, and other produce.[4]

The Communist Tudeh party's agrarian program of the 1940s was quite similar to that proclaimed by the shah in 1962. Even the party's arguments for agrarian reform had sounded very much like the later proclamations of development analysts, which stated:

After distribution of land among farmers:

1. purchasing power in general will rise and the market for home products will prosper;
2. agricultural production will increase as a result of the activities of agriculturalists, and the country will overcome the danger of famine and crisis;
3. as a consequence of prosperity in the internal market, home industries will advance and the industrial wealth of the country will grow;
4. once the agricultural and industrial wealth has increased, more taxes will be levied and the government's budget will be covered;
5. the middle class will expand, and as a result, class differences and internal social contradictions will be lessened and social equilibrium will be readily established.[5]

It is, therefore, not surprising that the Tudeh party much later declared that the shah's land reform was the expression of his retreat in the face of strong peasant demands for land and the change in relationships of power to the benefit of socialist and democratic forces during the period immediately after World War II.[6]

Groups less enthusiastic than the Tudeh party explained away the reform program as an imperialist conspiracy of one sort or another. These accounts ranged from crude conspiracy theories to more elaborate and careful political analysis. Among the former, one Maoist-Iranian group posited that American imperialism uses "grain as an instrument of neo-colonial subjugation."

> Agriculture is continually gaining importance in the world, certain food products have strategic significance, and those who have them can force the other side to kneel before them. . . . American imperialism does not sit passively. It does not wait for famine to hit a country and then appear on the scene as the angel of death, presenting its commodities. It acts actively on the world scene. That is, with the help of its allies in the less developed countries and through "land reforms" of the Iranian type or through other means it forces the bankruptcy of the agriculture of these countries; it deprives them of the production of their own sustenance; it threatens them with starvation until it achieves its aims.[7]

The more elaborate theories suggested that the object of land reform was to create a layer of well-off peasantry in order to defuse the revolutionary potential of rural uprisings. Under the influence of the Chinese revolution in particular, many political activists and a large stratum of intellectuals from Third World countries turned their attention to the peasantry and rural movements. In that context, the attention paid by the U.S. government, the United Nations (UN), and other international agencies to agrarian reform was seen as a competitive bid to win over the same constituencies by other means.

> Imperialists, as a result of the experience of liberation struggles of other peoples, know full well that if Iranian revolutionaries succeed in basing themselves on the peasantry and on a peasant movement, they will be finished and their satanic domination will be ended. It is for this reason that they try, in vain, (through such farces as the "land reform") to block a peasant revolution and to stop the revolutionaries from going among the peasants.[8]

The initial political skepticism reflected by these analyses blocked any timely understanding of these land reforms and has continued to mar most of the subsequent attempts to. Quite often analytical efforts have been geared to "proving" the failures of these reforms. Moreover, failure has been defined not so much in terms of the initial goals of these programs, as they were perceived by policymakers and governments at the time, but as they have later been analyzed by the critics.

More recent analytical and scholarly works, of course, do not suffer from such directly political and, to some extent, existential concerns. They do, however, have one thread in common with earlier analyses: they have tended to perceive the land reform as primarily geared to explicitly political ends. As one later writer put it, "The original idea was to distribute land among the cultivating peasants and thus create a rural bourgeoisie as a solid socio-political base" (Katouzian 1978:357).

Another political aim commonly mentioned in such literature is the necessity of breaking up the power of the landlords: "In terms of its political aspects, the land reform program had at least two aims: (1) to destroy the power base of the major landowning families and thus neutralize a potential source of opposition to the regime; and (2) to gain the support and allegiance of the peasants and hence forestall a revolution in the countryside" (Kazemi 1980:35).[9] A more recent and exceptionally thorough and insightful book on land reform in Iran by Eric Hooglund shares this political focus. Hooglund starts from the shah himself, arguing that his motivations for land reform were generally "to obtain some measure of popular legitimacy . . . ;

a desire to improve his domestic image; . . . idealism; a hope for national economic progress; a distaste for a system perceived as backward, rather than modern; sensitivity to world public opinion" (1982a:45). From this basis, Hooglund goes on to argue more particularly for a series of ideas about the political advantages inherent in the land reform policy already familiar to us. For Hooglund land reform would (1) break up the traditional dominance of landlords over rural areas; (2) neutralize oppositional forces on the left as well as among the intelligentsia and the urban middle class; and (3) create new bases of popular political support among the peasants themselves. Finally, Hooglund argues that "redistribution would certainly appeal to the United States government of John Kennedy, which was pushing land reform—despite the fact that the United States had never had a land reform experience of its own—with almost missionary zeal as a panacea to developmental problems in Asia and Latin America" (1982a:50). This line of argument poses several problems.

First, Hooglund presumes a desire on the part of the government of Iran during the 1950s to extend its authority to every pore of society. He then projects the landlords as a *potential* threat to this desire and resolves the problem by land reform:

> In the rural areas government control was very weak in the 1950's. For the most part, power in the countryside was monopolized by the large absentee landlords, especially those who lived in the major provincial towns. A program aimed at redistributing their holdings would erode their power. With their power reduced, if not eliminated, the opportunities for landlords to exert any independent challenge to the extension of governmental power would be considerably diminished (Hooglund 1982a:46).

But nowhere does Hooglund specify whom the government represented. As a matter of fact, his argument nearly conflates the person of the shah and the government as an institution. The concentration of power in the shah's hands, particularly in his later years, is undeniable. But even if the shah retained total political power, one would still need to explain what this power stood for, unless one argues that the state represented the shah's individual interests alone. Without an analysis of the Iranian state, it cannot be clear why a conflict between the central government and the landlords existed to begin with. After all, for a long time the state had been characterized either as "feudal" or according to other land-based categories. And there had been much truth in these categorizations. Since the Constitutional Revolution of 1906, the Majlis and other government institutions had been dominated by landlords.[10] Both Reza Shah and his son, before the latter sold off the royal estates in the 1950s, had been the largest landowners themselves. Throughout that period, including the 1950s, there in fact had been no challenge to the authority of the government by the landlords. Even after the land reform was initiated, the overwhelming majority of landlords adjusted rather quickly to the new situation, moving most of their wealth to industrial and construction projects. The initial resistance to land reform—for example, in the Majlis during the 1950s—and the subsequent clashes that occurred in some areas, arose as a response to the government's intentions and later as a result of its implementation of land reform. Resistance to the state by the landlords did not precede and cause land reform.

Second, even if one could agree about the presumed conflict between the government and the landlords, it is not clear why this particular method of resolving the conflict was chosen. Alternative choices were available. For example, military options might seem more in line with the previous experience of the country. When Reza Shah was intent on establishing the authority of his central government, he achieved his ends through military campaigns against tribes and various dissident movements in the provinces and through confiscating the lands of any landlord who seemed threatening. Nor was his son known for his aversion to military solutions. Why, then, if the government was seeking primarily to extend its authority, would it choose a reform as an alternative to simple raw force?

Third, attempts to explain land reform by the government's desire for centralization and extension of its authority tend to make for a circular argument. If the government needed land reform to gain authority, it is equally true that the government required authority to implement land reform measures.

Fourth, this type of reform program clearly was not unique to Iran. During the 1950s the UN launched its "decades of development" program, and many Third World regimes embarked on development projects, including land reform. Some explanation beyond the shah's megalomania and the mysterious desire of the government to extend its tentacles everywhere is required in order to relate events in Iran to this apparently global concern for development during this particular historical period.

Finally, strictly political explanations of the land reform ignore many of its important features. For example, land redistribution programs, in Iran as well as in other countries, invariably excluded certain categories of the rural population from gaining land. Hooglund poses this as an "unresolved question." Moreover, in Iran as elsewhere there was practically no limitation on the amount of mechanized farming land one individual could own. How can one reconcile these facts with a government's motivation to break the power of the landlords through eliminating their hold over landed estates?

To break out of circular arguments and provide an explanation that will account for all major phenomena, it will be fruitful for us to begin with certain more general considerations and to move away from the dichotomy between economic and political causes of land reform. If we note that development reforms in Third World countries during the 1950s and 1960s were not unique to Iran, we should be able to situate our analysis within this broader context and avoid basing it solely on the specifics of Iranian society. Moreover, it is evident that the political and social upheavals in many parts of the world in the post-World War II period created an international climate conducive to change; that is, the necessity for some modifications of political, social, and economic order was generally accepted. In this sense, "reform or revolution" became the agenda of the day. Within this political climate, however, the global nature of these reforms, their specific shape and impact, their achievements or failures, cannot be understood unless we consider the changing economic trends of this period on an international scale, taking into account the structure of the world economy and the place of each country within that structure.

The underlying thesis of this book is that although in a previous period both the internal level of development of most Third World countries and the general trends in the world economy happily coexisted with, and often reinforced, precapitalist social relations in agriculture, by the post-World War II period, and in some cases as early as the interwar period, the picture had changed. Both the gradual buildup of internal markets and the changing structure of the international economic order made an accelerated expansion of internal markets and commodity production in these countries not only possible but positively desirable. During the initial phases of capital accumulation the agricultural sector was thought to have a very special role to play: it was to provide the surplus for accumulation and to release the labor to be employed in the industrial sector. These ends could be achieved only by breaking up the old precapitalist agrarian relations, expanding monetary relations, producing for a larger market, and providing at the same time an internal market for the products of the growing manufacturing industries. The land reform programs of Third World countries were aimed at such transformations in the internal socioeconomic order of society.

To point out the socioeconomic aims of land reform within the development plans of the 1950s and 1960s is neither to deny the existence of political considerations nor to ignore that the exact timing of such reforms in each country was, for the most part, a political decision. To show that land reform in Iran was sought primarily for the sake of the political ends of creating a solid base for the regime, Katouzian, for instance, has pointed to the fact that "the Third Plan Frame prepared for the period 1962–67 makes no assumptions and allows no provisions at all for an imminent land reform. It is clear that when it was being prepared no one had an inkling that the adoption of such an important socio-economic policy was imminent" (Katouzian 1978:357). Leaving aside the haphazard nature of Iranian planning in this period and the notorious lack of coordination between various government departments in Iran, Katouzian's observation only proves that the decision in 1962 finally to push through the land reform program was political. But his observation is almost tautological: all government decisions are political, for decisions as to when and how to implement policies are always judgments about when it might be possible or necessary to carry them out. His statement says very little about why particular policies are perceived as necessary or desirable or about what they are to achieve.

Moreover, political considerations clearly weigh more heavily in certain instances. The victory of the Chinese revolution in 1949 had a particularly traumatic effect on American policymakers. The continued struggles of peasants for land in many Latin American countries and the later victory of the Cuban revolution added urgency to American decisions concerning land reform measures.[11]

The chief point here, however, is that the kind of changes proposed to "reduce social tension and create political stability," such as land reform, were compatible with and in fact were required by the economic developments of this period because of the growth of capitalism within many Third World countries and because of the new relations between these countries and the economies of the advanced capitalist countries of Western Europe and the United States.

It was these requirements that by and large shaped the type of land reform and development measures undertaken in the post-World War II period. The orientation toward industrialization, as opposed to other alternatives such as an agricultural development, is one such indicator. Certain key features of land reform measures, such as the exemption of all mechanized farming regardless of size, or the exclusion of large sections of the rural population from the benefits, would be incomprehensible or even counterproductive if the primary goal of such reforms had been to create social stability and to break up large holdings of land.

The failure of a figure such as Wolf Ladejinsky, with his broad political and intellectual influence on policymakers, to persuade the U.S. government to adopt his proposals for development plans and land reform points to the same considerations. During the 1950s, Ladejinsky's was, indeed, a lonely though loud voice which persistently argued for putting political considerations first in deciding on development strategies. In an article entitled "Too Late to Save Asia," he stated, "The only way to thwart Communist designs on Asia is to preclude such revolutionary outbursts through timely reforms, peacefully, before the peasants take the law into their own hands and set the countryside ablaze." Ladejinsky went on to argue that "an owner cultivator or a reasonably satisfied tenant would acquire a stake in society. He would guard that society against extremism. Private property would be strengthened where it has been weakest—at the huge base of the social pyramid. The common man of Asia would become a staunch opponent of Communist economics and politics" (Ladejinsky 1950).[12] It was on this basis that he repeatedly criticized what he saw as an overemphasis on industrialization. Instead, he proposed development plans based primarily on the agricultural sector:

Four fifths of the Asian continent's vast population are peasants. Agriculture, not industry, is the pivot of its economic life. Industry has made but a small dent in the character of Asia. The factory may bring material advancement to the Asians someday, but that day is in the distant future. The heart of the problem of Asia today lies in the countryside. It is on the farm where solutions must be sought and found. (Ladejinsky 1950)[13]

Ladejinsky also opposed what he saw as a bias toward the capital-intensive orientation of development plans:

Given the current state of all aspects of Indian economic development, any policy which has the effect of increasing the rural labor surplus before urban occupations can provide employment not only for the growing urban labor forces (which it cannot quite do today) but for rural workers also will only add to an unemployment problem already beyond the capacity of the economic and political system to cope with. (Ladejinsky 1965)[14]

Ladejinsky further argued painstakingly for developing "labor absorbing" rural projects to keep labor on land, to work for capital formation *within* agriculture instead of transferring capital to urban industries, and to raise production and productivity in the agrarian sector in order to provide food and raw material for later urban-industrial developments (Ladejinsky 1965).[15]

It is indicative of the general concerns of the 1950s that the model proposed by Ladejinsky for the Point Four Program was rejected. He was "discovered" and adopted by international organizations, such as the World Bank, only much later, in the 1970s, when limitations of and problems ensuing from the development policies of the previous two decades made substantive adjustment in rural policies necessary.

General considerations of the changing structure of the world economy during the 1950s and 1960s are not adequate for a thorough understanding of the specific pattern of development within each country, whether we are analyzing the overall economy of a given country or more specifically the agrarian sector within it. In this sense, the "prehistory" of each—how exactly a given region was integrated into the world economy over the past two or three centuries—cannot be set apart from the analysis of existing social formations within a particular country.

Looking at the case of Iran, one is immediately struck by the fact that the country's most recent political past — especially the fact that Iran had never been colonized by any major power — has molded its development throughout the twentieth century in ways quite distinct from those of Third World countries that have undergone a more or less prolonged period of colonial subjugation (e.g., the Indian sub-continent and the African countries). Primarily for geopolitical reasons — namely, Iran's location at the crossroads of the British colonial domain and tsarist Russia's projected area of expansion — the country was not colonized or annexed by either of them. Both Britian and Russia had recognized spheres of influence. Britain's was to the south and Russia's was to the north, and there was a central band between, recognized as neutral. Moreover, imperialist economic interest in Iran was not focused on agricultural products — as was the case in most colonies — but on another raw material — oil. The discovery of oil in Iran early in the twentieth century — the first oil concession dates to 1910 — marked the first serious economic concern in Iran by a colonial power.

Because of the very nature of the processes of its production and export, however, this principal economic link between Iran and the world economy affected the rest of the Iranian social formation in ways very different from those common in countries that had become major producers and exporters of agricultural raw materials. Typically in those countries, agricultural products issue from the labor of the vast majority of a population. The final produce is located at many millions of "production points." To reach a port of export, produce has to be collected and centrally processed by internal networks of circulation and trade. This process of production and trade by its very nature affects the mass of the population and the economic and social structure of an entire colony, not to speak of the impact of direct political subjugation.

It is this very complex, interwoven reality that has provided the material for the rich debates about India and Africa. Whether we decide that the initial impact of colonialism reinforces precapitalist modes of production or that a new and specific type of capitalist economy emerges from the colonial mode of production, the debate about these alternatives centers on the real and vast network of relationships generated by the production and export of agricultural raw materials.[16] No similar relationships ensue from the production and export of a raw material such as oil.

There are many reasons for this. To begin with, the production of oil is limited to more narrowly specific geographical areas than is agriculture, and it is extraneous or alien to the previous productive activities of the population even within the confines of those areas. Therefore, the production, processing, and export of oil bypass all the existing networks of production and trade. Trade in oil, then, has to establish its own infrastructure from scratch. In fact, in the initial phases of the Iranian oil industry, with the exception of the most unskilled jobs, all labor was imported into the country, as were the food, housing, and entertainment requirements of this imported foreign labor force.

The link between oil production and an indigenous economy and society occurs on a level totally different from that between agrarian production and indigenous structures. The revenues deriving from oil exports enable the state to have a steady rentier source of revenue. How this income is spent—on arms, court, luxuries, industrial, and agricultural development—is not at all related to the oil industry itself, but it is tied directly to the exigencies of state and general economy according to priorities established at the policymaking level. Only in this indirect way can we say that colonialism affected Iran over a historical period. This particular history meant that the population was spared the devastating effects of colonial policies, manifest in so many other countries of the Third World. On the contrary, it allowed Iran to slumber on to a good degree throughout the twentieth century, delaying the inevitable processes of dislocation and the disruption of the precapitalist social formations and holding back the emergence of a more developed capitalist economy for a long while. In this sense we can say that the development of capitalism in Iran occurred at a much slower pace and somewhat more "indigenously" than in many other Third World countries. Especially after the oil nationalization of the 1950s, oil revenues played an accelerating role in this process because of the effects of state expenditure of these revenues on the rest of the economy. From this standpoint the land reform of the 1960s in Iran was closely linked to the acceleration of capitalist accumulation and was similar to the Russian reforms of 1861 and the Stolypin reforms of 1906–1910.[17]

2

The Postwar Outlook on Development

In recent years many groups on the Iranian left as well as many Western scholars have begun to study and analyze the socioeconomic changes that occurred in Iran during the reign of the shah. Many of these attempts have been marred by what we might call a linear evolutionist concept of development. In general this style of analysis leads to one of two avenues of explanation.

Along the first of these avenues, analysts see the changes in underdeveloped countries, and in Iran specifically, as inevitable developments of the internal evolution of Third World economies. For example, M. Sodagar (1979a, 1979b) has argued that the growing internal level of capital accumulation necessitated the breakup of precapitalist relations in rural Iran. This approach is factually inaccurate as we shall see in detail later. The internal level of capital accumulation and class differentiation and the forms of subsequent development in capitalist relations have varied from country to country. In some countries, the state has had to carry a much heavier burden of initial capital expenditure than have private capitalists. As a matter of fact, owners of wealth have sometimes almost had to be coerced into becoming capitalists, for example, by transferring their wealth from landed interests to industrial investments. In many underdeveloped countries, and quite definitely in Iran, the drive for land reform and other development schemes did not come from native capitalists. Rather, outside agencies such as the UN and the U.S. government pressed for these changes.

Following the second avenue of explanation, other analysts have postulated a certain "historical incompatibility" between imperialist domination and precapitalist formations as the force generating and determining recent patterns of development and change. This approach carries only a dubious a posteriori significance: once socioeconomic changes have occurred, they can be attributed to some sort of presumed "historical incompatibility." But there is far less evidence for the existence of this "historical incompatibility" than there is either for the changes it is intended to explain or for alternative causal phenomena.[1] On the whole it is more helpful to analyze the actual changing structure of world capitalism over, say, the past century and to investigate the corresponding changes in the relations between underdeveloped and advanced countries during each period.

The period of the 1940s and 1950s marks a substantial change both in the internal economic structure of Third World countries and in the relation between them and the advanced capitalist economies. During the previous period, which corresponds roughly to the end of the colonial era, there had been little development of indigenous capitalism in Third World countries. Alavi's expression, "internal disarticulation and external integration," aptly characterizes that period:

> In the metropolitan economy capitalist development had brought about a complementary development in various sectors of the economy; though by no means an autarchic development. There was, however, a balanced development between agriculture and industry and between different branches of industry, in particular, between industries producing consumer goods and those producing capital goods. It was an integrated development in these terms. By contrast, in the colonies the pattern of production was progressively lop-sided, geared to the requirements of the metropolitan economy (i.e. exports), and also providing a market for the products of metropolitan industry (i.e. imports). Thus the circuit of generalized commodity production was not completed within an integrated and internally balanced economy but only by way of the linkage with the metropolitan economy, through dependence on exports and imports. (Alavi 1980:393)

On the other hand, Warren's general evaluation of the impact of colonialism on the emergence of indigenous capitalism in Third World countries seems rather one-sided:

> Direct colonialism, far from having retarded or distorted indigenous capitalist development that might otherwise have occurred, acted as a powerful engine of progressive social change, advancing capitalist devel-

opment far more rapidly than was conceivable in any other way, both by its destructive effects on pre-capitalist social systems and by its implantation of elements of capitalism. (Warren 1980:9)

To begin with, we have overwhelming evidence that there were cases, though few in number, of countries whose internal economies had been leaning toward the development of some sort of indigenous capitalism. For example, both India and Egypt were substantially deindustrialized under colonialism. But still more to the point, colonialism was destructive of indigenous precapitalist social relations and offered very little of a constuctive nature to replace them.[2] In countries where colonial rule had planted seeds of capitalism, very few signs of growth were evident for almost a century. What little growth there was of capitalist relations in certain sectors within some countries failed, in Alavi's words, to be an "integrated and internally balanced" growth. In fact, such growth brought with it few of the social and economic benefits that had been the products of capitalism in Europe. The later growth of indigenous capitalism during the 1940s and 1950s was greatly accelerated by internal changes within advanced capitalist economies themselves. In other words, indigenous capitalism grew not just as a result of slow cumulative changes in the colonies but also because of changes in the internal structures of the advanced industrialized economies. The confluence of both these trends during the 1940s accounts for two further trends of the postwar period: the push from the colonies for development, which roughly coincided with—and often was expressed in—the drive for political independence; and the zest with which the U.S. government and international agencies became advocates of development programs in underdeveloped countries.[3]

The Push for Industrialization

The first of these trends, gradual internal capitalist accumulation and the attempts by indigenous ruling classes to take charge of development, is ground that has been covered thoroughly and is not in dispute. The second trend, the interest of the advanced capitalist countries, and particularly of the United States during the immediate post-World War II period, in the development of Third World capitalism, is less widely acknowledged or is attributed primarily to political considerations. Programs such as Point Four are often viewed as "counterinsurgency," especially in light of the experience of the many lesser-developed countries of Asia and Africa, where the push for development quite definitely came more from the outside than from the indigenous ruling classes.

This focus on counterinsurgency has tended to obscure the strong economic interest that the United States, as leader of the capitalist world, and other Western countries had in the development of certain industries in Third World countries. During the period under consideration, Third World industrialization became not only acceptable but desirable to the metropolitan economies.

As early as the 1930s the Royal Institute of International Affairs commissioned a study of the effects of industrialization in the colonies on the British economy. This study was carried out with the cooperation of many British economists, several institutes in the colonies, certain private companies, and the International Labor Office. Its results were published in 1935 under the title *Eastern Industrialization and Its Effect on the West*. It concluded:

> First, the process of industrialization . . . would obviously involve enormous sums, only a portion of which can be supplied locally. . . . This process of assistance has a twofold effect—a financial and a "real" one. Financially, in so far as interest must be paid if the money is to be forthcoming, Eastern industrialization must involve a stream of income flowing to the West. . . . The "real" aspect of the industrialization process is provided by the circumstances that the further the process goes, the greater the demand for capital goods. . . . It thus appears erroneous to suppose that the process of industrialization will have no directly favourable repercussions on Western industries.
>
> Secondly, a rising standard of life and growing industrialization involves growing dependence on outside areas for raw materials and foodstuffs not available at all, or so cheaply, in the East. . . .
>
> Thirdly, a growth in the aggregate consumption of a given area . . . implies an addition to the existing volume of consumption. . . .
>
> There is not the slightest incompatibility, in *principle*, between the industrialization of the East and an increase in aggregate exports to the East (Gregory 1935:365–367).[4]

Later, in 1949, a U.S. government document echoed the same assessment of the necessity of industrialization and increased local production in underdeveloped countries:

Increased production in the underdeveloped areas will not only benefit the inhabitants of those areas but will have far-reaching effects on the world as a whole. The United States as well as other relatively advanced countries has a very real financial and commercial stake, as well as a humanitarian and political interest in the bringing about of progress in these areas. In the economic field there are four general lines of development which are likely to flow from such progress.

Trade. . . . Development of production facilities in these areas will . . . contribute to a general expansion of trade in which we and other nations can participate to our mutual advantage. . . .

Domestic Production. . . . By increasing domestic production . . . the foreign exchange now used in . . . purchase abroad could be devoted to the purchase of other types of goods which other countries are in a better position to produce and supply.

Capital Goods. . . . [T]he process of economic development means the existence of a long-term and expanded market for the sale of equipment and other manufactured products for capital installation. Growth in knowledge and skill in the installation and operation of machinery, equipment and facilities will result in a greater need and demand for such equipment. Facilitating the flow of capital for sound projects in the underdeveloped areas also will result in purchases by them of capital equipment which they cannot themselves produce but which the United States and Western Europe can manufacture in large quantities.

Raw Materials. . . . [T]he economies of many of the more developed countries are becoming more dependent upon the import of many basic minerals and raw materials. . . . The possibilities of great expansion in the production of these important commodities exist in a number of the underdeveloped areas of the world. This can be a process of great mutual benefit by increasing the world supply of these commodities while expanding purchasing power in the countries of origin. (USDS 1949:10–12)

The orientation toward encouraging Third World industrial development stemmed from a number of changes in the international pattern of capital accumulation and investment. First, the development of modern methods of producing raw materials, such as synthetic rubber and synthetic fibers, inside the industrialized countries themselves had tended to reduce the margin of superprofits previously enjoyed by monopolies engaged in production of these materials in Third World countries. Second, the slow but gradual spread of monetary relations within Third World countries drew attention to these regions as potential markets for consumer goods. Because of the exigencies of competition on a world scale and the collapse of empire and sharply defined "spheres of influence," the best way to cover such new markets was to move production of many consumer items to these countries. Finally, and most important, the accelerated growth of technological inventions, the rapid growth of the organic composition of capital, and the central role of the capital goods industries within the productive structure of the advanced capitalist economies all led to a tremendous increase in exports of equipment goods to the Third World.[5]

This increase in the export of machinery and the diversification of foreign investment from raw materials to local manufacture of consumer goods could not be realized were Third World countries to remain at their traditional levels of stagnation. From the standpoint of capitalism itself, at least a partial process of development seemed to be in order. The development literature of the 1950s reflects this genuine material interest in breaking through the low levels of capital accumulation and consumption in these countries. To view this crucial trend as primarily a product of the political ideology of counter-reform and counterinsurgency is to miss entirely its powerful material and financial base, the very source that provided it with such enormous global impact during the following two decades.

The development literature of the 1950s clearly indicates the economic preoccupations of development planners with respect to what they thought needed to be changed in the societies of the Third World.[6] Development planners and policymakers perceived the following as characteristic features of underdeveloped countries:

1. Low levels of accumulated capital, as well as low rates of productive internal savings.

2. Low levels of "human capital" in the sense that there were few wage earners compared with the number of peasant producers, who were primarily engaged in production for self-consumption. The low quality of the labor force, reflected in high levels of illiteracy and low levels of skill, was another feature of this labor force frequently emphasized. Planners further argued that a low standard of living, including a low intake of calories, was responsible for a low level of physical activity in the labor force.[7] Higher levels of food consumption

and a rise in the general level of living conditions and consumption were viewed by planners as necessary steps toward overcoming dietary problems and expanding internal markets (USDS 1949:1–9).

3. The limited size of internal markets was, of course, thought of as another feature of these countries that blocked investment opportunities. Moreover, as capital accumulation was historically considered the result of widening markets, these three features of underdevelopment did seem to constitute a circle that could be broken only from the outside.[8]

Therefore, at least initially, development planners argued that the "vicious circle of poverty" could be broken only by the injection of foreign aid. Over the next two decades the governments of the United States and Western Europe took on the increasing burden of this aid, hoping it would enable their own multinationals to market skills and equipment to the underdeveloped countries. Between 1956 and 1968 total official financial aid from the United States in the form of loans, grants, development aid, and so forth increased from $5.7 billion (U.S. dollars) to $13.4 billion. In the same period, private investment increased much more slowly from $2.9 billion to $5.8 billion (table 1.).

Even these levels of private investment might not have been reached had it not been for massive state-led aid. In the words of one company executive: "I must emphasize that there would be scarcely any investment if it were not for the infrastructure, the education, the training and the support provided by our [U.S. government] aid programs. We certainly would not be in India and very few investors

TABLE 1
Total Net Flow of Resources to Developing Countries
U.S. $ billions

Resource	Average 1950–55	1956	1968
Official development assistance	1.9	3.3	6.4
Grants and grantlike contributions	1.2	1.9	4.1
Loans	0.5	0.5	2.4
Total official flows	3.6	5.7	13.4
Private flows	1.6	2.9	5.8

Source: USDA 1970:56.

would be in any of the underdeveloped countries were it not for our effort at economic assistance" (quoted in George 1976:158). This trend in the composition of financial flows remained constant through the 1950s and 1960s and was reversed only in the 1970s: "A very big change has occurred in the composition of the total flows to the developing countries. In 1960, sixty percent came from concessional aid or Official Development Assistance (ODA). By 1977, more than two thirds was commercial, mainly from private bank loans, direct investment and export credits" (Brandt Commission 1980:222).

From the start, official aid was directed to projects that the United States and other developed countries believed would greatly expand world trade and help European recovery (USDS 1949:18–19). As a UN report noted in 1951: "We do not suggest that aid should be given unconditionally to under-developed countries. This would not be wise." The same report envisaged an International Development Authority "to decide upon and administer the distribution of grants-in-aid . . . and to verify their utilization. . . . To help in implementing development plans, especially in the procurement of scarce resources, e.g., capital goods, technical personnel." This report further recommended that "some part of the grants should be used for preparing development plans, and for speeding up the capacity of the underdeveloped countries to absorb capital" (UN 1951b:85–87).[9]

The emphasis by the U.S. government, the UN, and other international agencies on industrialization as a panacea for overcoming the problems of backward countries becomes most meaningful in this context. As noted in chapter 1, economists and policy advisers who argued for agricultural-based development planning remained ineffectual during this period.

Of course, these trends coincided with the growing self-confidence and intentions of local bourgeoisies and the governments of post-independence states in Third World countries. The local bourgeoisies had a definite economic interest in developing the manufacturing sector and benefiting from the expansion of domestic markets for consumer goods, even if such operations would initially involve nothing more than assembling imported packages.

Whether the local bourgeoisies had originally accumulated their wealth from landed interests, commercial, import-export ventures, or from the expansion of small-scale manufacturing did not matter. They were now at a point where the future reproduction of their wealth could diversify into at least a certain level of capitalization through industrial investments. Internal consumer markets could support such industries, especially if the state would undertake the vast infrastructural costs and the necessary structural modifications in an international climate that was no longer hostile and was encouraging such development. State-led planned industrialization, rather than laissez-faire capitalism, was thus more closely in step with the needs of capitalist development in these countries.

Even in those countries where internal development was meager and where there was practically no bourgeoisie to speak of, the emerging technocratic state bureaucracies shared this vision of development. For decades progress had seemed synonymous with railroads and steel mills. Agriculture meant backwardness, whereas industry signified civilization. Moreover, this conflation of development with industrialization had received powerful confirmation as a result of the Soviet experience, regardless of the varying political allegiances of Third World countries. The drive toward industrialization had, within thirty years, transformed one of the most backward countries of Europe, with its even more laggard Asian backwaters, into a prospering modern giant of superpower status. Whatever their politics, many Third World states could not help but look to the Soviet Union as a great success story and as a model of development. Industrial orientation in development appeared still more appealing to emerging states in the Third World because of the central role of the state in Soviet-type planning. And this was true despite marked differences between the Soviet and Third World economic systems. At all events, it was this conjunction of international and domestic interests and perspectives for the future that gave a powerful boost to post-World War II industrial development throughout the Third World.

The Perceived Contribution of Agriculture to Development

Since industialization was perceived as the primary goal of all development, the transformation projected for the agricultural sector during this same early period came to be defined in terms of agriculture's contribution to industrialization. Throughout the Third World, agriculture occupied a dominant position, with respect both to production and to the percentage of population engaged in it. Therefore, no development strategy could ignore the agricultural sector. Countries that had developed a significant manufacturing base far earlier saw much of it destroyed beginning in the nineteenth century by the flood of cheaper, industrially manufactured goods imported by colonial powers. Local capital thus turned to agriculture and the production of other raw materials. Frequently this new orientation aimed at production of a number of cash crops for the world market.

Many planners foresaw that the agricultural sector would make contributions of the following kind to development:[10]

1. As both population size and consumer demand for food increased, especially with an increase in urban populations, *increased total production and productivity in agriculture would become essential.*

2. Most underdeveloped countries depended on the export of agricultural produce *to earn the foreign exchange* necessary for the purchase of machinery, and other import items required for industrialization, as well as for both the servicing and repayment of foreign loans.

3. The agricultural sector would *supply the bulk of the labor force* needed in new industries.

4. In addition to transfer of labor, *agricultural surplus would also provide a significant share of the capital available for industrialization.* The means of transfer to the industrial sector would be state taxation, rental payments — including payment for land received through land reform — farmers' savings, and unfavorable terms of trade between agricultural products and manufactured goods.

5. Expanding cash incomes of the rural population were expected to provide an important internal market for the products of the new industries.

Development planners who advocated a more equitable income distribution were quite explicit in their arguments. Highly skewed income distribution prevented development at both ends: at the lower end, poor people had no incentive to produce more and no income to consume more; at the upper end, a high rate of luxury consumption slowed capital formation. Income redistribution would increase rural consumption of manufactured goods as well as farm inputs (Dorner 1972:82–84).

Many recognized that certain structural modifications might be required for development plans to work. In the words of the UN resolution,

> The social system may also deny to enterprises the resources they need for organizing new units of production. Thus it may not be possible to recruit labor, because it is tied to the soil by law, or because caste restrictions prevent labor from moving to new occupations. Or land may be concentrated in the hands of a small number of persons who are unwilling, often for reasons of political prestige, to sell it to persons outside their group (UN 1951b:15).

For strategies based on unlimited supplies of labor to work, surplus labor would first have to be released from where it traditionally was occupied: agriculture.

The Need for Land Reform

In addition to changes in the agricultural sector in general, land reform in particular was consciously thought of as a necessary precondition for industrialization: "Unsatisfactory forms of agrarian structure, and in particular systems of land tenure, tend in a variety of ways to impede economic development in underdeveloped countries" (UN 1951a:65). Land reform in these countries, the UN resolution on development urges, "would be the first step necessary for releasing the productive energies of the people" (UN 1951a:21).

Economic planners projected the contribution of land reform in a number of ways:

1. Reform was the mechanism that would achieve the separation of the peasant from his land, thus generating a reserve labor force.
2. Peasants who as sharecroppers or tenants had previously paid a large portion of their produce to landlords would now, as owner-cultivators, have the incentive to increase production and productivity, since there would be fewer people on the land. At the same time, the increase in urban and industrial demand for food and raw materials would encourage peasants to offer an increasing portion of their produce to the market.

In the words of the UN resolution: "peasants who have a permanent interest in the land and in its product, will often 'turn sand into gold'" (UN 1951b:40). Moreover, land installment payments to the government in return for land would oblige peasants to sell at least part of their product. Thus these payments would relate peasants to the monetary economy from the outset.

3. The accumulated wealth of landlords could now be redirected toward industrial investment through land compensation schemes that would be tied, at least partially, to industrial credit rather than being paid in cash (Eckstein 1955:660).

4. Under land reform, the state could collect taxes from the peasantry and thus centralize the surplus extracted from agriculture and spend it on necessary public investment in industry (Eckstein 1955:660).

5. The "release of surplus labor" from agriculture would also open up new fields for capital investment by industrializing agriculture itself, thus raising productivity and production even further.

Planners also foresaw that nationalization and privatization of common land and forests would prevent new settlements of the "released labor from land" as well as ensure that private investors had sole access to these resources (UN 1951b:14). It was further noted that in Middle Eastern countries, since large land ownership did not mean large-scale farming, land distribution would not decrease the scale of production and therefore would not impede increased production and productivity (Warriner 1955).

The "development strategies" of the 1950s and 1960s, as a model, were clearly, and in some cases explicitly, based on a generalization of the actual course of development of capitalism in Europe during the period of its agricultural revolution and early industrialization. As such, they were aimed at what Marxists refer to as primitive accumulation. Primitive accumulation in Europe entailed three interrelated processes: (a) the separation of the producer-proprietor from his means of production—peasants were separated from land, craftsmen from their tools—thus allowing the emergence of a free labor force; (b) the concentration of the means of production in the hands of the owners of capital, thus promoting development of superior techniques of production and a higher division of labor and (c) the expansion of the money economy, paving the way for generalization of commodity production rather than production for self-consumption.

The generalization of this historical course of European development into a model for planning Third World industrialization ignored many basic structural socioeconomic differences between the Third World countries of the present and a Europe of the past. The integration of many underdeveloped countries into the world market during the previous century had already shaped the internal structure of their economies in very particular ways. Where commercial agriculture had developed, it was integrated not with an internal market and domestic industries but externally with an already hegemonized *world* market. Moreover, the new manufacturing sectors were integrated with the capital goods sectors in the metropolitan economies and were not designed to encourage domestic "backward and forward" linkages in the former colonies. These particularities of Third World capitalism immediately tended to break down the applicability of the primitive-accumulation model and are at the root of many subsequent problems, both in the industrial development of these countries and with respect to the agrarian sector.[11] These problems had already been pointed out by the Latin American School of Development Economists and by many analysts in the 1950s and 1960s (Baran 1957:169–170; Tuma 1965:202–240). By the 1970s a vast body of literature was exclusively devoted to evaluating these problems and mapping out new strategies.

Recent Changes in the International Development Outlook

Beginning in the late 1960s the problems faced by Third World capitalist development in general, and the severity of the agrarian crisis in particular, forced a reevaluation of the early orientations sketched above. Marsden, for instance, writing for the International Labor Office (ILO) in 1973, notes that by the mid-1960s certain common development problems were emerging in the Third World:

> First, domestic food production had not kept pace with demand and in some cases not even with population. . . . Secondly, the new jobs created in the modern urban sector absorbed only a small fraction of the newcomers to the labor force. . . . Thirdly, the relative stagnation of

rural incomes restricted the growth of demand for industrial products. New plants, equipped with advanced technologies designed for mass markets, often did not reach the level of output needed to achieve economies of scale. . . . The need to boost output, employment and income levels in agriculture was readily apparent. (Marsden 1973:1–2)

This was the background, according to Marsden, for the introduction of the first "miracle seeds" and later for the "total package" approach designed to boost output and income in agriculture. Land reform as a specific and legalistically conceived panacea gradually gave way to more diffuse concepts such as "agrarian reform" and "rural development." Agrarian reform meant on the whole de-emphasizing distributive reforms and concentrating on "tenancy reforms" and other legal modifications with the primary purpose of stabilizing, and not changing, the issue of who owned property. This was intended to encourage agricultural investment to advance with the Green Revolution. By the end of the 1960s, the emphasis on agriculture's contribution to economic development had turned 180 degrees from the original emphasis on releasing labor from the land for industry. Agriculture was now to "provide a large part of the additional employment that will be needed over the period up to 1985" (FAO 1969:11).[12]

The late 1960s and early 1970s also marked the beginning of a shift away from blaming all evils on population growth. As massive and forceful family-planning operations conspicuously failed to tame and control the rural millions in the Third World, it became evident that "the population problem" was not a question of numbers but of social and economic policies. As Erich Jacoby, an influential figure in Food and Agricultural Organization and ILO circles, pointed out, "As a matter of fact, the underutilized labor, covered by the term *excess population*, is to a considerable extent an effect of the economic policy carried out in underdeveloped countries." (Jacoby 1971:30).

The problems of slow industrialization and lack of employment were all too obvious. Between 1950 and 1970 the manufacturing sector in the developing countries grew at an annual rate of about 4 percent, while manufacturing employment globally absorbed less than one-fifth of the Third World's approximately 200 million person increase in the size of its labor force. (McNamara 1981:156).

The "population problem" of Third World countries, then, came down to the fact that industrialization could not employ enough people profitably, even though, in the words of McNamara, "the bitter irony of unemployment is that there is enough unfinished business on this planet to keep everyone employed to the maximum of his ability." (McNamara 1981:86). But it is important to note that institutions such as the World Bank, its investors and its clients, were not at all inclined to see themselves as "charity clubs." In his speech at the Bond Club of New York in May of 1969, McNamara emphasized just this point: "the World Bank is not only a financial institution — it is a development agency. . . . But having said that, I must make equally clear that the World Bank is a development *investment* institution, not a philanthropic organization and not a social welfare agency" (McNamara 1981:55). What is more, McNamara forcefully assured prospective investors from the Bond Club that the bank's combination of assets included "a portfolio of loans for projects which bring high economic returns to the borrower — returns which can run as high as 100%" (McNamara 1981:60).

Was it possible to invest profitably in the poor, in particular the multimillion masses of the rural poor? The idea began as an extension of the Green Revolution. But by the early 1970s, planners generally noted that only a tiny layer of already prosperous rich peasants were taking advantage of the Green Revolution, and they realized that it might be desirable to invest in small farming:

> More recently, as the implications of demographic changes have become clearer, the principal virtue seen in small-scale family farming is that it can provide employment and, to a lesser extent, can economize on purchased inputs. If small holdings tend to be more socially-productive than large holdings — in that they produce as great an output per unit area using more of the abundant and less of the scarce resources — the conflict which many have perceived between an equitable distribution of land and efficiency in farming may be largely illusory.[13]

The conflict of small-scale versus large-scale agriculture marked the debates of the 1960s. Proponents of small-scale family farming had long pointed to the labor-intensive nature of such farming and had shown empirically that through the labor of the whole household, many small farmers make up for their technical and investment disadvantages in comparison to larger farms with higher levels of capital expenditure, and often their production per unit of land is higher. The supporters of large-scale agriculture had emphasized that much of the small farmer's output never reached the market, and therefore, with respect to meeting urban demands and planning options, small farming was too awkward to deal with. Once it became evident that investing in small farming need not be philanthropy, the advocates of a labor-intensive small-farm development policy ceased being radical critics of hitherto official policy and became instead the respectable advisers and policymakers of international agencies and state bodies, eventually reaching the upper levels of the World Bank itself. Under their influence, land reform was granted a new lease on life as part of what was now being termed "rural development packages."

On the whole, "rural development" now became concerned with the domestic market problem. Planners increasingly felt that economic growth could only become "self-sustaining" if the standard of living of the mass of the population still on the land could be raised. In a 1975 World Bank study, Lele reflects well how rural development had turned into a new panacea, charged with solving two major problems simultaneously: controlling unemployment by keeping the population on the land and providing an expanding market for industries:

> [U]rban employment has not been increasing rapidly enough to absorb the flood of rural migrants, partly because of the particular enclave nature of industrial development. . . . Improving living standards of the subsistence rural sector is important, not only as a holding operation until industrialization can advance sufficiently to absorb the rural exodus, but frequently as the only logical way of stimulating overall development. This approach is also essential for purposes of improving the general welfare of an extremely large section of the low-income population. (Lele 1975:5)

Early pilot projects reaffirmed the initial hopes:

> In recent years, considerable progress has been made in getting the beneficiaries of agricultural investment down to the small farmer through use of commercial banks, cooperatives, input suppliers, etc. The scope for profitable agricultural investment has also been notably expanded by the technological advances of the "green revolution" . . . as a result,

the Bank has been able to increase its lending for agriculture substantially.[14]

The eventual public declaration of this shift in policy came in McNamara's famous Nairobi address to the Board of Governors of the World Bank in 1973. Much to the surprise of his radical critics, McNamara said:

> There is no viable alternative to increasing the productivity of small-scale agriculture if any significant advance is to be made in solving the problems of absolute poverty in the rural areas. . . . Without rapid progress in smallholder agriculture throughout the developing world, there is little hope either of achieving long-term stable economic growth or of significantly reducing the levels of absolute poverty.[15]

To achieve this, the bank would introduce rural-development programs specifically for small-scale subsistence farmers, changing the composition of its agricultural credit distribution.

Within a year McNamara reported that the World Bank had invested $2 billion in fifty-one rural development projects in forty-two countries with the expected return on these investments to exceed 15 percent. This turnaround in the bank's policy toward small-scale agriculture has continued ever since.[16] But it is important to point out here that this new international orientation toward small-scale agriculture bypasses a major problem, that of increasing *labor* productivity. Indeed, it has been argued that since Third World countries have an abundance of labor and a scarcity of capital, it is desirable to concentrate on labor-absorptive projects. This view of the Third World's development dilemma attributes the problems of the post-World War II drive toward industrialization to an overemphasis on capital-intensive projects. The problem in Third World economies, however, is not that labor is being replaced too quickly by machinery but that this replacement takes place under conditions where the machines are largely not produced within the same national economy because these economies generally lack a producer-goods sector.

> In the United States, for example, the mechanical cotton picker displaced workers by the tens of thousands. Many of the workers displaced (though certainly not all) and especially their children did find employment among the complex of industries involved in the production, sale and servicing of cotton pickers—steel, rubber, oil, machinery manufac-

ture, transport, farm implement sales and service, etc. But what about Nicaragua, which imports cotton pickers from the United States? Most of the industries linked with the cotton picker do not exist in Nicaragua; they remain in the United States. (Dorner 1972:138)

This is another point at which the Western model of industrial development and economic growth from primitive accumulation has proven recalcitrant to application in the Third World.

Without a producer-goods sector, all the classical linkages between the various parts of manufacturing that lead to a secular expansion of all markets, and not just or even primarily the consumer market— from increased employment, training, and development of a modern workforce to innovations and techniques whose development and production expand net employment—all such linkages simply never come into existence. It is this profound structural dilemma of industrialization in underdeveloped agrarian countries that lies at the root of the pauperization, as opposed to the proletarianization, of peasants and other petty producers.[17]

3

Land Reform and Primitive Accumulation

Let us look more closely at the three levels on which the perceived structural changes in agrarian relations were to have an impact: (a) the creation of a paid labor force; (b) the accumulation of capital; (c) the commercialization of production and consumption. I will focus most sharply on those general issues that are of particular moment for this study of Iranian land reform.[1]

The Creation of a Paid Labor Force

The early studies prepared by national and international development agencies and study teams make it clear that a major concern of planners regarding land reform was to facilitate the release of "surplus labor" from agriculture to produce a steady flow of labor for urban industries and infrastructural services. Planners repeatedly calculated and concluded that in most underdeveloped countries as much as 50 percent of the population could be removed from the land without any adverse effect on the level of agricultural production and productivity per unit of land, even at existing levels of technology.

The chief problem here was how to remove this "surplus population" from the land. After all, one simply cannot open a factory and expect peasants to turn up at the gates for work. As a matter of fact, no one thought it would be either historically or logically rational to depend on a *voluntary* mass change in the structure of the labor force. A peasant whose forebears have made a living from the land for generations—no matter how meager and under what oppressive conditions that living has been made—knows that somehow he can always survive. His very conservatism is his defense mechanism. A peasant will not give up the security of this experience for a haphazard or occasional opportunity to work in the city unless he observes over a prolonged period that it is possible to make a more secure and better living as an urban worker. In other words, the voluntary migration of peasants into an urban labor force presupposes an already existing and thriving paid labor market, and what the economists call "the pull factor" cannot operate until such a market exists. Any first generation of workers, if it is to be created on a large scale and within a short period, generally has to be called into existence by application of some "push factor."

This had been the historical experience of Europe, as is well known. Clearly the changes that land reform programs brought about in the agrarian structures of the underdeveloped countries during the post-World War II period also set the push factor into operation. These changes were often introduced by new legal definitions of land ownership, including the elimination of common land and use rights, that deprived at least part of the rural population from access to land use and thereby forced them to seek alternative employment.

It may be objected that the natural growth of urban populations would have provided more than enough applicants for the limited jobs created through industrial projects and that, at least in part, development strategies were based on a notion of the availability of "unlimited supplies of labor," crying out for efficient utilization. The factual basis for the first point became evident only in the late 1960s. By then both the limitations of industrial employment and the massive rural-urban exodus of the 1950s—which itself was at least a partial result of changes in the countryside—had posed the problem of urbanization without industrialization. As for the notion of "unlimited supplies of labor" (Lewis 1954), the point was not the mere existence of large numbers of working human beings; the problem was that this working population had to be "free" in the double sense pointed out by Marx. It needed first to be free from precapitalist bonds—whether tribal, feudal, caste, or other—that would tie it down to the land or to a cottage industry as in feudal Europe or to specific labor categories as in India. But it also had to be free from access to any means of making a living other than wage labor.

The result of freeing labor had been achieved through private appropriations and successive enclosure acts in the England of the seventeenth to nineteenth centuries and through mass eviction and delimitation of the indigenous peasantry to "reserve lands" in southern Africa at the end of the nineteenth century, and it had its post-World War II counterpart, at least to a certain extent, in the land reform measures adopted in Third World countries.[2] All such reform measures excluded certain segments of the rural population from obtaining land. The form of this exclusion varied, depending on the agrarian structure of particular countries. But in no country did the reforms encompass the whole of the rural population. Rather they introduced a universal differentiation between that sector of the peasantry who now had a more secure and well-defined legal relation to the land they cultivated, and those who were, for all practical purposes, cut off from attaining any such rights.

Because part of the rural population lost its traditional access to the land under land reform and had to be prevented from establishing new subsistence settlements, these legal changes often had to be forcefully implemented. In many countries forests and pastures were nationalized at the same time land reform was enacted in order to prevent future claims to new lands by the landless. Such dual enactments made urban employment the only alternative for the landless. They also made it possible for forests and pastures to be leased out to agro-industrial concerns.

Both the expansion of monetary relations and increased dependence on them were encouraged by land reform, affecting even those peasants who retained access to land. Monetary arrangements, such as payment of rent and taxes in cash and monetary installment payments for land bought through land reform, provided the classical mechanism for keeping newly landed peasants integrated into the national economy. Once a peasant *needs* a certain amount of cash income, he has to obtain it by selling produce to the market, by working to some extent for a cash wage, or by renting out some portion of his land.

Although land reforms of the postwar era have largely been successful in altering land ownership patterns and in formalizing tenancy agreements, their impact in terms of introducing a shift in the occupational patterns of the working population has been far from revolutionary. Prereform agrarian relations often entailed some sort of sharecropping arrangement between peasant and landlord, coupled with a recognition of land-use rights for the peasant. As a consequence of land reform, large precapitalist estates or villages have either been broken up and sold to peasants, changed to new forms of peasant tenancies, or changed to capitalist farms.[3]

In some cases, the change to capitalist farming, based on paid labor, may have gotten under way as a legal loophole allowing escape from complete and comprehensive land reform: a few tractors and a nominal categorization of sharecroppers as wage workers to be paid in kind were often sufficient provisions to allow landlords to claim exemption under "mechanized farm" clauses. Once initiated, however, this process had a logic of its own: "wage workers" could no longer claim traditional use rights to land, and even limited mechanization did improve output, especially with the aid of often generous government grants and loans. The formal change in landlord-peasant relations frequently meant eviction of large numbers of former peasants and their replacement by new tenants or paid agricultural workers.

The fact that under land reform in many Third World countries a substantial part of the cultivated land—and often it was the best agricultural land—remained outside the reform legislation, both through legal exemptions and semilegal loopholes, is sometimes cited as proof of the failure of these reforms and of a lack of change in the agrarian structure, but this is not true. It is undeniable that in many cases only a small percentage of land was distributed. Under the Egyptian land reform, for example, the percentage was as low as 12 percent of the total area under cultivation (Abdel-Fadil 1975:9). Even under the Iranian land reform, which distributed one of the higher percentages, the land covered by various acts was still less than half the total cultivated area. Still, by effecting changes in the old *property* relations through elimination of absentee landlordism of the old type, institutionalizing tenancy in place of sharecropping, and so forth, the old agrarian structure was transformed into one more attuned to potential capitalist development. Consequently, a growing sector of Third World agricultural production now consists of capitalist farms, and in at least some countries a sizable middle peasantry has begun to produce for the market, often on the basis of family labor.

Wherever sharecropping has continued, it is significantly different in character from what it was before land reform. First, sharecropping is no longer a traditional land-use right that peasants can claim year after year. Rather it has become an annually negotiable contract. Second, sharecropping agreements in more prosperous circumstances are often transitory in either of two directions: the previously absentee landlord employs skilled farmers on sharecropping agreements while he develops managerial efficiency and eventually runs the enterprise on a capitalist basis, or the sharecroppers establish themselves as a successful farming enterprise and move to a cash-rent arrangement.

Although the extent of the breakup of the old landed property relations and the scale of existing precapitalist relations such as sharecropping vary from country to country, it is nonetheless the case generally that today's picture of the Third World countryside from this point of view is substantially different from that of the 1950s before enactment of land reform.

With regard to the introduction of changes in the occupational patterns of the working population, the results of land reform are more problematic. On the one hand, reforms have been more than successful in contributing to an "overflow" of rural migrants: the population in the millions of pauperized shantytown residents in almost all major Third World cities speaks for itself.[4] By the end of the 1960s, rural migration accounted for more than half of all urban growth (McNamara 1981:86). Yet at the same time, contrary to the classical development of capitalism, the number of people remaining on the land has continued to increase, while the percentage of the labor force still engaged in agriculture has decreased only very slowly. There are even a few cases where this percentage has increased.

Even for the more industrializing Third World countries, such as Mexico and Brazil, where there has been a radical decrease in the agricultural labor force as a percentage of the total labor force—from two-thirds in 1949 to just over one-third in 1980—the absolute number of people living on cultivated land has continued to increase (table 2).

TABLE 2
Agricultural Labor Force as Percentage of Total Labor Force

Country	Year	Total population (millions)	Total labor force	Agricultural labor force (millions)	Agricultural labor force as % of total labor force
Mexico	1949	24.4	5.9	3.8	65
	1959	33.7	10.5	6.1	58
	1969	48.9	13.4	7.0	52
	1980	70.0	20.2	7.3	36
Brazil	1949	49.3	14.0	9.5	67
	1959	64.2	17.1	9.9	58
	1969	90.8	25.9	12.4	48
	1980	126.4	39.8	15.2	38
India	1959	402.6	101.8	71.8	71
	1969	536.9	209.3	146.5	70
	1980	693.9	266.0	168.1	63
Iran	1949	18.4	—	—	—
	1959	20.1	—	—	—
	1969	28.0	7.5	3.6	48
	1980	38.1	10.6	4.1˙	39
Thailand	1926–39	18.0	6.8	6.0	88
	1959	20.9	10.2	9.0	88
	1969	34.7	16.0	12.5	78
	1980	47.7	21.3	16.1	75
Egypt	1926–39	20.0	6.1	4.3	70
	1959	25.4	6.5	4.1	64
	1969	32.8	8.8	4.8	55
	1980	42.0	11.8	6.0	50

Source: Food and Agricultural Organization, *Production Yearbook,* for 1949, 1959, 1969, 1980 (Rome).
Note: Dashes indicate data not available.

Capital Formation and Land Reform

Historically the transfer of resources from agriculture to industry, because of unfavorable terms of trade, taxation, and bank interest, has played a significant role in capital formation. It is generally agreed that the industrial revolution of the eighteenth century was preceded by an agricultural revolution and that to a large extent the resulting increase in the production of agricultural surplus formed the basis for capital accumulation, particularly through the intermediary of country banks:

> When the landlord's estate began to be transformed from a purely natural economy into a money economy or semi-money economy, when the landlords thereby promoted trade on a large scale, and when the growth in their demands stimulated an increase in extortion from the peasantry, they entered into a certain kind of unconscious co-operation with merchant capital. Everything that was plundered in the countryside, except what was consumed on the spot, was sold to merchants. In return, the merchants supplied the landlords with the products of urban or foreign industry, which served to satisfy their growing and increasingly refined demands. Merchant capital sold these products at a profit of 100 percent, and more. Then it lent money to the ruined gentlefolk at usurious rates of interest. As a result, the feudal lords were in this period in a certain sense agents for merchant capital, transmission pumps for the plundering of small-scale rural production in the interests of primitive capitalist accumulation (Preobrazhensky 1967:85–86).

The transfer of capital from agriculture to industry can also take place through state taxation. Japan is a classical example:

> Particularly in the earlier decades of the country's [Japan's] modern economic growth, taxation of the agricultural sector represented the principal mechanism by which resources were transferred from agriculture to the more rapidly growing sectors of the economy. Agriculture's share of government tax revenue was approximately 85 percent during the years 1888–1892 and still accounted for some 40 percent in 1918–1922.

> It is apparent that agriculture's contribution was significant even if we confine our attention to government flows. Investment by the government represented about 30 percent of gross domestic fixed capital formation during the extended period from 1887 to 1936; and that figure excludes military investment (Johnston and Kilby 1975:213).

During the second half of the twentieth century, land reform has served a similar function for the Third World both because of payments by peasants to the state for the land they have received and because of partial state compensation to landlords, accompanied by institutionalized "encouragement" for them to channel these compensation payments to industry:

> Payments [by governments] to the landlord are made mostly in interest-bearing bonds spread over a period of years, with cash seldom exceed-

ing 10 percent of the fixed price of the land. . . . Payments through bonds, extended over periods of twenty years or more and bearing an interest rate of 3.5 to 5 percent, have eased budgetary difficulties and . . . served to avoid the inflationary impact of large cash disbursements. In some countries the bonds are negotiable and redeemable in equal annual installments; or the bonds can be used for the purpose of industrial and commercial investment, for the payment of taxes and such.

[In Taiwan] an estimated 40 percent of the total compensation found its way into industrial and business investments. (Ladejinsky 1964)[5]

In Iran, however, the figures have been much lower. Various calculations show that at most about 10 percent of the compensation payments were reinvested in industrial or modern agricultural ventures (see appendix A).

The fact that land reform payments did not contribute significantly to capital formation in Iran is related to the inordinate contribution of oil revenues to the Iranian state budget. These high oil revenues rendered unnecessary any strict controls over such subsidiary sources of investment capital. As one analyst has noted:

In Iran and Iraq the direct effect [of oil revenues] was the provision of capital for large irrigation and drainage projects and the construction of dams which enabled the Government to expand land settlement projects and solve water problems in land reform areas. The importation of machinery and financing of industries for agricultural requisites such as fertilizers and insecticides were other favorable effects of oil revenues. It was also reported that oil revenues helped in the payment of compensation to landlords whose lands were expropriated by land reforms in both countries. (El-Ghonemy 1966:13)

In these special cases, not only did agriculture not contribute to national capital formation, it did not even have to come up with enough surplus for accumulation and capital formation within the agricultural sector itself. I will discuss the implications of this peculiarity for agricultural production and productivity at greater length later. Here it is important to note that, despite this fact, in Iran and in other oil producing countries, peasants were still required to make their cash payments for the land they acquired under reform. If popular support among the peasantry had been the overriding criterion in launching the land reform, as so many observers have tended to argue, it would surely have been much more attractive to waive such payments, especially since the state no longer really needed the financial contribution they provided. That this was not done in Iran or in any other country that I know of has to do with another dimension of capitalist development in the countryside, the expansion of a monetary economy and the generalization of commodity production.

Monetization of Production and Consumption

Subsistence production cannot be left alone until it withers away while the capitalist sector gradually grows in breadth and depth. As long as money has not penetrated the natural economy of the peasant household, peasants will have no point of contact with capitalism.

> Natural economy simply does not accept battle, as long as it is not dragged into money-commodity exchange. Capitalism then resembles an athlete who vainly calls on a weak opponent to fight while the latter remains silent and does not answer. Only when this weaker opponent is dragged into the capitalist arena by the development of commodity exchange does it get thrown on its back in the process of free competitive struggle. (Preobrazhensky 1967:125–126)

This "dragging" of the peasant producer into the money economy is often achieved by the imposition of money taxes and cash rents in place of payments in kind or labor. Installments paid by peasants to the state for land acquired under land reform programs fulfill a similar function:

> Whenever the socio-economic system in effect requires payment in money of state taxes, of the services due to landlord, and of debts, the situation changes radically. We can then observe a phenomenon which could be called the "obligation to commercialize". The peasant is compelled to sell in order to obtain the money he needs to meet these financial obligations and not lose his plot. His reaction to the incentives of the market is diametrically opposed to what bourgeois economic science would expect: if prices go up, he sells less, and if they go down he has to sell more. The fiscal burdens to which he is subject are basically fixed; therefore, the amount sold (often at the expense of what is available for his own personal consumption) is inversely proportional to the price level. It often happens that a high level of prices brings about a relative return to "natural production" of such plots, and vice versa. (Kula 1976:43)

Unlike the formation of an ordinary commercial surplus—which is regularly marketed by richer peasants and responds positively to price fluctuations and other market incentives—this kind of "obligatory" sale in part finds its way back to the peasant. At harvest time the peasant has to sell some of his crops to pay his cash debts, but at a later time and at higher prices he has to buy back food and seeds. Moreover, if the village community is left to itself, whatever benefits might arise from these transactions tend to go primarily to the local landlord, the money lender, and the trader. Precisely for this reason, land reform programs included the setting up of cooperatives to facilitate services made necessary by commercialization in the wake of land reform (El-Ghonemy 1966:9).

Agricultural cooperatives were quite explicitly projected as vehicles for the further commercialization of agriculture and the integration of peasants into the national economy. They were to buy surplus produce from the peasants, sell consumer and production goods back to them, and provide short-term credit, directing interest paid on such credit to the national banking system and away from unproductive usurious channels. Indeed, under land reform in many countries, including Iran, membership in the local cooperative society was a precondition for peasant acquisition of land.[6]

Finally, there is another important way in which the peasant household copes with monetary obligations: one or more members of the household work at least some of the time for wages. This phenomenon has often been observed and documented in transitional situations. It can sometimes take the form of commuting daily to industrial centers close to the peasant village. At other times it may involve migration for a few months at a time, with the peasant worker returning to the village at peak agricultural work times. Transnational migrations fulfill a similar function. The size of this "floating mass of temporary migrants" is often very large. It derives its economic rationale both from the peasant's monetary needs and the inadequacy and insecurity of urban industrial employment. The former forces the peasant to become a worker; and the latter continues to keep him a peasant.

4

Pre-Land Reform Agrarian Relations

Throughout recent centuries various forms of landed property have coexisted in Iran.[1] No'mani (1980:146) lists the following categories: (a) common peasants' lands; (b) state lands; (c) conditional land rights, such as *Iqta'* or *toyul*, that is, circumstances where revenues from agricultural land were given to local governors or military officers as a salary of sorts for their current services, which sometimes included collection of the state's share of agricultural revenue; (d) unconditional land rights, such as *soyurqal*, that is, circumstances where revenues from agricultural land were bestowed as a reward for previous services rendered to the state; (e) Crown lands; (f) private lands, including large landed estates, as well as small peasant properties; (7) *awqaf*, or religious endowments; (8) tribal pastures.[2]

The relative amounts of lands within each category, particularly of lands held privately or under state control, varied from period to period, depending on the relative balance of forces between local powers and the central state (F. S. Khamsi 1968:14–19).

Changes during the Nineteenth Century

Certain important developments during the nineteenth century, all related to the increasing integration of the Iranian economy into the world market, led to a new phase of consolidation of large private landholdings that lasted up to the eve of land reform in the early 1960s.

The Qajar period (1785–1925) at first witnessed a new consolidation of landed property by the central government (Lambton 1953:134–135). This did not last very long, however, and soon the indirect management of agricultural surplus extraction through tax farming—called *toyul-dari* in this period—began to reemerge (Lambton 1953:139–140). Furthermore, the preoccupation of the central government under Fath-Ali Shah (1797–1834) with the wars against tsarist Russia allowed the tax farmers to treat their holdings as essentially private land.

Two new factors distinguished this phase of decentralization of control over the agricultural surplus from all similar periods in the past. The first of these was the growing need of the central government for income in cash to cover its expenditures, primarily for the import of modern arms and court luxuries. This need in turn brought about the custom of selling government offices, including toyul rights, to the highest bidder. The custom further strengthened the tendency of the toyul to remain in the same family. The need for cash also forced the government to begin selling the state lands themselves, rather than paying out revenues from the land.

The second factor distinguishing this phase of consolidation was that merchants and other wealthy families began to pay increasing attention to acquiring land as private property for two basic reasons. First, all attempts at setting up indigenous manufacturing industries had met with bankruptcies because of competition with manufactured goods imported from the industrialized countries, particularly Russia and Britain. The commercial companies importing these goods pursued dumping practices. They also enjoyed the financial support of their banks. Moreover, far from favoring the native manufacturers, the Iranian government actually gave advantages to foreign importers (Ashraf 1970:322–327; Kolagina 1980:55–58). Second, the increasing integration of Iran into the world market led to an increase in the export of certain agricultural products, such as opium, tobacco, rice, cotton, dried fruits, and spices (Gilbar 1978:314–355).

The big merchants, by increasingly buying land to acquire control over production and by financing production of certain crops, encouraged such changes in patterns of cultivation. Often the sale of very large tracts of land to wealthy merchants was arranged in an attempt to ease the financial stringency under which the central government was operating (Gilbar 1978).

These changes in the agricultural production and property relations were formalized and consolidated through a series of legal measures. In 1887, Nasser ed-Din Shah issued the imperial order to sell as private property all state lands, except those in the vicinity of the capital city Tehran (Kolagina 1980:57). In 1907, the first Majlis, the Iranian parliament, abolished the granting of land assignments — toyuls — altogether:[3]

> Two other measures were taken affecting taxation and the methods by which the state financed its operations. The first was the abolition of the use of conversion rates and premiums (*tas'ir*) in assessing taxes. It was customary to assess the land tax in kind, but its payments were often demanded in cash; by manipulating the conversion rates or adding a premium to the basic assessment, it was possible to raise the rate of taxation. The second was the abolition of the levy taxes, known as *tafavut-i 'amal*, by the governors and others for the expenses of the local administration over and above the regular taxes. These measures did not materially alter the structure or personnel of the landowning classes; but they ensured greater security of tenure to landowners, prevented, in theory at least, the alienation of large areas of land from the control of the central government, and were a necessary preliminary to the establishment of a modern tax administration (Lambton 1953:32–33).

As a modern judiciary and legal system was taking shape in the first decades of the twentieth century, particularly after Reza Shah's accession to power, other new legislation further consolidated private ownership in land. Land Registration Acts, passed between 1921 and 1929, required all titles to be registered with a special office. De facto possession of the land, and even of whole villages, for the previous twenty years was recognized as proof of ownership (Mo'meni 1980:32).[4] In 1934 sale of state agricultural lands was resumed for the specific purpose of initiating modern agricultural development. Much of such land, particularly in Gorgan, Mazandaran, and Khuzistan, was taken over by Reza Shah himself, who by the end of his reign in 1941 had become the largest single landlord in Iran, with more than 2,000 villages wholly or partly owned by the Crown (Lambton 1969:49).

The State of Rural Society in the 1950s

By 1956, when the first national census was carried out in Iran, there were a total of 51,300 villages, with state lands accounting for 10 percent, Crown lands 4 percent, *waqf* (endowment) lands another 10 percent, and private lands 76 percent (Ajami 1976a:190).[5]

TABLE 3
Distribution of Landholdings, by Size, 1960

Size of Holding (ha.)	Number of Holdings (thousands)	% of Total Holdings	Area (thousands of ha.)	% of Total ha.	Average Size of Holding (ha.)
0–2	748.8	40.0	571	5.0	.8
2–5	474.5	25.3	1,554	13.7	3.3
5–10	340.0	18.1	2,413	21.2	7.1
10–20	223.8	11.9	3,054	26.9	13.6
20–50	77.7	4.1	2,209	19.5	28.4
50–100	8.4	0.4	564	5.0	67.1
100–500	3.8	0.2	684	6.0	180.0
500 +	0.3	0.02	307	2.7	1,023.3

Source: OAS 1960: vol. 15, table 101.

The first comprehensive Agricultural Census of Iran was carried out in 1960. It provided information on the size and number of landholdings, defining a holding as an operational unit of cultivation (table 3). It also provided information about various types of tenure but not on the concentration and distribution of land ownership. Various sources offer somewhat different estimates of ownership distribution. According to Hadary,

> In 1949 . . . a sample survey of 1,300 villages in the Tehran and Demavend areas . . . revealed that 60 percent of the rural families possessed no land at all; another 25 percent owned less than one hectare, and about 10 percent owned between one and 3 hectares. In other words, the 95 percent of the rural families surveyed who held 3 hectares or less owned only 17 percent of the total land. One percent of the land holdings were 20 hectares or larger; of this top group, one-fifth were 100 hectares or more and included 34 percent of the land surveyed. (Hadary 1951:185)

A later U.S. Department of Agriculture report, dating from 1958, traced the following picture:

> Of the claimed land, four main types are found:
>
> (1) Big estates; some 55 percent of the land belongs to about 100,000 wealthy families.
> (2) Small holdings; about 20 percent of the land belongs to individual peasants.

(3) State domains; 10 percent belongs to the Shah or to the state.
(4) Religious endowments (*waqf*); nearly 15 percent of the claimed land has been dedicated in perpetuity for the benefit of religious organization. . . .

About 60 percent of the farmers work as tenants. Of those cultivators who own their land, 63 percent have less than 2½ acres, 25 percent have 2½ to 7 acres, and only 12 percent have more than 7 acres. (West 1958:5)

F. S. Khamsi (1968:47) refers to the ownership by 5 to 20 percent of the wealthy families during the prereform period of between 70 and 90 percent of all land. McLachlan (1968:686–687) refers to the ownership by 1 percent of the agricultural population of 56 percent of all cultivated land, of which 33.8 percent was owned by only 0.2 percent. He also states that "smaller holders and peasant owners" held 10 to 12 percent of the total cultivated land. Salmanzadeh (1980;58) suggests yet different figures: 90 percent of the arable land owned by less than 5 percent of the population, while at the other extreme 60 percent of peasants owned no land and another 23 percent owned less than one hectare of cultivated land.

Since most of the sources do not indicate the basis for their estimates, it is not possible to determine their accuracy. They do, however, all point to a system of concentrated large land ownership, typical of many Middle Eastern countries during this period. The dominant form of tenure was sharecropping.

TABLE 4
Number and Size of Holdings,
by Type of Tenure, 1960

Type of Tenure	No. of Holdings (thousands)	% of Total Holdings	Area (thousands of ha.)	% of Total Area
Sharecropping	814	43.4	6,222	54.8
Rented	235	12.4	844	7.4
Owner-operated	624	33.2	2,976	26.2
Mixed tenure	203	11.0	1,315	11.6
Total	1,876	100.0	11,357	100.0

Source: OAS, 1960: vol. 15, table 101.

TABLE 5

Distribution of Type of Tenure in Different Categories
of Landholding Size, 1960

Size of Holding (ha.)	Share-cropped Holdings		Owner-operated Holdings		Rented Holdings		Mixed Tenure		TOTAL	
	% of No.	% of Area	% of No.	% of Area	% of No.	% of Area	% of No.	% of Area	% of No.	% of Area
0–5	33.7	44.9	40.0	31.8	16.9	15.0	9.4	8.3	100	100
5–10	59.4	60.0	22.6	22.5	5.0	4.8	13.0	12.7	100	100
10–20	66.1	66.4	18.8	18.4	4.5	4.2	10.6	11.0	100	100
20 +	63.3	48.5	22.2	32.1	4.4	7.8	10.1	11.6	100	100

Source: OAS 1960: vol. 15, table 101.

TABLE 6

Distribution in Each Tenure Category according to Size
of Landholding, 1960

Size of Holding (ha.)	Share-cropped Holdings		Owner-operated Holdings		Rented Holdings	
	% of No.	% of Area	% of No.	% of Area	% of No.	% of Area
0–5	50.0	14.6	77.8	22.2	87.0	36.6
5–10	24.7	23.2	12.3	17.2	7.2	13.6
10–20	18.2	32.8	6.6	17.9	4.2	15.8
20 +	6.9	29.4	3.3	40.6	1.7	34.6
Total	100.0	100.0	100.0	100.0	100.0	100.0

Source: OAS 1960: vol. 15, table 101.

The area of mixed tenure holdings shown in table 5 can further be subdivided into 63.4 percent sharecropping, 18.6 percent owner-operated, and 17.9 percent rented. *This gives a final figure of over 62 percent of all agricultural land under sharecropping in 1960.* Since the future land reform legislation applied only to sharecropping land, the above figure constitutes roughly the area under consideration in this book with the marginal exclusion of all orchards and nurseries that were exempted from land reform, regardless of their tenure status.

Tenure types varied somewhat in various size categories. Significantly, there was a much higher percentage of owner-operated units among the smaller holdings of less than five hectares: 40 percent of such holdings and 32 percent of the area. Among the large holding categories of more than 20 hectares, 22 percent of holdings, covering 32 percent of the area of such farms, were owner-operated (tables 5 and 6). On sharecropping land, the share of the landlord varied greatly, from one-fifth up to four-fifths, depending on whether the land was irrigated or not and what other production inputs were provided by the landlord.[6]

Owing to the recent history of private ownership, much agricultural land and most holdings, whether in villages wholly owned by one landlord or owned by several landlords, were not physically demarcated. In other words, the physical demarcations on the ground corresponded to various crops and various peasant work units. In villages owned by more than one landlord, the relative size of the land owned determined the relative division of the final share of the crop accruing to the landlords.[7]

Production was mostly organized through work units, each composed of several peasant households. In the work unit there were both peasants with traditional use rights to the land and those who simply contributed their labor. Some would also lend their animals for plowing. At the time of harvest, first the landlord's share would be set aside, sometimes along with the following season's seed, then the shares of those members of the village community with some sort of communal responsibility would be separated out, such as those of the *mirab* (the person in charge of the division and rotation of water), the miller, the ironmonger, and the carpenter. The remaining crop would then be divided among the peasant households according to traditional land-use rights, that is, in proportion to the amount of land to which each peasant held use rights. Additional crop shares would be accrued if work animals were contributed by a household.

Over time this collective work organization brought about the emergence of two types of peasants: those with traditional land-use rights, the *nasaqdars*, and those without them. By 1960 close to 1.3 million peasant households, 41 percent of the total number, were without land-use rights. The significance of this division becomes clear when we remember that only *nasaqdars* were to become land reform beneficiaries.

The peasant with *nasaq*, or traditional, rights would receive a share of the final crop proportional to the amount of land to which

TABLE 7
Average Number and Size of Plots per Holding, 1960

Size of Holding (ha.)	Average No. of Plots per Holding	Average Size of Each Plot (ha.)
0–2	3.4	0.2
2–5	5.4	0.6
5–10	7.9	0.9
10–20	10.8	1.3
20–50	13.3	2.1
50–100	16.0	4.2
100–500	24.1	7.5
500 +	26.0	39.4
Country average	6.1	1.0

Source: OAS 1960: vol. 15, table 101.

he held use rights. A use right *was not tied to a specific piece of land*. All land was cultivated in common, or by work units comprised of several households, and even these units were rotated annually. The origin of this kind of land rotation may lie in considerations such as different sections of land having different points of access to water sources. As a matter of fact, each work unit generally would cultivate several sections of land per year, and these sections would change the following year. Later, with the emergence of private ownership of land on a large scale during the late nineteenth and twentieth centuries, the landlords, fearing possible claims of ownership in the future, most likely developed an interest in preserving this system in order to prevent attachment of peasants with nasaq rights to any specific piece of land. This meant that even peasants with land-use rights had many scattered pieces of land for their use (table 7).

Another survey, carried out in twelve regions in the mid-1960s, indicated a similar problem (Khosravi 1976:168). This problem began to be felt more acutely after the land reform, since during the reform each peasant was to buy exactly the same piece of land he happened to be cultivating at the time of the reform provided that the land did not fall outside the jurisdiction of the reform. That is, those peasants who were enabled to purchase their nasaqs ended up in possession of several small plots of land, often separated from one another by long distances.

TABLE 8
Number of Tractors Imported, 1926–1947

Year	Number of Tractors Imported
1926–1930	77
1931–1935	8
1936–1940	327
1941	15
1942	45
1943–1945	0
1946	101
1947	46
Total	622

Source: Overseas Consultants, Inc. 1949: vol. 3, p. 62.
Note: Approximate number in operation in 1949: 240.

With the exception of a few regional developments in the 1940s, notably in Gorgan and parts of Khuzistan, agricultural production remained labor-intensive.[8] It was carried out with age-old traditional instruments and with little use of mechanical power and other modern inputs: "Mechanization is uncommon, as evidenced by the Ministry of Agriculture's estimate that only about 900 tractors, 100 combines, 40 threshing machines, 100 discs, and 60 sowing drills and harrows were in operation at the end of 1950" (Hadary 1951:183). Another report put it in these terms: "The Iranian farmer has a very low investment in farm equipment. A special village study showed an investment in equipment of only Rls. 467 [$6.20] per farmer, and all pieces were hand tools except a plow for two oxen" (OCI 1949:vol. 3, p.61). The same report provided the information in table 8 concerning the import of tractors into Iran. As the table indicates, the level of mechanization was very low. By 1960 only 3.8 percent of all holdings were completely mechanized, while another 5.9 percent used both mechanical and animal power (OAS 1960:vol. 15, table 129). Thirty-two percent of the mechanized farming was concentrated in the provinces of Gorgan and Mazandaran and another 48 percent in the Central Province, Tehran, and in Fars (see tables 9 and 10).

The distribution of the ownership of animals was also uneven. Of all holdings smaller than one hectare, 53.3 percent had no cattle or buffalo, and of all holdings between one and three hectares, 22.9

TABLE 9
Sources of Work Energy, by Location of Holding, 1960 (in percent)

Location	Draft Animals Only	Machines Only	Machines and Draft Animals	Human Labor Only
Tehran	60.2	12.7	11.1	16.0
Gilan	88.5	.4	1.5	9.7
Mazandaran & Gorgan	60.9	11.8	15.0	12.3
East Azarbaijan	86.8	3.4	1.1	8.7
West Azarbaijan	74.8	6.5	6.7	11.9
Kurdistan	91.5	.3	1.0	7.0
Hamedan and Kermanshahan	82.2	1.0	7.4	9.4
Khuzistan	85.4	.9	1.9	11.8
Bakhtiari and Charmahal	90.2	2.8	2.8	4.1
Fars	66.3	2.6	10.3	20.7
Kerman	73.7	2.2	5.9	18.0
Sistan and Baluchistan	90.6	2.1	1.6	5.3
Khorasan	80.8	.6	6.0	12.6
Isfahan	34.9	2.6	4.2	58.5

Source: OAS 1960: vol. 15, table 130.

TABLE 10
Sources of Work Energy, by Size of Holding, 1960 (in percent)

Size of Holding (ha.)	Draft Animals Only	Machines Only	Machines and Draft Animals	Human Labor Only
0–2	58.7	3.0	2.0	36.2
2–5	85.8	4.7	6.5	3.0
5–10	88.4	2.9	8.0	0.7
10–20	86.1	4.3	8.9	0.7
20–50	75.2	5.7	19.0	0.2
50–100	71.4	4.1	24.2	—
100 +	35.4	34.5	30.2	—

Source: OAS 1960: vol. 15, table 130.
Note: Dashes indicate that numbers are negligible.

percent had none (OAS 1960:vol. 15, table 118). Similarly, 49.9 percent of the former category and 49.5 percent of the latter had no sheep or goats (OAS 1960:vol. 15, table 120); 73.3 percent and 36.5

percent, respectively, had no draft animals (OAS 1960:vol. 15, table 125). For all holdings less than one hectare, the average number of livestock per household was 3.5, while for those holdings of more than twenty hectares, the average was 21.3 head per household (OAS 1960:vol. 15, table 117). This uneven distribution of ownership of animals is also reflected in the fact that of all holdings that rent plowing animals, 57.0 percent are less than three hectares in size (OAS 1960:vol. 15, table 125). Moreover, of all holdings that depend on human labor alone, 96.3 percent belong to this same category (OAS 1960:vol. 15, table 129).

Use of chemical fertilizers was practically unknown. Even in Mazandaran and Gorgan, the most advanced areas of agricultural development, chemical fertilizers were used on about 3.5 percent of all land under cultivation, mainly on rice and cotton fields. The primitive level of agricultural technology accounted for a very high percentage of fallow land: 37 percent of irrigated land and 42 percent of dry land in the agricultural census year (OAS 1960:vol. 15, table 105). Predictably, the highest percentage of fallow land belonged to the sharecroppers, 40.7 percent of their irrigated land and 46.1 percent of dry land, while the lowest was that of rented land, with only 19.4 percent of irrigated and 25.1 percent of dry land left fallow (OAS 1960:vol. 15, table 105). Most of the land under cultivation was set aside for annual crops. The ratio was highest for the rented land: 90.5 percent of irrigated land under cultivation and 95.6 percent of dry land. Only on irrigated owner-operated land was the percentage of perennial crops significant, 15.7 percent (OAS 1960:vol. 15, table 104). The bulk of the area under annual cultivation, 87.2 percent on the average for the whole of Iran, was in subsistence crops.[9] The bulk of land under wheat and barley, 69 percent and 63 percent, respectively, was cultivated on a sharecropping basis, while 55 percent of land under rice cultivation was rented (OAS 1960:vol. 15, tables 108 and 110). Regionally, the only province with a low ratio of land under annual cultivation was Kerman with 70.4 percent of land under annual cultivation (OAS 1960:vol. 15, table 113). This low ratio can be accounted for by the nature of date and pistachio cultivation, which predominates in this province. The only provinces with a high percentage of annual commercial crops were Mazandaran, Gorgan, and Khorasan: 22.4 percent of land in

TABLE 11
Indexes of Agricultural Production (AP) and Per Capita Agricultural Production (PCAP) in Iran, 1935–1939 and 1957–1961

Year	AP[a]	PCAP[a]
1935–1939	85	118
1957–1958	117	106
1958–1959	119	108
1959–1960	123	106
1960–1961	118	96

Source: F. Khamsi 1969: table 1.
[a]1952–1954 = 100

annual crops in Mazandaran and Gorgan was in cotton, accounting for 55.8 percent of all land under cotton cultivation and 65.3 percent of all cotton production in Iran; corresponding figures for Khorasan were 7.5 percent, 20.9 percent, and 15.7 percent, respectively (OAS 1960:vol. 15 , table 111). This province also accounted for 44.5 percent of all land in sugar beets, 53.3 percent of all land in melons, and 96.5 percent of all land in spices.

The average yields of all major crops remained rather low. For the two major subsistence crops, the Agricultural Census of 1960 reported an average yield for the entire country of 729 kg per hectare for wheat and 678 kg per hectare for barley (OAS 1960:vol. 15, table 108).[10]

Total agricultural production grew very slowly in the few decades prior to land reform, while agricultural production per capita declined (table 11).

No satisfactory information is available on what percentage of agricultural production reached urban markets. It is generally assumed that there was a high degree of self-consumption of subsistence crops, such as wheat, barley, rice, and pulses. Production of these crops was predominantly carried out under sharecropping agreements. The landlord's share of such crops would reach the urban cereal market through the intermediary of his bailiff, or mobashir, and through local agents of the grain merchants. It is doubtful whether much of the peasants' share would reach the market. Commonly peasants practiced foreselling on very disadvantageous terms. Perpetually in debt to local shopkeepers, peasants would pay back their loans and

TABLE 12
Size and Source of Loans to Agricultural Holdings, by Size of Holding

Size of Holding (ha.)	% Receiving Loans	Loans from Governmental Sources		Loans from Landlords		Loans from Gavbands		Loans from Moneylenders and Shopkeepers		Average Total Loan Received per Holding (rls)
		Quantity (millions of rls)	%	Quantity (millions of rls)	%	Quantity (millions of rls)	%	Quantity (millions of rls)	%	
0–2	34.2	368.9	9.6	185.9	8.8	78.5	1.7	2,193.3	85.7	6,582.7
2–5	47.5	198.0	10.7	164.3	11.1	28.0	2.2	1,645.7	85.9	9,036.8
5–10	46.1	170.4	10.9	126.3	11.5	16.4	1.9	970.9	84.4	8,199.2
10–20	42.7	236.2	10.7	154.4	15.2	4.6	.6	950.5	83.1	14,091.1
20–50	45.3	144.3	11.9	133.0	18.2	5.0	.9	644.5	79.5	26,329.5
50–100	42.9	48.0	16.7	27.3	25.0	9.6	5.6	65.1	77.8	41,299.6
100+	41.5	154.7	42.3	12.1	19.6	5.0	12.2	150.7	40.8	197,610.3

Source: OAS 1960: vol. 15, tables 201 and 202.

interest by giving up a large part of their crop share at harvest time, when prices were low. By midwinter, they would run out of grain for consumption and would borrow grain from the shopkeeper at high prices against the next year's crop. (Lambton 1953:306–329 and 379–392; Hooglund 1982a:12–22).

As for cash crops, such as cotton, fruits and vegetables, oil seeds, and nuts, the ratio of owner-operated units was higher. Even on landlord estates, there was a tendency to use paid labor in orchards, albeit these wages were paid in kind, in order to avoid any nasaq rights on land under cultivation in perennial crops. This is related to a generally accepted Iranian tradition linking lasting things on the land, such as perennial crops, fruit trees, and buildings, with possible claims to ownership. On annual crop land, the landlord would avoid any attachment of peasants to particular sections of land through the system of rotation we have already mentioned earlier in this chapter. In any case most cash crops were sold to agents traveling through the countryside and prebuying the harvest through the landlord's bailiff or directly from peasants on owner-operated units. On landlord-owned farms the peasant's share was normally sold together with the landlord's share. In this case peasants received their share in cash after all common expenses and their previous debts had been deducted.

Very litle data are available on changes in the living conditions of the peasantry. Prior to the 1960s there were no household expenditure statistics. The only available data for the 1950s, with no comparative material for any earlier period, are on peasant indebtedness.

According to the 1960 Agricultural Census, 40 percent of all landholders borrowed money in that year. Only 10.4 percent had received loans from governmental sources. Of the rest, 10.9 percent had borrowed money from landlords, 1.8 percent from *gavbands* (those who rent out plowing animals), and 85 percent from moneylenders and shopkeepers (OAS 1960:vol. 15, tables 201 and 202). The quantity of money borrowed from nongovernmental sources was several times that borrowed from governmental sources (see table 12). The interest rate of the former often exceeded 60 percent annually.

In summary, the integration of Iran into the world market economy led to the emergence of large private landholdings. This integration did not predominantly take the form of the introduction of capitalism into agricultural production, and unlike in many other colonial and former colonial countries, did not take the form of producing predominantly for the world market while preserving the old precapitalist social relations. Rather, the appropriation of land by an emerging landowning class in Iran was primarily a means of access to a high rentier source of income, secured through the sharecropping system that could yield to the landlord a share of the crop as high as 80 percent. Production of agricultural crops for the world market remained marginal, both in terms of the area of land devoted to export as well as the variety of crops produced. Production for export affected only a few regions. Even in these areas, only a small percentage of production was carried out through the employment of paid labor or by owner-operated units. For example, 50 percent of the irrigated land in cotton and 60 percent of the land in tobacco was sharecropped. According to the 1956 general census, 68.6 percent of the population was rural, and 56.5 percent of the economically active population was engaged in agricultural production, contributing 27.1 percent of the national income. Over 40 percent of peasant households had no use rights to land whatsoever. Almost half of the rest were sharecroppers with traditional use rights. Agricultural productivity was very low.

5

The 1962 Land Reform:
History and Legislation

Prior to the 1950s, land reform had not figured much in the political and economic life of Iran. Although some radical factions of the Majlis had raised the issue of land reform during the postconstitutional period, it had remained marginal (Abrahamian 1982:86–89, 102–106). The actual record of the first Majlis (1906–1908) and its subsequent sessions as well as of various cabinets favored abolition of the toyul and enforcement of land-title registration, leading to a formal consolidation of large landlordship. With the consolidation of a strong merchant-landlord merger in the formation of the ruling class during the late nineteenth and early twentieth centuries, the urban classes had no incentive to promote any kind of land reform. Neither was there or had there ever been any strong peasant movement on a national scale striving for agrarian change (Abrahamian and Kazemi 1978:259–304).

By the 1940s this situation had changed somewhat. There were still no peasant upheavals to force land reforms. The only exceptions were the land reform measures taken by the government of the Democratic League of Azarbaijan (DLA) between 1945 and 1946. These measures basically amounted to a distribution among the peasants of all land belonging to landlords who had fled. In many places it was, in fact, the peasants who took over these lands, and the government simply sanctioned their actions after the fact. After the defeat of the DLA government, however, this sanction was withdrawn. Nonetheless, the political memory of this land reform process cannot have been completely erased, and the choice of Azarbaijan as the first province to implement the later 1962 land reform program was probably related to it.

The New Outlook on Economic Planning

Of great national significance before the 1950s were the cumulative changes resulting from Reza Shah's building of a modern centralized state. Although there had been no comprehensive economic planning during Reza Shah's period, the totality of his policies and achievements basically amounted to the formation of a new state. The birth of this state was shaped by all the various new ministries and government departments, the first functioning national bank and monetary system, the building of a strong central army, the establishment of the police force and the judiciary system, the construction of bridges and other transport and communication projects on a monumental scale, and a thoroughly new educational system (Banani 1961). As a result of these cumulative changes it became possible during the 1940s for a new generation of government officials and men of wealth to begin to think in somewhat different terms and to acquire somewhat wider perspectives than earlier. In 1944 the government began to think for the first time of economic planning and development plans. It set up a special commission to work on a long-term plan and sought international advice, primarily from the United States. Here is how one participant reports on the birth of the first development plan:

> A series of political shuffles stalled action for a year, but when the strong Qavam government assumed office [in 1946] it approved a decree establishing, within the Ministry of Finance, a "Commission for Drafting Plans for the Development of the Country" [April 1946]. The draft plan produced by this Commission in the summer of 1946 was really the first draft of what became three years later, the Seven Year Plan Law. During this three-year period of preparation, four foreign influences were to play a major role in shaping the final result — the World Bank, the American Embassy in Tehran, two American consulting firms and Max Weston Thornburg, a private U.S. citizen (Baldwin 1967:25).

The two consulting firms referred to by Baldwin were Morrison-Knudsen International Company and the Overseas Consultants (OCI), of which Max Thornburg was the president. Both firms produced voluminous reports of a development program for Iran. None of these plans was implemented immediately, but they remained influential in the drafting of all subsequent development plans.[1]

It was as part of the discussions on development plans that the first references to agriculture occurred. At this early point, however, there was no talk of land reform. On the contrary, the *Report on the Seven Year Economic Development Plan*, prepared in 1949 by OCI, ruled out any tenure changes:

> Landlords in Iran, as in other countries of the world, render an economic service and should not be abolished. . . . In planning for the improvement of agriculture in Iran, the landlord as an institution should be retained, but practices should be promoted which will bring about better conditions for the peasants and an increased agricultural production for the nation (OCI 1949:vol. 3, p. 12).

The report further warned in strong terms against attempts to change the tenure system:

> The system of land tenure in Iran has undergone little change over the centuries. To say that it is archaic is an understatement. However, this system is now so embedded in custom and in the life of the people that it cannot wisely be changed overnight. To attempt this might bring famine, chaos in agricultural relationship, and in the long run would not benefit the peasant (OCI 1949:vol. 5, p. 239).

The emphasis in the OCI report was on the mechanization of agriculture to increase the work output of each peasant family and the productivity of lands then left fallow. The report argued that by bringing more land under cultivation mechanization would not replace peasants, although it also noted that in the long run, "some rural workers must be transferred to non-agricultural occupations to produce and merchandise the products which will be demanded when the income of rural farm families increases." For the time being, however, the problem was seen as one of getting "the machinery into the hands of the peasants rather than the landlords. Many landlords are now buying tractors to be used only for plowing. Their use for this purpose will increase crop yields, but since no provision is made for harvesting, which is the bottleneck in agricultural production, no peasants will be replaced and the area worked per family will not be increased" (OCI 1949:vol. 3, p. 13).

The Political Shifts of the 1940s

In 1941 the Allied forces occupied Iran. With the end of the war and the emerging rift between the Soviet Union and its Western allies, Iran became the scene of the first Cold War clashes. Subsequent to the conflict over the withdrawal of the Soviet army from the northern provinces of Iran in 1946, Iran became increasingly important to the United States policy of formalizing alliances against the Soviet Union along the latter's southern borders. America's increasing military and economic aid to, and involvement in, Iran dates from this period. A recent United States government document summarizes this history.

> Despite the current and substantial United States involvement in the Middle East it is important to recall that this is primarily a post-WWII phenomenon and developed even later in the Persian Gulf.
>
> World War II converted and enhanced the American interest from its pre-war focus on commercial and philanthropic activity. During the War, American forces were active in the region and the United States developed political and strategic concerns. Iran was a route for supply of an American ally — the Soviet Union — to its north and Iran itself was declared eligible for lend-lease in 1942. The Persian Gulf Command (the forerunner of MIDEASTFOR) was created. Oil became a military/political concern and other factors made the strategic value of the area more obvious. Soviet and Soviet-sponsored activity in the northern tier immediately after World War II contributed to the United States concern and led to the formulation of policies designed to contain the perceived Soviet threat.
>
> Iran became a focal point of this United States activity, which was reflected in various bilateral arrangements and agreements as well as in such concepts as the Truman Doctrine which, although it was formally linked to Greece and Turkey, was based on many of the same principles that animated and motivated the United States bilateral arrangement with Iran. A series of arrangements were devised with Iran which provided economic and military aid and the United States established important and close ties with the regime of the Shah (U.S. Congress 1980:6).

The interest of the United States in Iran coincided with, and in fact was in part given impetus by, a change in previous Iranian political orientation away from the European powers and toward the United States. Indeed, as late as 1948–1949, it was Iranian politicians, including the shah, who were eagerly trying to encourage U.S. commitment to Iran.[2] In their attempts to secure this commitment and to obtain American military and economic grants, these Iranian politicians tried to use reference to Iran's geopolitical position to persuade the United States to treat Iran on a par with Turkey and Greece, countries that were receiving substantial military and economic aid under the Marshall Plan.[3] This attitude of attempting to cash in on Iran's geography in the developing Cold War climate is evident in official exchanges of this period. In an official note, dated June 7, 1949, Iranian Prime Minister Saed wrote to John Wiley, the American ambassador in Tehran:

> During your period of residence in Iran and as a result of your studies of Iran's geographical position, Your Excellency has well realized the delicate situation of Iran. You have learned the importance of Iran not only so far as her domestic situation is concerned but also (because of) her impact in international affairs. You know well that Iran in this part of the world is the advance guard of the democratic and free nations of the world. This being the case, the Iranian nation has the right to expect from the great people of the United States who are the protectors and supporters of human freedom and civilization, immediate and gratuitous assistance in order to protect her integrity and independence and fulfill her international duties.
>
> You will notice that the appendix to this letter is a list of the immediate essential military needs of Iran. The minimum articles which may be used in one year have been noted therein. It goes without saying that in view of the speed with which progress is made in military techniques, every year the quality and quantity of such needs will naturally change and other lists should be prepared for future years in consultation with experts. (USDS 1977:528)

The Americans, of course, found this attitude — and the accompanying veiled threats that Iran might disassociate itself from the United States and "look elsewhere" if enough aid was not granted — irritatingly arrogant and unacceptable and made it quite clear that the U.S. government was the one to decide "where and when its assistance might be accorded" (USDS 1976:183).

Over the following three years, however, international and internal Iranian developments worked toward a shift in U.S.-Iranian relations. Internationally, intensification of the Cold War deepened American involvement in fortifying a southern "sanitary" zone that included Iran. Internally the growth of a nationalist mood against the Anglo-

Iranian Oil Company and the expansion of an organized labor movement under virtual hegemony of the Tudeh party convinced the American government that it had to commit further military and economic aid to stabilize Iran politically. In retrospect one wonders about the accuracy of the reports on the internal situation in Iran during this period. The strength of the Communist movement and anti-American xenophobia of the nationalist forces seem often to have been highly exaggerated in order to serve prior policy determinations.

Whereas during the 1947–1950 period the United States pursued a policy of limited military assistance combined with continuous pressure for economic development, based on the Seven-Year Plan prepared by OCI, by mid-1950 it came to the conclusion that it had to take more aggressive responsibility to prevent Iran from "falling under Soviet dominance." Thus, Iran's demand that it be treated like Greece and Turkey received a cold response from the United States throughout 1948 and 1949, and into early 1950. Iran was politely "advised that before it could receive any assistance of the type granted to Greece and Turkey, political, economic and military considerations must be weighed and Congressional approval obtained." (USDS 1977:547) A memorandum prepared for the secretary of state, Dean Acheson, for his talks with the shah when the latter visited Washington November 16–20, 1949, argued in these terms:

> Since preparation of the Background Memorandum, Iranian Ambassador Ala has suggested that upon the departure of the Shah, a joint statement be issued reaffirming the principles of the Tehran Declaration on Iran, promising Iran further military and economic assistance and "extending the Truman Doctrine" to include Iran. If the Shah raises this point, it might be pointed out that our position regarding the maintenance of the independence and territorial integrity of Iran is well known, that we will consider a public reiteration of it in connection with his visit here, but that we cannot make any commitments towards further financial, military, or other aid at this time. (USDS 1977:570–571)

The initial push for a change of attitude naturally came from the American ambassador in Iran, John Wiley. Increasingly he argued that economic aid to Iran must be increased immediately and that military aid must be changed from "token" and only "provocative" levels to substantive and "preventive" levels. He ended his letter of February 15, 1950, to Dean Acheson with the following anecdote:

> Once I had a friend who saved up enough money to buy a dress suit to take the girl of his choice to a dance. The great moment arrived. But he had forgotten to buy the white tie; everything, therefore, went askew. In our policy towards Greece, Turkey and Iran, Iran is, I think, the white tie we forgot to buy. (USDS 1977:471)

Wiley eventually succeeded in persuading Acheson to buy the white tie. A paper prepared at the Department of State in April 1950, "The Present Crisis in Iran" (USDS 1978:509–518), was quite alarming. "Recent events in Iran have indicated that the time of collapse may not be far away." After an extensive review of the political and economic situation in Iran, it concluded:

> It is worthy of note that Iran is the only free country on the periphery of the Soviet world not receiving or about to receive direct United States economic assistance designed to keep it outside of the iron curtain. The situation in Iran has reached the point where, whatever its causes and whatever the Iranians technically could do themselves to correct it, the United States cannot take the chance of seeing Iran surrender to communism and must take every reasonable step within its power to make sure that another country directly exposed to the threat of Soviet aggression, internal or external, does not fall into the Soviet orbit.

> Aid to Iran is not recommended primarily because Iran needs economic aid, but because it offers the most effective means of forcing the Iranians in spite of themselves to put their house in order (USDS 1978:516).

This paper further argued that for the increased aid "to obtain the desired effect it will be necessary to impose certain rather rigid conditions upon any economic assistance the United States extends" (USDS 1978:517). These conditions included internal reforms and the administration and control over the aid by a U.S. official sent to Iran, and they required the shah to appoint a prime minister who could carry out effective reform: "If necessary, the United States should be prepared to name the Iranian official who it believes most effectively could meet these requirements" (USDS 1978:517).

This new turn, "give aid and demand reform," became the hallmark of U.S. policy in Iran over the next decade. What kind of reforms should become the subject of policy discussions and decisions now had to be considered. Originally State Department documents casually mentioned land reform as a possible political expediency. As "development economics" became more clearly formulated, land reform as an urgent transformation necessary to pave the way for capital transfer and an economic "take-off" found its own independent economic life, as discussed in chapters 2 and 3.

The Distribution of Crown Lands: An Important Precursor

In May 1950 the foreign ministers of the United States, the United Kingdom, and France met in London. In preparation for this meeting the U.S. Department of State drafted a position paper on Iran for discussion with the British delegation alone. The paper aimed at two points: first, traditional British influence in Iran should be used to convince "the still appreciable circle of Iranians who look to the British for leadership" of the need for reforms; second, in response to Iranian "informal suggestions," the British should be persuaded to concede to "justifiable Iranian demands" concerning increased royalties from the Anglo-Iranian Oil Company, greatly needed for the implementation of the Seven-Year Development Program (USDS 1978:529–532). On May 17, 1950, in a telegram reporting on the London talks, James E. Webb, the acting secretary of state in Washington while Dean Acheson was in London, noted: "UK considering urging Shah take action on redistribution crown lands; interference with free trade unions; absentee landlordism; better labor legis; anti-corruption campaign" (USDS 1978:545). This appears to be the first official reference to land reform in Iran. It was far from the last. From this time forward, practically every discussion of reforms in Iran included a reference to land reform in particular.[4] Here it is important to note that the Point Four agricultural extension programs got off the ground later this same year.

Eventually, on January 27, 1951, the shah issued an imperial decree declaring the sale of the Crown lands.[5] The actual sale and distribution of the Crown lands started in Varamin, near Tehran, in March 1951 and proceeded very slowly for the first year. Varamin had been the site of the first modern agricultural center set up shortly after the end of the war by a group of American agricultural extension officers under the auspices of the Near East Foundation. Such privately initiated extension programs received a boost from the state only after January 1949, when the American president, Harry Truman, announced the willingness of the United States to launch a "bold new program" of aid to underdeveloped countries. This new program became known as the Point Four Program:

> [T]he first Point 4 agreement was signed on October 19, 1950, at Abayaz Palace in Tehran by Ambassador Henry F. Grady and General Ali Razmara, prime minister of Iran. This agreement, creating an Iranian–United States Joint Commission for Rural Improvement, called for co-operation in a program under which American experts in agriculture, health and education would work with Persians to train the peasants and villagers of Iran (Warne 1956:18).

The most significant influence of Point Four, however, did not lie in its local programs, such as improvement of cattle breeds, the introduction of new poultry production techniques, and malaria eradication campaigns. Rather, it was most instrumental in putting land reform on the development agenda for Iran. Point Four achieved this first through working out the sale of Crown and state lands and second by clearing the way for the drafting of the land reform acts of the 1960s. Of course, by then the Point Four project itself had been terminated, and its work had been absorbed by the Agency for International Development (AID).

The Point Four involvement in the sale of Crown lands was quite direct. First, it contributed heavily in financial terms. In September 1952 the shah established the Rural Development Bank (Bank-e Omran-e Rusta'i). A U.S. State Department press release, dated September 18, 1952, announced that the Point Four Program:

> would contribute $500,000 — half the initial capital — to get the bank started. Point Four will also provide an American financial adviser to assist the bank in developing its policies. . . . Ultimately, the bank will receive nearly 25 million dollars from the proceeds of the land sales. No part of these proceeds is to revert to the Crown, nor are they to be used for general economic or industrial development. All of the money from the sale of lands is to be devoted to rural services and other benevolent purposes for the direct benefit of the peasants (Alexander and Nanes 1980:246–247).

The press release also noted that "this marks the first major step by the United States to implement in the Middle East its policy of cooperating with other governments in carrying out programs of land reform which they initiate themselves." Additional funds were also made available from the Plan Organization, Bank Melli, Government Insurance Fund, and other similar sources (Kristjanson 1960).[6]

The second and most important aspect of Point Four involvement was that technicians and consultants, sent by the U.S. Operation Mission (USOM)—Point Four—and later by the Ford Foundation, played an influential role in policy formulation and implementation. One such figure, Paul V. Maris, a consultant on land reform and rural development, served first on USOM/Iran and then as a consultant to the Ford Foundation in Iran. He first went to Iran in the spring of 1952, and during the next two and one half years, he became the single most influential person in working out detailed policy on land reform and rural development.[7]

When one reads the documents of this period, two facts become quite evident. First, the sale of the Crown lands was seen as a first and exemplary step toward further sales of state lands and toward the eventual sale of all large landed estates. Second, land reform was seen as a necessary means to rural development and more generally the transformation of Iran from an agricultural to a more diverse economy based on manufacturing.

In an address delivered at a luncheon of the Organization of Professional Employees of the United States Department of Agriculture on February 15, 1955, Paul Maris summarized his evaluation of the Iranian scene in these terms:

> First, Iran has a very lopsided economy. It leans all too heavily upon agriculture. About three-fourths of the population gain their livelihood from cultivating the land or tending herds and flocks. It would appear to be a good thing if Iran could be put through the industrial reform wringer and come out with a substantially higher percent of its labor force engaged in trades and industries and a substantially smaller percent in cultivating the land.

> Second, rural poverty is the great millstone around the neck of the nation's economy. Producing capacity per man is low. Purchasing power per man is correspondingly low. Lack of land, water, capital, credit, marketing facilities, transportation facilities and technical knowledge and skills all contribute to the perpetuation of this poverty.

> Third, there is much unemployment and underemployment in Iran's 40,000 villages. That is a costly thing measured in terms of total national economy.

Fourth, Iran has a small ruling class consisting of people of wealth and education, a small middle class consisting of professional people, merchants and the like and a very large class of poor and illiterate people. The corollary to this is, of course, an inefficient government since there is an absence of an enlightened middle class to exercise a restraining influence.[8]

To put Iran through "the industrial reform wringer," a new Seven-Year Plan (1956–1962) focused on infrastructural projects, such as building high dams, increasing the country's hydroelectric output, building roads and other communication networks, and expanding such services as electricity and telephone lines, while at the same time, joint efforts by the Ministry of Agriculture, USOM/Iran, and the Ford Foundation concentrated on "rural development." "Rural development" quite definitely had a real content. It aimed for an integrated approach that included not only tenure changes but also the establishment of village industries, the extension of credit, the improvement of marketing of agricultural produce and the sale of manufactured goods within rural communities, and the improvement of agricultural techniques. But in addition, "rural development" also became a politically expedient euphemism, especially in the aftermath of the 1953 coup, when the government, having just alienated the nationalist middle class and having clamped down on the Communist and labor movements could hardly afford the animosity of the landlords. For example, in a letter of December 21, 1953, to Mostafa Zahedi, the deputy minister of agriculture and the nephew of General Zahedi, who had led the coup against Mosaddeq and replaced him as prime minister, Paul Maris wrote:

> The program contemplated is one of such broad and comprehensive nature that it can most suitably and accurately be described as a rural development or rural improvement program. Land reform is not a good descriptive term for the program for the reason that it is not sufficiently inclusive to cover its many aspects and is mistakenly thought to mean compulsory sale, or expropriation, of private lands. Its use in Iran, therefore, arouses unnecessary and undesirable opposition.[9]

A number of institutional measures were taken to establish the rural development program on firm footings. A survey team, composed of representatives of the Ministry of Agriculture, the Ford Foundation, and USOM/Iran, was set up to carry out a "Reconnaissance Survey":

> The purpose of the Reconnaissance Survey is to provide an overall picture of the present distribution of farming population on the arable lands of Iran, particularly to delineate the distinctly over-populated and the distinctly under-populated areas, and to indicate the desirable sizes of farms in the different geographic and types of farming areas under a policy of equitable distribution of available land resources. The basic background information obtained in the course of the survey should serve as a guide in working toward a better distribution of farming population within farming areas, as well as between farming areas. It should provide an indication as to the number of cultivators, who can be profitably employed on the arable lands of Iran both as these lands are now developed by irrigation and by improved farming methods.[10]

The survey was carried out in 1954. Although the results were never published in final form, its findings were extremely influential in later policy formulations.[11] The basic presumption of the survey, confirmed by its findings, was that there were too many people on the land. This meant that farm sizes were so small as to perpetuate low income and low productivity. It was, therefore, necessary to determine the minimum farm sizes for different areas of Iran, and if enough additional land could not be brought under cultivation, to move "the surplus families" to other areas, to employment outside of agriculture, or, if need be, "provide some form of public relief for surplus families for a few years." Presumably there eventually would be other kinds of employment for surplus families on relief.

From the outset, even in the immediate aftermath of the 1953 coup, the objectives of land reform were spelled out in clear terms of developmentalist economics: national economic prosperity depends on the purchasing power of rural people; therefore the prevailing system of land tenure must change to allow for increased production and improved agriculture, with the costs of such improvement coming out of the increased productivity of the land itself. The potential purchasers of land should be required to agree to cooperate with technical specialists and in the purchasing and marketing of products. They must also be required to meet their payments on the purchase price of the land and to repay all operating and capital outlay loans.[12] These developmentalist concerns were more clearly spelled out as general development economics matured during the latter part of the 1950s. By the end of the decade B. H. Kristjanson, a member of the Harvard Advisory Group in Iran (1958–1959) under the Ford Foundation project, would argue that "An accelerated rate of capital formation must emerge as the primary consideration [in land reform] with recognition that better living conditions will evolve slowly" (Kristjanson 1960:1).

Similarly V. Webster Johnson of the Near East Foundation would write:

> A basic need in Iran is a country-wide program that stresses increased agricultural production by the introduction of improved farming practices and the gradual removal of institutional barriers that prevent the growth of owner operated family farms and improved tenure conditions. . . .
>
> The economic development of Iran depends upon the physical and human resources available for production; how effectively these are used; and the institutional organization framework in which economic activity is carried on. In Iran, about 75 to 80 percent of the population is engaged directly in agriculture and another 8 to 10 percent is associated closely with the handling of agricultural products. As the labor force is engaged predominantly in agricultural activities, it should follow that in the economic development of the country, a basic requirement is an increase in agricultural production. Poverty is associated with the low income derived from agriculture; and in turn, this makes for low purchasing power, and a restricted expansion of purchasing power, for goods produced within the country. . . .
>
> The large landowners in Iran hold an immensely important position in society, and through their political power are able to exert great influence in the economic field and in the type of institutions established to serve the needs of farmers. This power needs to be exercised wisely; and, admittedly, this is difficult in the presence of a concentration of land ownership. For instance, it is reported that many of the large landed proprietors are not interested in improvements in agriculture; that the status quo is more favorable to their interests. To the extent that this is a fact, or that it is not conducive to change, steps are throttled for the improved position of existing family farm operators and the tillers of small landholdings.
>
> The relative high return to large landlords from their holdings affords a good life and even luxuriant living, but may restrict capital accumulation since the income may be spent substantially for consumption goods rather than investment. The result is that wealth flows to cities, eco-

nomic development is deterred by the curtailment of venturesome capital into local industrial pursuits, and the stores hold large stocks of imported goods. The result is a type of exploitation of man by man, which springs from the relation of landlords to villagers.[13]

Another important institution that owes credit to the energetic Paul Maris was the Rural Development Seminar. This was not a gathering for academic discussion. It maintained strict criteria for membership. For instance, absence from three consecutive meetings without notice was construed as withdrawal from the group and, aside from the initially invited members, new participants had to be proposed by three members and receive a majority vote of the entire seminar. The group met fortnightly and had an elected steering committee that chose discussion topics and discussion leaders. The seminar's recording secretary took notes and kept an attendance record. The group's initial invited membership included A. H. Adl, minister of agriculture, Asadollah Alam, Mostafa Zahedi, and other high government officials, as well as members of the USOM/Iran and of the Ford Foundation and the Near East Foundation missions to Iran. In other words, it was far more of a ministerial body than a seminar. Although it modestly declared its purpose to be the enlightenment of "its members on the social and economic aspects of basic problems related to rural welfare and development in Iran," it was directly involved in policy formulation and in drawing up the actual land reform legislation for the government to submit to the Majlis.[14] One such piece of legislation concerned the sale of the public domain land.[15]

As pointed out earlier, from the outset, the sale of the Crown lands had been regarded as the first and testing step of a comprehensive program. During Mosaddeq's premiership, USOM/Iran had already drawn up plans for distribution of the public domain lands and had presented these to the prime minister.[16] However, because of the political crisis of the period, the general distrust of Mosaddeq by the American administration, Mosaddeq's own alternative legislation on the reduction of the landlords' share (see chapter 1), and his political dispute with the shah, the whole program ground to a halt. Immediately after the August 1953 coup, the program gained fresh momentum. At a meeting with the new Iranian prime minister,

General Zahedi, on October 29, 1953, Kenneth Iverson, the Near East representative of the Ford Foundation, indicated that

> with the change in Government the Foundation was prepared to further assist Iran if the Government was interested in the type of assistance which it could provide. He referred to (1) the Shah's land distribution program in which Mr. Maris was one of the principal drafters; (2) and to the public domain lands which the Foundation understood are to be granted to the peasants of Iran following the general procedure developed in connection with the Shah's lands.[17]

Iverson also said that he understood the government was considering a land reform program which would directly affect large private land owners, noting that some discussions pointed to a voluntary program, while others had indicated that the government might be considering a program to compel division of the large estates. Iverson then went on to offer the services of the Ford Foundation in the working out and implementation of such a plan.

In response Zahedi confirmed that

> the Government had a plan of land reform under consideration. He explained that the public domain lands would be handled in the same manner as the Crown lands; that confidentially the Government was planning a program whereby the large land owners would be divested of all lands above that which they can farm personally; and that the excess lands would be sold to small farmers or peasants, payments to be made by the small farmers over a period of 15 to 20 years. A bank would be established by the Government which would purchase the lands from the large landowner and pay the large landowner in 5 to 10 years and the recipient of the land (the small farmer) would pay the bank in 15 to 20 years.[18]

One could argue that Zahedi was saying what he thought the Americans would be pleased to hear, but this would be difficult to substantiate. None of the available documents points to any reluctance on the part of Iranian government officials to proceed with such programs. What the documents do reflect, to the frequent irritation of the Americans directly involved, is much administrative laziness and bureaucratic inefficiency. Reading through them, one gets the impression that the shah and the Iranian government felt that in 1953 they had "delivered" Iran to the Western camp, and in return for this political commitment, they expected the Americans to carry out a program of social and economic development for them. By the end of the decade, the Americans had grown tired of footing the bill given that there had been such slow progress on the Iranian side. With a new political crisis looming, the Kennedy administration changed strongly to a "self-help" line.

In a report made on November 18, 1953, Iverson confirmed that the Ford Foundation had been asked to advise the government of Iran in its formulation of a national land reform policy and program and suggested that Maris would remain in Iran until legislation had been considered and adopted. He emphasized that "the interest of the Government at the highest level in carrying out a vigorous land reform program appears to be very real," and that they are "concerned with formulating an economic development program in which land reform is a major plank."[19]

The original projection, as far as large private holdings were concerned, was that sale of Crown and public domain lands would encourage enlightened landlords to sell their lands and divert their capital to investment in industrial development. It was repeatedly warned that the government should not "resort to compulsion in the distribution of large private holdings unless experience demonstrates after a fair trial that voluntary purchase by the Government and resale to peasants will not provide land as fast as it can be properly subdivided and settled."[20]

Few enlightened landlords volunteered to sell. Eventually, the government opted for compulsion. In September 1959 the minister of agriculture formally and confidentially asked the AID mission to draft comprehensive land reform legislation. Article 2 of this draft would have limited ownership of agricultural land to 200 irrigated hectares or 600 hectares of rain-fed land. By the time the legislation was modified and passed by the Majlis in March 1960 and by the Senate in May of that year, the land ceilings had been increased to 400 hectares and 800 hectares, respectively.[21] Moreover, article 3, point 3, and article 4 of the modified legislation allowed landlords to transfer ownership of land above the legal maximum to their legal heirs within two years after passage of the legislation and to sell additional land to third parties, so long as they paid a 50 percent sales tax on such transactions. All such transfers and sales had been specifically outlawed in the original draft.

This legislation was never implemented. Aside from the legal loopholes, which would have made it ineffective, and the enormous technical obstacles, such as the nonexistence of any cadastral surveys or land registration according to hectarage, a new period of economic crisis and political instability prevented enactment of any comprehensive land reform program.

The Second Seven-Year Development Plan had been initiated in 1955. Increased oil revenues and foreign loans were to finance the plan, which concentrated heavily on infrastructural projects by the government and encouragement of private capital toward consumer goods industries. To help finance the plan, the International Bank for Reconstruction and Development extended a $75 million loan to Iran in January 1957 and concurred with the Iranian government to devalue the rial from 32.25 per U.S. dollar to 75.75 (effective May 22, 1957). This devaluation effectively more than doubled the rial funds available from foreign loans and oil revenues. This Devaluation Loan Fund was to be used as credit extended to private entrepreneurs for industrial projects. Loans were easily obtained against "paper projects," over which the government exerted little supervision. As a result, much of the money was spent in property speculation and private consumption or found its way to foreign bank accounts. Soon Iran was faced with a huge inflation problem and was running out of foreign reserves with little industrial development accomplished. By September 1960 Iran was forced to institute a stabilization program imposed by the International Monetary Fund (IMF) in exchange for a $35 million emergency line of credit. Extraordinary cash grants by the U.S. government became necessary in 1961 to finance development expenditure and foreign loan repayments (Benedick 1964:14–15; Bharier 1971:90–95). The cash grants were accompanied by political pressure on the Iranian government.

These pressures seem to have also been precipitated by a new period of political instability in Iran. Political discontent surfaced in the country around the issue of elections for the twentieth session of the Majlis in the summer of 1960. The shah had promised free elections within the confines of the two loyal legal political parties, the Melliyoun and the Mardom parties. The National Front protested the elections with public demonstrations, demanding the cancellation of the election results. Eventually Prime Minister Eqbal was compelled to resign on August 27, 1960, and the shah cancelled the election results on September 1, 1960. New elections, held in January 1961, produced no more legitimate results and sparked a new wave of antigovernment demonstrations focused on the universities and the bazaar. The new prime minister, Sharif-Emami, failed to gain political credibility, and after a wave of labor unrest culminating in the famous May 2, 1961, teachers' strike and demonstration (in which one teacher was shot dead in front of the Majlis building), he was forced to resign. The shah appointed Ali Amini as the new premier on May 6, 1961, and dissolved the Majlis on May 9, 1961 (Ladjevardi 1985:215–223). Amini had served in the mid-1950s as the Iranian ambassador to Washington and was widely believed to be America's choice for the job.

The nature of relations between the United States and Iran at the end of the 1950s is ambiguous. Three chief issues are involved. First, how much pressure did the United States exert on the Iranian government, and how successful was it? Second, what exactly were the issues at stake? Finally, was land reform undertaken as a result of these pressures?

There is no doubt that by the end of the 1950s the United States had grown impatient with financing Iran's budget deficits without seeing much progress made by the Iranian government on internal reforms (Rubin 1980:100–101). The attitude of the U.S. government was consonant with a general shift in American foreign policy at about the same time. In the immediate aftermath of World War II, the demise of the major European powers left an open vista for the United States to fill politically and economically. The Marshall Plan in Europe and the Point Four Program in underdeveloped countries were both marked by the traditional missionary spirit of "us helping them." More than a decade later it became necessary for the United States to take an accounting. With respect to many Third World countries, the United States was now finding it necessary to insist on "self-reliance." To paraphrase John F. Kennedy, the American motto became: "Ask not what America can do for you; ask what you can do for yourself . . . and for America." Indeed, the Foreign Assistance Act of 1961 made self-reliance and reform criteria for the availability of loans from the United States. Loans would now be given based on "the extent to which the recipient country is showing a responsiveness to the vital economic, political and social concerns of its people, and demonstrating a clear determination to take effective self-help measures" (USDS 1965:1269–1270).

In the case of Iran, increasing political instability and economic crisis made this push for self-help more urgent and more problematic. As a National Security Council position paper of February 24, 1961, noted:

> In 1953 when the Shah led Iran away from its traditional neutralist position into the Western camp, he felt that he was henceforth entitled to virtually unlimited military support from the U.S. . . .
>
> The U.S. problem, then, is one of giving the Shah strong moral support and reassurance while at the same time inducing him to turn his efforts and thoughts towards the solution of the pressing problem of domestic unrest. . . .
>
> . . . He should be assured that U.S. military and economic aid programs will continue, but with some change of emphasis and objectives. (USNSC 1961b)

The main points on which the new American administration sought a change were two. First, it wanted the shah to scale down the growing size of the army; Iran, it argued, needed an army capable of maintaining internal security and guerrilla activities, not an army poised for regional conflicts and still less one that could stave off a Soviet attack.[22] Second, in the political field it wanted the shah "to draw the pro-Mosaddeq nationalists and other non-Communist opposition groups into the fabric of political life." This could be achieved by "appointing respected moderate Mosaddequists to positions such as those of Minister of Finance and Head of the Plan Organization, where they could assume responsibilities without being able to reverse policy."[23] The changes the new U.S. administration was interested in for the economic field were much less controversial and involved an emphasis on sticking with the IMF's stabilization program and a reform of the tax system to enable the government to raise revenues internally. As far as land reform was concerned, the U.S. administration seemed fairly resigned to the slow steps already under way. There is certainly no evidence in the available documents that the land reform legislation of 1962 was undertaken as a result of direct pressure on that specific issue by the Kennedy administration.

On February 11, 1961 — barely three weeks after Kennedy's assumption of office, and only three months prior to Amini's assumption of the Iranian premiership, under whose cabinet the land reform legislation took effect in January 1962 — a National Security Council paper on Iran already noted that "new regulations, based on the 1960 Land Distribution Act for landlord-tenant relationship are now in process" (USNSC 1961a). The American attitude toward land reform, moreover, was more "tokenistic" than the Iranian land reform proved to be. One U.S. official of the period, William Gaud, assistant administrator of AID for the Near East and South Asia, claims the 1962 program took the United States by surprise:

> As far as land reform is concerned, yes. We had been working on the government of Iran for some time on this business of land reform. . . . We made very little progress on land reform, then all of a sudden, more or less out of the blue as far as we were concerned, the Shah announced his own land reform program. . . . And it was a fairly broad-scale attack on the problem, not terribly well thought out, but it was his. It was Iranian; it was Persian, as they said. It was their own home-grown product. (Interview recorded by Joseph E. O'Connor Feburary 21, 1966:41, Oral History Program, John F. Kennedy Library)

Allowing for exaggeration of the degree of surprise, it seems unlikely that, if the 1962 land reform had been "ordered" by Kennedy, an important AID official would see it as coming "out of the blue."

This still leaves the question of the Amini cabinet. Amini took office on May 6, 1961, and it has often been thought that the shah appointed him reluctantly and under pressure from the Kennedy administration. Indeed, the shah himself wrote:

> The U.S. wanted . . . its own man in as Prime Minister. This man was Ali Amini, and in time the pressure became too strong for me to resist, especially after John F. Kennedy was elected president. . . . I remember so well my first meetings with the Kennedys at the White House: Jacqueline Kennedy spoke of Amini's wonderfully flashing eyes and how much she hoped I would name him Prime Minister. Eventually I gave Amini the job (Pahlavi 1982:22–23).

No matter how comforting it may have been for the deposed and ailing shah to blame Americans for his own failures, his memory did not serve him very well. In fact, the shah visited the United States during April 10–18, 1962, eleven months after Amini had taken office. Indeed, since Amini resigned on July 19, 1962, it can be more convincingly argued that after his visit to the White House, the shah felt confident enough of American support to get "their man" to resign and to appoint his own man, Asadollah Alam, his close friend and confidant, in his place. Having done that, the shah was to take over the reform program directly, putting the seal of "the Revolution of the Shah and the People" on it.

U.S. documents on this period either are not publicly available or are inconclusive on the issue of Amini's appointment. The archival material at the John F. Kennedy Library, for instance, is heavily sanitized wherever there seems to have been a reference to the nature of Amini-U.S. relations.[24] Nevertheless, the same documents indicate total U.S. backing of Amini's program, as if Amini was, indeed, "their man." A National Security Council document dated May 15, 1961, that is, nine days into Amini's term of office, speaks of American policy being "directed towards the support of the Iranian Government rather than support of the Shah personally." It goes on to emphasize that

> the goals which we envisage and which we believe to be in the long-term interests of Iran and Iranian people are wholly consistent and almost identical with those which the new Prime Minister has publicly declared as his program. It is recommended that our purpose be to give full encouragement and support to the Government of Iran in carrying out this program. (USNSC 1961c)

Amini's program included land reform, but at the time of his declaration hardly anyone took it seriously. Too many governments for too long had talked about it and had done nothing further. This time around, however, it proved to be a different story. For one thing, Amini appointed Arsanjani, a long-time advocate of land reform, as minister of agriculture. He immediately took charge of the issue. Several conferences were organized by the government over the summer of 1961 to revitalize and amend the old land reform legislation; new legislation was finally issued in January 1962 as an amendment to the original legislation of 1960. By this time, the Majlis and the Senate had been dissolved; the cabinet was ruling by decree and was directly responsible to the shah. In the new legislation, significant changes were introduced, which I shall discuss in a later section.

The 1962 Land Reform: The Indigenous Reformers

This survey of the land reform program in Iran concurs with the judgment of a number of authors. Kazemian (1968:38) states:

> The pressure on the Iranian Government for reform did not come from the peasants. On the contrary, it was external rather than internal pressure which persuaded the ruling class of Iran to do something about the nation's rural population.

Baldwin (1967:93) expresses a similar point of view:

> During the late 1950s the attempt to extend land distribution beyond the Shah's Crown Lands program was mainly an American objective. The strongest source of pressure for doing anything on this front came from Point IV, which had supplied several advisers to Bank Omran to help it administer the Crown's program.

Still, it would be false to portray the land reform, and other economic development plans of the 1960s, as purely "external" projects imposed on the Iranian government and on an unwilling ruling class. The concurrence of these reforms with the Kennedy administration in the United States has often been used to demonstrate the "American character" of these reforms, but it is clear from our previous section that the American involvement in the Iranian land reform predates the Kennedy administration by more than a decade. More important, however, was the confluence of interest between the global developmental policies of the United States and the orientation of a significant sector of the Iranian ruling class.

Already by the 1950s an important sector, though numerically a minority, of Iranian men of wealth had turned their interest to manufacturing industries, and new concepts of how to generate wealth were beginning to take the place of old ones.[25] Land rent and commercial profits, though still the dominant form of wealth, were giving way to industrial profits. This itself was closely tied to new governmental policies:

> In the mid-1950s a series of laws was passed evidencing the government's desire to encourage the private sector. Legislation offered tax benefits to new companies and export producers, granted tariff waivers on imports of productive capital goods, and set down basic guarantees to foreign investors. Perhaps the most important single factor was the government's Revaluation Loan Fund Program, the significance of which can only be

fully appreciated in comparison with the state-industry policy of Shah Reza. It must, of course, be admitted that businessmen were readier to accept this stimulus in 1957 than they might have been two decades earlier. . . .

Although there is neither an industrial index nor detailed statistics, there are indications of a great upsurge in manufacturing since 1956. Plan Organization estimated that total private investment more than doubled in the four years to March 1960. In the same period, capital goods imports increased almost sixfold, the number of mechanized factories and workshops rose from 2,300 to over 8,200, and industrial employment grew from 82,000 to 134,000. Output has been increasing at an estimated average annual rate of over 10% since 1955–1956 (Benedick 1964:20).[26]

The attention paid to the problems of Iranian agriculture and to the necessity of land tenure reforms was part of this new general economic orientation. The new orientation was initiated and encouraged primarily by the state—most clearly by the shah himself. It gained its first advocates in a new layer of Iranian technocratic state planners and reformers; eventually, by the early 1960s, it found an echo within a certain layer of Iran's entrepreneurs.[27]

The shah's views have been thoroughly covered and publicized by official Iranian sources of his regime. They were also articulated in his own two books (Pahlavi 1961 and 1967). Although because of the general tone and quality of prose of these two books, as well as their publication dates, one tends to assign them propagandistic value alone, the shah expressed similar views throughout the 1950s, and he did so in various contexts. Minutes of cabinet meetings with the shah reflect his early preoccupation with land reform. For instance, in the meeting on April 8, 1957, the shah stated: "The government should put into effect the distribution of State lands as soon as possible and submit to the Majlis the legislation on limiting [land] ownership. We started this social and land reform from 1950. We will continue it till the last piece of Crown and State lands [are distributed]. Then large landed estates will have to be distributed" (Ahmadi 1962:vol. 1, p. 62). This theme was repeated in numerous cabinet meetings throughout the 1957–1960 period.[28] A similar point of view was expressed by the shah in his press conferences and public speeches of the time. In a January 25, 1959, press conference, he said:

As I have repeatedly stated, I would have liked to see the work of land distribution over and done with overnight. But unfortunately it takes time. Undoubtedly, after the distribution of Crown and State lands, it will be time for limitation of [private] land-ownership, limitation and not elimination. We want to limit ownership and to increase the number of owners. We will then investigate the local situation, we will see how much land each person is able to cultivate. What we aim at is a situation whereby each owner should be in a position to manage his own land. This system in which landlords sit in Tehran, New York and Paris and the local manager [*mobashir*] delivers their land revenues to them annually should be eradicated. In this system neither the landowner benefits from his land, nor does the sharecropper [*ra'iyat*]. But perhaps if the landlord himself manages part of his estate directly his income will increase many fold (Pahlavi 1962:719–720).

Toward the end of the 1950s the government put sustained effort into drawing up land reform legislation and preparing various governmental agencies for a land distribution program, which at the time was still projected as a further generalization of the Crown and state lands distribution programs.

In November 1959 a conference, "Agricultural Credit and Rural Cooperatives," was organized by the government. Representatives from the Ministries of Agriculture, Industries and Mines, Customs and Monopolies, Interior, Commerce, Culture, the High Council of Cooperatives, the Plan Organization, the National Bank of Iran, the Rural Development Bank, the Economic High Council, the Agricultural Bank, and a host of other state institutions participated in this two-week event. Various committees discussed agricultural development, the credit system, measures to expand cooperatives, and land reform. The final report of the conference stressed that:

Economic development of the country is largely dependent on development of agriculture.

1. Agriculture provides the source of income for about 80 percent of the Iranian population. Agricultural development is, therefore, the most effective way of raising the standard of living of this four-fifths of the population.

2. Increases in agricultural income and productivity will be of public benefit, since a larger part of internal demand for food and raw material for industries will be thus provided, reducing imports of such material and increasing exports.

3. Considering the rapid growth in population, as a result of better general health, nutrition and cultural conditions, the increase in food production becomes ever more important. This requires higher levels of investment in order to expand the area under cultivation, as well as to increase agricultural production and productivity. Considering that food items constitute half of urban consumer expenditures and over two-thirds of rural consumer expenditures, increasing agricultural production will have an anti-inflationary impact and will facilitate economic growth.

4. Agricultural and industrial development are interdependent. Higher incomes of farmers will increase their purchasing power, providing a good market for domestic agricultural and manufacturing products. Agriculturally related industrial development, in turn, provides a secure market for many agricultural products.

5. Increases in agricultural productivity will provide an incentive for farmers to release agricultural producers—who are not efficient enough—from agriculture toward industries (*Tehran Economist*, December 4, 1959).

The report further argued that to achieve these aims and to carry out land reform, a much higher allocation of financial resources for agriculture was required. It concluded:

In order to stabilize the farmers' situation, as well as the overall economic situation, a land reform program will be launched in which land, in viable economic units, will be allocated to farmers and measures will be taken to stabilize agricultural prices and to secure internal and export markets for agricultural products (*Tehran Economist*, December 4, 1959).

This growing concern among an important new layer of state planners about general economic development and about land reform in particular found its most eloquent spokesman in the person of Arsanjani, the minister of agriculture, who was ultimately in charge of the 1962 land reform. Arsanjani had been an advocate of land reform ever since the 1940s, and once he was put in charge, he used every possible occasion to explain and expand on the aims of land reform. On the eve of the ratification of the 1962 legislation, he declared in a press conference on January 14, 1962:

We do not aim to assault landlords or to harm anyone. We want the farmer, that is, the person who works the agricultural land, to own the product of his labor. We also would like to release much of the capital, now locked up in villages, and to get it into other productive activities or even into agricultural production itself, but in mechanized farming. In this way, landlords will benefit more from their wealth, farmers will get their rights, and our agricultural economy will find a more solid basis (Ministry of Agriculture 1962:34).

A day later, in a radio interview, Arsanjani emphasized: "This law aims to save 15 million people in Iran. It aims to serve the landlords themselves. It aims to rescue their capital from scattered land, left idle and unproductive" (Ministry of Agriculture 1962:59).

During the following months, Arsanjani spent much effort elaborating the aims of the land reform program:

> I have heard that in some villages, adventurist elements or perhaps some landlords, who do not like to see the implementation of land reform, are provoking the peasants, spreading rumors that the land reform will trample upon their rights. [They say these things because] the law gives land to peasants who hold land-use rights. But we have other provisions for non-holders [*khoshneshins*] and agricultural workers. That is, after existing land has been distributed among rightful peasants, we will see what extra land is available in villages to be allocated to agricultural workers. We will help them through cooperatives to bring such land under cultivation and become its owners. But our progressive aim, in implementation of land reform, is to remove surplus population from villages and move them into other branches of production. . . . In America nine percent of the population works on agricultural land and delivers the highest, historically unprecedented, level of production to American society. [Why?] Because they employ mechanized means and modern farming [techniques]. The rest of the population has left the countryside and works in industrial and productive branches. So, one of our aims must be to become a progressive society. We must strengthen and develop agriculture along with agriculturally related industries in the first place. Then gradually we must move to heavy industries. For this we need experienced workers. The increase in the growing population of the villages should satisfy this need. (Ministry of Agriculture 1962:98)

Arsanjani also elaborated repeatedly on what he foresaw as the positive effects of land reform on the general economic development of the country:

> If the land reform is implemented in the country, it will have several aims. First, an economic aim, that is, to increase national income and production. Second, to raise agricultural purchasing power to help

national economic prosperity in agriculture and agriculture-related industries. . . . Third, a social and political aim, to create political and social stability in a developing country, such as Iran. . . .

. . . We aim at several things, combined with giving land to the peasants: formation of cooperative societies and equipping them with technical farming equipment and the means to mechanize farming, and to evaluate soil conditions, to give fertilizer to peasants, to guide them in proper irrigation. . . . The combination of these measures will increase peasant production in a short span of time; within a year or two peasant income will double or triple. . . .

What effect has the increase in peasant's purchasing power had on industries and other productive branches[?] This year, more generally over the past few years, production of textile factories, and domestic sugar factories, has gone up. What has caused this increase? [The answer is] the increase in consumption. . . . The peasant, instead of wearing home-spun cloth, now uses annually several meters of cotton, buys this for this wife and kids. He cannot buy more than a few meters yet. But even the purchase of these several meters of cotton has meant that our factories can go into production. . . .

If we raise the peasant's purchasing power, as I have indicated, if instead of one thousand Tumans [$133.00] a year he earns five thousand Tumans a year, his purchase from the market of clothes, food, and even his expenditures on traveling will multiply several-fold. The impact of this will show up in the towns. That is, factories that produce textile, sugar, etc., will produce more; new workers will be employed in industries; a period of economic prosperity will set in, in which traders, merchants, grocers, etc., everyone that holds a job in the cities, will indirectly benefit. . . . Workers will benefit, ironmongers, carpenters, metal-craftsmen, all of those whose profession is somehow related to agriculture will greatly benefit. To overcome the crisis in the industrial sector, people's purchasing power must go up.

How does this happen? By increasing the salaries of state-employees, who number about 200,000 in all of Iran? Never. By increasing the incomes of the urban population, who number only seven million? Absolutely not. To increase the buying power of the population, we must turn to the overwhelming majority of the population, to the 15 million peasants. (Ministry of Agriculture 1962:105–112)[29]

In another interview, he pointed out:

In 1961, there was an unsold stock of 50 million meters of cotton textile in the country. The government was forced to extend 350 million Tumans ($50 million) credit to help manufacturers. . . . Do we have

surplus production, over and above consumption, in the textile industry? No, this is not the case. People have no purchasing power. If they
did, if every peasant would buy 5 meters instead of 3 meters, of textile
for himself, and another additional 5 meters for his wife and children,
we would get rid of this 50 million meters. The textile industry would
flourish. . . . If in Iran the purchasing power of the 15 million population who are involved, directly or indirectly, with agriculture is not
increased, the country's economy would go bankrupt. No matter how
much the gentlemen factory-owners spend and borrow money and build
factories, no matter how much we borrow from foreign banks, all this
money would go to nothing. If the purchasing power of the peasant is
doubled, then the textile factory would not be idle, it would increase
production. The peasant would consume more sugar, he would build a
house for himself, etc. (*Keyhan*, August 13, 1962).

A later report by an official of the Iranian Land Reform Organization for the UN confirmed the same thinking:

Economically as well as socially, share-croppers and tenants were living
and farming in a subsistence condition unconducive to high level agriculture production and to the growth of self-reliance among the people.
The rural sector lacked a middle-class income group. As a result, market of industrial goods was restricted, and manufacturers and other
producers were discouraged from expanding their output to take advantage of the cost savings through mass production. In such a situation,
land distribution and agrarian reform seemed to be the key factor not
merely for establishing social justice in the villages and introducing
economic incentives for higher agricultural productivity but also for
expanding the market for industrial goods in the rural areas. (Khatibi
1972:62–63)

What is significant is that it took more than a decade, as well as
substantial international pressure, for the Iranian government — the
shah particularly — and many men of capital to be won over to the
more insightful viewpoint of people such as Arsanjani. This is reflected
in the changes in the successive development plans of the 1950s. The
Second Seven-Year Development Plan of Iran, 1955/56–1961/62,
prepared by the Plan Organization, had no references to tenure
changes whatsoever. Even a revised 1960 report made only a vague
reference to tenure changes:

Agricultural progress depends on institutional as much as on technological changes. The most important institutional factors presently holding back Iranian agriculture are the traditional arrangement for land

tenure, marketing and credit. In the past, Plan Organization has neglected institutional factors almost completely. . . . This attitude reflects a mistaken belief that institutional changes will take care of themselves. (Plan Organization 1960:33)

It further argued that some sort of distributive income reform "is needed to develop the mass purchasing power upon which a successful program of industrialization must be based" (Plan Organization 1960:33).

It was only in the third plan, prepared for the 1962–1967 period, that some of the international consultants' recommendations were reflected:

The process of development will require a large-scale movement out of agriculture and into other fields of employment, which will be principally of an industrial nature. . . .

Side by side with the excess labor in agriculture there is an acute shortage of trained manpower in other sectors of our economy. This shortage impedes the pace of industrialization and the absorption of surplus agricultural labor by other sectors of our economy. (Plan Organization 1961:vol 1, pp. 21–22)

Although land tenure was recognized as a central problem, even in this report, which was prepared only months before the 1962 Land Reform Act, references to tenure reform remained quite vague:

The land tenure structure is one of the major obstacles to realizing the agricultural development objectives of the plan. The major tenure program during the Plan, however, will be to grant individual cultivators the right of continuous cultivation on particular plots of ground by written contracts, eliminating the present widespread practices of changing each year the plot an individual cultivates. By fixing cultivation rights, the tenant family will have much greater incentive to direct its energies to proper cultivation, crop rotation, fertilizer use, irrigation improvement, and the building of needed structures. (Plan Organization 1961:vol. 2, pp. 116–117)

The final "change of heart" from "fixing cultivation rights" to selling the land to the peasants seems to have occurred in the last months of 1961. Quite possibly, the economic stagnation of the late 1950s and the increasing political instability of the 1959–1962 period, combined with renewed pressure from the Kennedy administration, convinced the shah and at least a segment of the ruling class that more substantive changes would be less costly and more effective as a basis for rule in the long run.

This general and gradual reorientation of wealth and restructuring of capital investment from land to manufacturing accounts for the acquiescence of the big landlords to land reform. Although much evasion, legal and illegal, took place, there was very little organized resistance or opposition by the landlords once the aims of land reform were spelled out and it became evident that ultimately it would not conflict with their interests.[30] In fact, along with Iranian industrialist entrepreneurs, some of the big landlords themselves became advocates of land reform, although they formulated a different approach to the problem.

The *Tehran Economist*, for instance, the voice of Iranian industrialists and technocrats orientated to industrialization, favored some form of agrarian change as early as the mid-1950s. In an editorial dated September 22, 1955, it stated: "Although the principle of [private] ownership should be respected, if certain landlords don't know how to manage their estates, and leave huge farm properties in a state of decay, they must be forced to develop their lands. If they refuse, their ownership must be limited." At a time when political relations between Iran and Nasserite Egypt (and later Iraq under Qassem) were very tense, the *Tehran Economist* published favorable reports on the Egyptian land reform. Favorable reports were also published throughout the 1950s on land reform programs in India, Pakistan, Morocco, Japan, and Syria. For example, one editorial during this period argued:

> Those who think their interests will be threatened by a land distribution program are totally mistaken. If we look at the life and work of such people — mostly big landlords — we will see that for several reasons, including their inability to manage big estates . . . they cannot produce as much as is feasible from their lands. . . . If they would put their capital into any other field, their revenue would be far greater.

> We do not have complete statistics, but from experience and popular estimates, it is said that the return on big estates today is less than 10 percent, while the return on land speculation in several cities is over 100 percent, and industrial returns are over 20 percent. Therefore, it isn't clear why a big landlord, even if he does not care about the people of this country, doesn't at least care for his own interests. Don't our landlords know how to calculate? Or maybe they know arithmetic but

don't know how to adjust their situation. (*Tehran Economist*, May 18, 1959)

At one point, the *Tehran Economist* proposed that, since the government seemed hesitant to introduce limitations on land ownership and since there was no sign that major landlords would sell and distribute their estates voluntarily, the government should introduce progressive taxation on agricultural lands (*Tehran Economist*, August 21, 1959). Indeed, when the original land reform legislation was submitted to the Iranian parliament in December 1959, even before the parliament watered down the bill, the *Tehran Economist* severely criticized the many loopholes in the proposed legislation. It argued that the bill would be ineffective in changing landlord-peasant relations in Iran "from a feudal to a capitalist system" and that "the only practical and progressive solution" would be for the government to take over all land swiftly and courageously and then proceed to allocate such land to landlords or farmers depending on who could develop how much land. The development of the land was to be the only criterion in such a program (*Tehran Economist*, December 11, 1959). When the legislation was passed by the parliament and the Senate in the spring of 1960, the *Tehran Economist* observed that despite the many modifications that had rendered the legislation ineffective, its very passage had set the stage for acceptance of land distribution and the uprooting of feudalism (*Tehran Economist*, May 28, 1960).

Apart from the general tone of its commentary, the journal also gave much attention to the alternative viewpoint voiced by "developmentalist landlords." This group, represented most eloquently by Arsalan Khal'atbari—himself a landlord, a practicing lawyer, and a member of the parliament at the time—argued that the only way for Iranian agriculture to develop in a modern capitalist direction would be for the government to provide adequate credit and infrastructural support for landlords to change their ancient ways. Alternatively, if adequate compensation was offered, uninterested landlords would voluntarily sell their estates and move into more profitable ventures.[31] In an article entitled "Land Reform and the Economy," Khal'atbari argued:

> In my view, large landownership is condemned only because that small number who own such vast estates cannot manage them; thus they rel-

egate management of land and peasants to tenants or to local managers [*mobashir*]. Their villages are often not doing well. Such a state of affairs is to the economic disadvantage of the country. Otherwise, owning large estates per se is not a crime.

In America there are landlords who own hundreds of thousands of hectares of pasture, or fifty to one hundred thousand hectares of farm land. The crime is to keep estates underdeveloped to the economic detriment of the country and in decay, while others can develop such lands.

But among big landlords, once in a while, you do find persons who put their life, energy, and capital into developing their estates; they develop barren deserts into vast fields or orchards. They have provided the livelihood for hundreds of families and thousands of individuals who would have otherwise lived in poverty and unemployment. This minority of landlords is different from all those who abandon their estates to decay. . . . Shall we treat both types of landlord in the same manner?

No, we must definitely make a distinction so as not to discourage people who think about development in the future. We must encourage such people. . . .

When the land reform bill was submitted to the Parliament, I talked to the Minister of Agriculture. I proposed that instead of this barely practical law, the government should establish a special bank to buy land. Often landlords know that in the future they will not be able to manage their estates. Many of them would volunteer to sell out. If there is a bank that would guarantee payments, all landlords would sell. Because land revenues compared to other economic activities, such as manufacturing, construction, and commerce, are quite low. Landlords prefer to go into other businesses. A bank could act as an intermediary to buy land from landlords and sell it to farmers. In this way, quite peacefully, many farmers will come to own land, and because many landlords will volunteer to sell their estates, the price of land will drop. . . . But the Minister of Agriculture said that the government had no such money. I said that the government did not intend to pay a fair price, otherwise it spent hundreds of millions of Tumans on useless buildings and spurious purchases. . . .

Therefore, in order for landlords to be persuaded to sell, they must receive a fair price; if cash payment is not possible, guarantees must be made so that landlords could spend the money from their land sales in other productive activities, in manufacturing, mines, housing construction, etc. This type of re-investment program must constitute a fundamental economic policy of the government. This type of capital investment will benefit the country economically and industrially. . . . If land payments are made in installments over many years, they can only be used for consumption, with no value to the country. . . . There is no cause for hurrying things like this. The talk about [the danger of] revolution in the countryside is fabricated by foreign journals and the foreign press. . . . It is undeniable that, despite many problems in our country, there is no place in the Near and Middle East as secure and calm as ours. It is this that has encouraged people to invest in agriculture and other productive activities. (*Tehran Economist*, May 10, 1961)

In other articles Khal'atbari argued that the only way Iranian agriculture could be developed would be through the private capitalist sector (*Tehran Economist*, November 18, 1961). He repeatedly pointed to the United States and Britain as models of successful agriculture, with Italy and Turkey as possible alternatives, while Iraq and Syria were pointed out as negative examples. Khal'atbari's articles reflect clearly that the landlords *as a class* were on the defensive. But they also show that the landlords' reaction was not one of outright opposition but of cautious adaptation.

It was against this background of discussion on the future of Iranian economic development that the Amini cabinet, once it took office on May 6, 1961, revived the issue of land reform. The choice of Arsanjani, a long-time advocate of land reform, as the minister of agriculture was itself extremely important. Arsanjani immediately made land reform the top priority of his ministry. A conference on land reform was held in Tehran, under the auspices of the ministry of agriculture, from May 20 to June 3, 1961. The ostensible aim of the conference was to investigate the possibility of amending the old 1959–1960 legislation (*Tehran Economist*, June 10, 1961). In practical terms, however, the conference was geared toward mobilizing the government bureaucracy and the technocrats for an impending implementation of new land reform measures. It was attended by directors of the Department of Agriculture from all provinces, and in its final resolution it called for the establishment of a separate office to take charge of the implementation of land reform. The conference discussed various shortcomings of the old legislation with a view to finding practical solutions to some basic problems, such as the role of rural cooperatives, the land ceilings to be set, and the possibility of paying landlords in government bonds to be cashed in the form of credit for industrial and other "productive activities" (*Journal of Chamber of Commerce*, June 1961).

In August 1961, Mahdavi, the former minister of agriculture and governor of Khuzistan Province at the time, published a long essay entitled "A Practical and Useful Way to Implement Land Reform."[32] The essay was dated May 6, 1961, that is, two weeks prior to the Land Reform Conference. It contained a blueprint for a revised land reform legislation that had some of the essential hallmarks of the 1962 act. It proposed, in place of limits defined in hectares, to set the land ceiling allowed big landlords at "one village" in order to avoid problems arising from the absence of cadastral surveys in Iran.[33] It also proposed to leave current land-use patterns untouched, by selling to each peasant the land he was cultivating at the time of reform. As for payments to landlords, it proposed that payment should be made in ten annual installments, with the provision that the bonds could be cashed in for credit allocated to "productive activities." Since the Majlis and the Senate had both been dissolved by the shah on May 9, 1961, the final bill was submitted to, and ratified by, the cabinet in January 1962. It bears a remarkable resemblance to the document written by Mahdavi and published the previous May.

The 1962 Act and Later Amendments

The legislative acts that constitute the Iranian land reform are made up of the original 1962 act as well as of a number of amendments and subsequent further enactments. The most important of these dealt with the second and third stages of the reform and with the reforms related to the transfer of waqf or religious-endowment lands. We will now consider the details of the legislation, its amendments and the later enactments.[34]

The most important points of the 1962 act included, first, an upper limit set on the ownership of agricultural land. This limit was one whole village, to be chosen by the landlord (1962 Land Reform Act, article 2). The landlord could select either one single village, or portions of various villages totaling one village. Traditionally, Iranian villages were, for purposes of ownership and tenure, divided not according to independent measurements of area, such as acres, hectares, and so forth, but as portions of a total village taken as a unit of area. Each village was composed of six *dangs*, one dang being one-sixth of the village land. Often when ownership changed hands, through either inheritance or sale, the actual physical layout of the village would remain the same. Ownership would only signify the landlord's share of the final crop. For instance, if three landlords owned equal shares of two dangs each in a village, at harvest time each would have claim to one-third of the total landlords' share of the crop. As the 1962 act sought to leave cultivation patterns unchanged, while maximizing the landlords' options, this provision of the legislation allowed landlords to choose various dangs, or portions of them, in the various villages they owned, so long as the total did not exceed six dangs.

In the original 1962 legislation, the wife and children of a landlord were not granted an independent legal status. Two amendments passed in September of 1963 and February of 1964, however, enabled the wife and each child to hold land up to the upper limit set by the land reform law. These amendments increasèd tremendously the amount of land which effectively remained exempt from the reform. The 1962 act also did not deal with religious public endowments [*waqf 'am*], but private endowments (*waqf khass*) were treated as privately owned lands (1962 Land Reform Act, article 2, addendum 4).

Second, in addition to what was within the land limits just mentioned, all orchards, tea plantations, and nurseries were exempt provided that the land, water, and plants all belonged to the same person (1962 Land Reform Act, article 3, part 1). What is more, all mechanized farmland was exempt (1962 Land Reform Act, article 3, part 2). The latter included land which, at least one year prior to the reform, had been plowed by tractor and employed labor paid either in cash wages or by fixed wages in kind but not land farmed on a sharecropping basis. Later, in 1964, a limit of 500 hectares was set for ownership of mechanized land. If land in excess of this limit had been brought under mechanized cultivation at the direct initiative of the landlord and with his capital, however, it would also remain exempt and in his ownership for as long as it was farmed by mechanized methods (1964 Land Reform Regulations, article 19).

Third, in the first stage of the reform, all land above the limits and outside the exemptions was to be sold to the government, which would sell it back to the peasants (1962 Land Reform Act, article 15). The methods of payment, and its quantitative and qualitative significance to the overall process of capitalist development in Iran are discussed in appendix A).

To carry out the reform, it was envisaged that a separate government department, the Land Reform Organization (LRO), would be set up (1962 Land Reform Act, article 7, addendum 2). The director of the LRO would be proposed by the minister of agriculture and appointed by a royal decree.

Throughout the various stages of land reform all irrigated land was transferred with its traditional water rights (1962 Land Reform Act, article 17, addendum 1). Deep wells and other sources of irrigation that required power pumping were exempt from such transfers (1964 Land Reform Regulations, article 35). The 1962 act also devoted a full chapter (1962 Land Reform Act, articles 20–25) to the regulation of relations between landlord and sharecroppers on land exempt from distribution. These regulations formalized in legal terms the traditional arrangements involved in sharecropping.

The generous exemptions granted to the landlords and members of their families in this first stage, combined with well-known administrative "flexibilities" favoring the landlords, meant that on the whole only a very small percentage of land was actually affected by this reform. According to the *Statistical Yearbook of Iran* (Plan Organization, Statistical Center 1973: chapter 12, table 63), even by the end of all land reform operations in 1971, only 3,967 whole villages and 10,995 parts of villages, out of an estimated total of some 60,000 villages, had been divided under the provisions of the first phase:

> The Land Reform Law enforcement was not effective in preventing many illegal transfers of title of villages from owners to relatives or others by falsely dating the transfer documents. Although many such cases were identified, few were reversed. The same thing happened in regard to mechanization, with many complaints being received of tenants ousted or arbitrarily or falsely listed as wage laborers by landlords after the law went into effect. (Platt 1970:97)

This state of affairs led to the introduction of the second stage of the reform, introduced in January of 1963 as the Additional Articles and implemented from 1964 onward, subsequent to the passage of the new Implementation Regulations in August of 1964.

These additional articles, known as the second stage of land reform, reduced the upper ceiling of holdings from one whole village to 20 to 150 hectares, depending on the region, the quality of the land, and the type of crop farmed on it (1964 Land Reform Regulations, article 45).

In the second stage, landlords were no longer required to sell their extra land to the government. The Additional Articles of 1963 envisaged three options: (a) the landlord could, on the basis of the revenue of the three previous years, work out a rental fee and rent the land on a thirty-year lease to the peasants working it, with rent adjustments every five years; (b) the landlord could sell the land to the peasants working it; (c) the landlord could divide the land between himself and the peasants working it in proportion to traditional share-cropping divisions, and the peasants would then pay the landlord two-fifths of the price of such land in equal installments spread over a period of ten years (1963 Land Reform Articles, article 1, points a–c).

The 1964 Land Reform Regulations added one more option to the above three. If the majority of peasants and the majority of land-lords agreed — with the majorities defined not according to the number of individuals involved but according to the area of land culti-vated, in the case of peasants, or owned, in the case of landlords — they could form a joint stockholding unit in which each would hold shares proportionate to their traditional share of crops (1964 Land Reform Regulations, article 17; 1965 Land Reform Regulations Con-cerning Article 17 of the 1964 Regulations, article 1). Such units would be managed by a board of directors composed of one repre-sentative of the landlord(s), one representative of the peasants, and a third person agreed upon by both sides. If they failed to reach an agreement on the third person, the Ministry of Agriculture would appoint the third member (1964 Land Reform Regulations, article 17). Furthermore, on lands within the 20- to 150-hectare ceiling, the landlords were allowed to buy out any traditional use rights held by the peasants and could cultivate such land directly (1964 Land Reform Regulations, article 45).

The second stage of land reform also dealt with public endowments. These lands were to be leased to the peasants on ninety-nine-year terms, with rent adjustments every five years. It also allowed the government to buy private endowments and sell such lands to peasants, allocating the revenue of the sales to the original purposes of the endowment (1963 Land Reform Articles, article 2).

The implementation of the second stage did not lead to large-scale sales of land to the peasants. The overwhelming majority of landlords chose the rent option: 213,172 landlords as compared with 3,283 landlords who chose either to sell their land to the peasants or to divide it according to sharecropping ratios (Central Bank of Iran, *Annual Report for 1970*, table 61).

In March of 1969, the government introduced yet a third stage, requiring landlords who had chosen to rent their lands or to set up joint units, either to sell to the peasants at that time or to divide the land according to sharecropping ratios. Under the latter option the landlords would receive two-fifths of the price of the land. Under this stage 316,372 landlords chose to sell all excess land, while 35,403 chose to divide such land (Plan Organization, Statistical Center, *Statistical Yearbook of Iran for 1973*, chapter 12, tables 65 and 66).

As far as beneficiaries of land reform are concerned, throughout the various stages, the law gave priority to *nasaqdars*; that is, whatever land fell under the law's jurisdiction was to be sold to those peasants who held traditional cultivation rights over such land (1962 Land Reform Act, article 16, part a). Peasants without such rights, such as sharecropping laborers and paid agricultural workers, had the next priority (1962 Land Reform Act, article 16, parts c and d). But given the fact that not even all agricultural land became subject to redistribution, there were very few cases where peasants without cultivation rights became even minimally entitled to purchase land. Much less did they end up actually owning land. This differentiation between various layers of the rural population was quite logical within the overall policies of the government at the time, and this, as we have already argued, was done to encourage migration from rural areas to the urban centers.

Default on three consecutive annual payments would lead to loss of the title and the resale of the land to other beneficiaries (1962

Land Reform Act, article 28). Membership in rural cooperative societies was a precondition for receiving land (1962 Land Reform Act, article 16, addendum). The cooperatives were to take charge of all common agricultural affairs, such as the repair of *qanats* (the underground water canals) and irrigation canals, the use of common farm machinery, pesticide operations, and veterinarian services.

6

Results of the Land Reform

CHANGES IN PROPERTY RELATIONS

Land Ownership

In any discussion of land reform, the first question that frequently arises is, How much land was affected? After 1962 the Iranian land reform underwent three legislative phases and a decade of implementation. In September 1971, the government declared the land reform complete in all its stages. Yet to date no official figures exist for the exact hectarage of land redistributed through this program. Ajami (1976b:146) estimates that "under the three phases of the land reform program, between 40 and 50 percent of the cultivated land was transferred to some 70 percent of Iran's rural population." Ashraf (1982:11) offers a somewhat different estimate:

> Since the land reform legislation only covered absentee-landlords' [arbabi] lands — that is, approximately two-thirds of all cultivated land — and since about one-fourth of such land was retained by the landlords under the provision of dividing the land between landlord and peasants, if we assume that all farmers and sharecroppers who worked on such land benefitted from the land reform, then we could say that one-third of the rural population received close to half of all land under cultivation.

All sources agree that large tracts of land in each village, as well as many whole villages, remained under the ownership of previous landlords. In part, this was a consequence of the provision for dividing the land between landlord and peasants, one of the major options

TABLE 13
Pattern of Land Distribution in Selected Villages

Name of Village	Land Remaining with Previous Landlords (ha.)	Land Sold (ha.)	No. of Peasants Buying Land	No. of Households without Land
Aloo-sajard	800[a]	250	255	45
Kadouyeh	300	100	20	3
Bergan	900[a]	300	66	64
Madouan	820[a]	180	72	80
Shamsabad	537[a]	79	35	25
Khasvieh	375	385	239	60
Haram	500	100	50	65
Doulatabad	270[b]	392	109	0
Tang-karam	740	84	32	370

Source: See footnote 1, this chapter.
[a]Two owners.
[b]Three owners.

of phase two. But much more important, it was a result of the provision for exempting all mechanized farming throughout all the phases of the land reform. This latter option provided a very flexible loophole. Using tractors for plowing and registering peasants as laborers, rather than as sharecroppers, was sufficient for exemption. One source reported that in the western provinces alone a minimum of one million hectares had remained under the ownership of previous landlords (*Economist Intelligence Unit* [*Iran*] 1, 1973).

Data from individual village reports confirm similar patterns. According to field reports prepared by the Ministry of Cooperatives and Rural Affairs (MCRA) and the Institute for Social and Economic Research of Tehran University, in a total of thirty-nine villages, 14,900 hectares had remained under the ownership of 63 landlords; 1,613 peasants had received 9,580 hectares; and 1,434 households had remained landless.[1] A few examples in table 13 show typical ownership figures emerging from the land reform. Nevertheless, compared with many agrarian reforms of this period in other Third World countries, the Iranian program affected ownership of a relatively large proportion of agricultural land. The Egyptian land reform, for instance, covered only 12.5 percent of all cultivated land and only 9 percent of the rural population (Abdel-Fadil 1975:9). This difference between Iran and other countries is related to the overall pattern of capitalist development in Iran. The availability of large and growing oil revenues to the state made possible an accelerated and profitable growth of the manufacturing sector.[2] Low-cost infrastructural support and services, low-interest loans, and long tax holidays for industrial investment started Iranian manufacturing off at a rate of profit of 20 percent (*Tehran Economist*, May 18, 1959). By the 1970s, rates of return of up to 40 or 50 percent were reported (Halliday 1979:154). There was no possibility that land rent could match such rates. Former landlords very quickly became a significant component of the newly emerging Iranian bourgeoisie (Halliday 1979:151).

Concentration of Ownership

Today, as before the reform, no official data exist on the concentration of land ownership in Iran. The 1974 Agricultural Census data are categorized on the basis of the size of unit holdings only. Unit holdings are defined as units "of agricultural production in which one or several activities takes place under a single management, while economic and technical direction [of production] may be carried out individually or jointly by several people" (Plan Organization Statistical Center, 1977:h). The resulting data, therefore, do not correspond exactly with ownership distribution, since many units are rented, many landlords own a number of holdings in various villages, and many owner-households operate their lands jointly as one unit. Still, the 1974 census data are useful in other ways. A comparison with the 1960 Agricultural Census reveals important tendencies (table 14).

Before we discuss these tendencies, one problem in dealing with the 1974 Agricultural Census must be pointed out. The size categories in the 1974 census data include only a single breakdown for the 10–50-hectare range. This immediately introduces a purely statistical discontinuity in the data. For instance, as is evident from table 14, the percentage of landholdings drops from 17.3 percent in the 10–50-hectare bracket to 0.66 percent in the 50–100-hectare bracket. Similar discontinuities will be seen in other statistical results of this census as we review them throughout this chapter. Since the results of the censuses for 1960 and 1974 are quite comparable, a look at the 1960 data, which include further breakdowns between the 10–20-hectare range and the 20–50-hectare range, shows that the discontinuity is a purely statistical problem. In the 1960 data, the percent-

TABLE 14

Number and Size of Agricultural Holdings, by Plot Size, 1960 and 1974

Size of Holding (ha.)	1960					1974					1960–1974	
	No. of Holdings (thousands)	Area (thousands of ha.)	% of Total Holdings	% of Total Area	Average Plot Size (ha.)	No. of Holdings (thousands)	Area (thousands of ha.)	% of Total Holdings	% of Total Area	Average Plot Size (ha.)	Change in No. of Holdings	Change in Area (%)
Total	1,877.3	11,356.3	100.0	100.0	6.05	2,479.9	16,479.2	100.0	100.0	6.62	+32.1	+44.6
0–1	492.3	198.9	26.2	1.7	.40	734.3	259.9	29.6	1.6	.35	+49.2	+30.7
1–2	256.5	371.8	13.7	3.3	1.45	322.2	443.7	13.0	2.7	1.38	+25.6	+19.3
2–5	474.5	1,553.9	25.3	13.7	3.27	541.6	1,732.9	21.8	10.6	3.20	+14.1	+11.5
5–10	340.0	2,413.0	18.1	21.2	7.10	427.9	2,953.4	17.3	18.0	6.90	+25.9	+22.4
10–20	223.8 ⎱ 301.5	3,054.5 ⎱ 5,263.7	11.9 ⎱ 16.0	26.9 ⎱ 46.4	13.65 ⎱ 17.46	428.1	7,500.7	17.3	45.7	17.52	+42.0	+42.5
20–50	77.7 ⎰	2,209.2 ⎰	4.1 ⎰	19.5 ⎰	28.43 ⎰							
50–100	8.4	563.8	0.45	5.0	67.12	16.3	1,073.7	0.66	6.5	65.87	+94.0	+90.4
100–500	3.8 ⎱ 4.1	684.2 ⎱ 991.0	0.20 ⎱ .22	6.0 ⎱ 8.7	180.05 ⎱ 241.71	9.6	2,452.9	0.39	14.9	255.51	+134.1	+147.5
500+	0.3 ⎰	306.8 ⎰	0.02 ⎰	2.7 ⎰	1022.67 ⎰							

Source: OAS 1960: tables 101 and 301; Plan Organization, Statistical Center 1977: tables 1 and 15.
Note: Total number of rural households: 1960 = 3,218,500; 1974 = 3,264,800 (an increase of 1.4%).
Number of holdings without land (e.g., animal husbandry, etc.): 1960 = 507,600; 1974 = 513,400 (an increase of 1.1%).

TABLE 15
Distribution of the Added Land under Cultivation among Various Size
Holdings between 1960 and 1974

Size of Holding (ha.)	Increase in Area (thousands of ha.)	Increase in No. of Holdings (thousands)	% of Total Area	% of Total Holdings	Weighted Average Increase (ha.)	% of Change in Average Plot Size since 1960
0–1	61.0	242.0	1.2	40.2	0.25	−37.5
1–2	71.9	65.7	1.4	10.9	1.09	−24.8
2–5	179.0	67.1	3.5	11.1	2.67	−18.3
5–10	540.4	87.9	10.7	14.6	6.15	−13.4
10–50	2,237.0	126.6	44.2	21.0	17.67	+ 1.2
50–100	509.9	7.9	10.1	1.3	64.50	−3.9
100 +	1,461.9	5.5	28.9	0.9	265.80	+ 10.0
Total	5,060.9	602.6	100.0	100.0	8.40	+ 38.8

Source: Table 14.

ages decline from 18.1 (5–10 ha.), to 11.9 (10–20 ha.), to 4.1 (20–50 ha.) to 0.45 (50–100 ha.), and to 0.22 (more than 100 ha.) percent, respectively. Personal inquiries at the Statistical Center of Iran (Plan Organization) indicate that finer classification of the 1974 census data is not available. This difficulty makes the data already unsatisfactory because the only landholding classification is in accordance with farm size, even more problematic. For instance, the 10–50-hectare category clearly lumps together vastly different types of agricultural holdings. The lower end of the bracket includes mostly peasant family farms, while the higher end of the bracket would in all probability be composed of commercial farmers and capitalist enterprises. Nonetheless, with these problems and limitations in mind, we will now look at the trends that can be derived from a comparison of the 1960 and 1974 data.

A first tendency, evident from table 14, is increased concentration of landholdings. Whereas the number of small holdings—less than 1 hectare and between 1 and 2 hectares—increased by 49 percent and 26 percent, respectively, between 1960 and 1974, the amount of land under each category increased by only 31 percent and 19 percent. At the other end of the scale, the very large holdings of more than 100 hectares increased in number by 134 percent, and the amount of land in this category increased by 147 percent. The average size of holdings in this category increased from 241.7, to 255.5 hectares.

Alternatively, we can observe the same phenomenon in the distribution of the total land under cultivation (from 11.4 million hectares in 1960 to 16.4 million hectares in 1974) in various holding-size categories during the period in question (table 15). A comparison of table 15 with table 14 shows that only in two size categories was the weighted increase in average size larger than the original average plot size: (a) the 10–50-hectare category, where the increase was marginal, 17.67 hectares as compared with 17.46 hectares in 1960; (b) the larger-than-100-hectare category, where the increase was substantial, 265.8 hectares compared with 241.7 hectares in 1960. The group most adversely affected was in the under-10-hectare categories.

The reasons for this increased concentration of landholdings are manifold. At the lower end of the scale, among small holders, one reason, related to the very nature of the reform legislation, was that many peasants received only a portion of the land they traditionally cultivated. For instance, in cases where the landlord chose to divide the land according to traditional sharecropping ratios, under option *c* of the second phase, the peasant received between one-fifth and four-fifths of the land. Moreover, since poorer peasants were not in a position to bring new land under cultivation, they suffered more than others from the fragmentation of land through inheritance. At the upper end of the scale—and this is probably the most important factor—large tracts of land of several hundred to several thousand hectares, lying downstream from the dams constructed in the 1950s and 1960s, were rented out by the government to large agro-industrial concerns. Because of the size of these allocations, even a small number of such ventures would have a major effect on the distribution pattern of landholdings.[3]

The second point to be drawn from table 14 concerns the scale of landlessness among rural households. At first glance table 14 indicates a substantial decrease in landlessness in rural Iran. In 1960, 833,600 rural households were neither engaged in animal husbandry nor were they landholders. This figure decreased to 271,500 households in 1974. This decrease of more than half a million would seem, on the face of it, to contradict the statement that land reform excluded a large proportion of rural households from access to land.

The contradiction resolves itself, however, once we take into account the rural-urban migration during the same period.

It has been estimated that about 47.5 percent of all rural households, that is, about 1.5 million households, did not receive land (Keddie 1972:387). Their exclusion was, of course, the result of the provision that only those peasants who held traditional land-use rights, nasaq, would receive land. It was generally assumed at the time that large portions of those without such rights—commonly referred to as *khoshneshins*—would migrate to the industrial and urban centers to provide the necessary urban labor force. This they did. Indeed, it is the success of this projection that accounts for the fact that while 1.5 million households were in fact excluded from land reform benefits, by 1974 there were fewer landless households left in the countryside.

The land reform introduced an irreversible change in the position of the landless khoshneshin. Prior to land reform, he participated in work teams (*boneh*) along with the nasaqdar peasants and he received a share of the final crop. Although the khoshneshin's position was not as secure as a nasaqdar peasant's, he could hope that some day the landlord might grant him land-use rights, possibly as a result of the misfortune of another peasant. But in the same way that the right of a nasaqdar peasant to his land was secured through the land sales, the hope and possibility of access to land for a khoshneshin peasant were forever dashed once he was excluded as a beneficiary of land reform.[4]

In the early days of land reform, the khoshneshins still hoped that the government might eventually sell them land previously held by landlords. These hopes have now been renewed under the new regime, whose policy encourages a return to the countryside. Present discussion of new land reform legislation could now affect ownership of land by the khoshneshins (Ashraf 1982). But between 1962 and 1980, the lot of the khoshneshin who remained in the countryside deteriorated sharply. Small cultivators tended to hire less agricultural labor and depended more on family workers. As a matter of fact, the families of small cultivators often competed with the khoshneshins for the work available on larger farms. Increased mechanization also reduced demand for agricultural laborers. In a detailed study of one area, Hooglund (1975:157) calculated that on a per capita basis each agricultural laborer worked fifteen fewer days in 1970, an average of thirty-five, than he had in 1962–1963, when each worked an average of fifty days. All had to seek supplementary employment to make ends meet:

> By 1970 all 24 *khwushnishin* laborers were earning at least half their gross annual incomes from work in localities other than the three villages under discussion. In fact, eight men no longer participated in the local summer labor force; three commuted daily to larger villages near Zanjan and Sultanabad; two were employed on farms in the Qazvin area (149 kilometers to the east) and returned to their villages one day each week; two worked in Gilan (over 350 kilometers to the north-east) from mid-May through mid-August during which time they were absent from their families; and one went to the Hamedan region for six weeks at the beginning, and again for six weeks at the end, of the summer. (Hooglund 1975:159–160)

In time more and more khoshneshins, as well as vast numbers of peasant small landowners, migrated to the urban centers (Kazemi 1980). During the decade between the most recent national population censuses (1966–1976), more than 2 million peasants migrated from the rural areas to the cities. The sample census on manpower, carried out in 1972, indicated a total of 3,974,434 internal migrants in Iran, of which more than 2 million had stated rural areas as their last place of residence before finally settling in a city (Kazemi 1980:28).

In the survey carried out by Kazemi among heads of migrant households in Tehran, nearly 85 percent said they had left the villages as a result of unsatisfactory employment and inadequate income (Kazemi 1980:44). Once in a town, they had no intention of returning to the countryside despite the problem of insecure employment, shantytown living conditions, and much larger income differentials.

> Although they had contact with the middle and upper classes of Tehran through the media, kin relations, and service agencies, they often compared their situation with less fortunate kin in the village, with whom they probably had more consistent and personal interaction. They perceived rural work to be a drudgery and unhygienic and town life to be more exciting than the farm. Despite disappointments, few seriously intended to return home. (Bauer 1983:145)

In sum, then, the land reform introduced a basic split within the mass of the peasantry: on the one side were those who became property owners, with secure access to land; on the other were those whose hopes for land appeared to be dashed forever. The latter group did not manifest itself socially by mass landlessness in the countryside; rather, this group migrated to the urban areas.

Land Tenure

Even though a substantial percentage of land remained under the ownership of previous landlords, the land reform dramatically altered the tenure situation throughout the country. This change also affected land held by landlords (table 16). A comparison of table 16 with the prereform 1960 figures of table 15 shows that owner-operated holdings grew from 33 percent of the total number and 26 percent of the total area to 92 percent and 91 percent, respectively. Although there is a generally high level of uniformity, the percentage of owner-operated units is lowest among the two largest categories, units consisting of fifty hectares and more (table 17). According to definitions provided by the census results of 1974 (Plan Organization, Statistical Center 1977:h–i), an owner-operated holding is one in which the person who is in charge of economic and technical management of agricultural production, and who is the recipient of the profits or losses of such an operation, is the owner of the agricultural land. Now, it has been estimated that a peasant and his family can cultivate between 1.5 and 5 hectares of land, depending on type of crop and region.[5] If tractors are used for plowing instead of oxen, and for such crops as wheat and barley, one family can handle as many as 50–65 hectares. For crops such as cotton and rice, which require intensive labor throughout the production cycle, if mechanization is limited to the use of tractors for plowing, the area that a single family can bring under cultivation does not rise significantly.

These figures mean that holdings of 10–100 hectares would have to at least use tractors, and holdings above 100 hectares would have to be fully mechanized, if they are genuinely owner-operated farms. Tractors were not used on some 1.8 million hectares of land under cultivation and on 2.0 million hectares of fallow land in the size categories of 10 hectares and more (table 18). How can this inconsistency with respect to owner-operated holdings be explained?

One possible explanation is that although the owner may declare himself to the census reporters as the manager of his holding, he may not be involved in actually administering agricultural produc-

TABLE 16
Number and Size of Holdings, by Type of Tenure, 1974

Type of Tenure	Holdings		Area	
	No. (thousands)	%	No. of ha. (thousands)	%
Owner-operated	2,282	92	14,878	91
Rented	54	2	516	3
Part rented, part owned	63	3	482	3
Others	80	3	541	3
Total	2,480	100	16,417	100

Source: Plan Organization, Statistical Center 1977: table 88.

TABLE 17
Type of Land Tenure, by Size of Holdings, 1974

Size of Holding (ha.)	Owner-operated		Rented		Part Rented, Part Owned		Other	
	% of Total No.	% of Total Area	% of Total No.	% of Total Area	% of Total No.	% of Total Area	% of Total No.	% of Total Area
0–1	92	91	2	2	2	3	3	3
1–2	91	91	2	2	4	4	4	4
2–5	91	91	2	2	3	3	4	4
5–10	93	94	2	2	2	2	3	3
10–50	93	92	2	3	3	3	2	3
50–100	88	88	5	5	4	4	3	3
100 +	80	83	8	7	5	5	6	6

Source: Plan Organization, Statititical Center 1977: table 88.

TABLE 18
The Use of Tractors for Plowing, by Size of Holding, 1974

Size of Holding (ha.)	Total Ha. under Cultivation (thousands)	Tractorized Ha. (thousands)	Non-tractorized Ha. (thousands)	Total Ha. Left Fallow (thousands)	Tractorized Ha. Left Fallow (thousands)	Non-tractorized Ha. Left Fallow (thousands)
0–1	145.7	36.8	108.9	29.6	5.6	24.0
1–2	290.1	87.8	202.3	82.0	20.9	61.1
2–5	1,155.8	519.2	636.6	464.0	130.5	333.5
5–10	1,837.7	1,039.2	798.5	1,013.6	375.0	638.6
10–50	4,499.6	2,909.5	1,590.1	2,846.1	1,284.0	1,562.1
50–100	610.6	521.5	89.1	428.6	257.3	171.3
100 +	1,296.7	1,224.3	72.4	1,091.5	785.7	305.8

Source: Plan Organization, Statistical Center 1977: tables 15 and 260.
Note: All figures for land under cultivation exclude land in perennial crops.

tion as such. Rather, he may be "managing" his holding by leasing it out in smaller plots to peasant families. One such type of arrangement is *nesfe-kari*, in which the landlord and the peasant share equally in all current expenditure, but without calculating any remuneration for the labor of the peasant and his family, and also share in the final output. Here is how one author describes a nesfe-kari arrangement in a village near Qazvin:

> Contrary to expectation . . . the new system of production was not capitalist production in its usual form. The landlord was not in a position to act as a real capitalist (with sufficient capital and necessary management). Nor were the peasants from the surrounding villages prepared to work as "day-laborers." . . . Consequently, a different mode of production was worked out that has become prevalent not only in the Qazvin area but all over Iran. It often marked the transition from the former sharecropping regime to capitalism. This method of production is called *nesfe-kari* [half-half cultivation]; the operators are often from Qom, Yazd, and Isfahan. . . . They provide half the necessary capital for production, are skilled in plantation of expensive cash crops, organize the production without involving former [local] peasants, . . . manage the whole operation and accounting, . . . in short, they run the job for the landlord in a way that is profitable, controllable, and without headaches. Under the terms of the agreement between the landlord and *nesfe-karan*, the landlord provides land and water, plus half the current expenditure on seeds, plowing, insecticides, etc. There are three middlemen who are in charge and bring in a group of *saifi-karan* [experts in summer crops, such as melons] for six months. They divide the output between themselves and the landlord on a 50–50 basis. These middlemen have their own agreement with the *saifi-karan*; they pay them either in cash or a share of the crop. (Mahdavi 1982:54–56)

Another indication of farming-out practices is the existence of large holdings on which agricultural labor is carried out primarily by family members. Only a very small (7.3) percentage of the 10–50-hectare holdings depend "primarily on wage labor" (table 19). For the 50–100-hectare holdings the figure rises to 36.7 percent, leaving 63.3 percent of holdings on which labor is "wholly or mostly family labor." Even on holdings of 100 hectares and more, 36.0 percent of holdings depend on family labor, wholly or partially.[6]

Given the fact that more than 4 million hectares of land in categories of 10 hectares and larger are *not* mechanized, such heavy dependence on family labor would make sense only if large plots

TABLE 19
Type of Labor Employed by Size of Holding, 1974

Size of Holding (ha.)	Family Labor Only	Family Labor for Major Part of Farm Work	Wage Labor for Major Part of Farm Work	Total
0–1	74.8	20.8	4.4	100.0
1–2	61.1	34.6	4.3	100.0
2–5	61.2	34.1	4.7	100.0
5–10	55.0	40.8	4.2	100.0
10–50	44.2	48.5	7.3	100.0
50–100	17.9	45.4	36.7	100.0
100 +	8.9	27.1	64.0	100.0

Source: Plan Organization, Statistical Center 1977: table 7.

were being cultivated by many peasant families, supervised either directly by the landowner or by middlemen working for him.

There is one other possibility, however. In some areas of Iran, villagers pool their land together for cultivation purposes. If such units are reported as single holdings, but are jointly operated, then large units of land could be cultivated by traditional techniques and by utilizing family labor. Saedloo provides many examples of this:

> The 90 peasants of the village of Dowlatabad are divided into six groups of fifteen. Each individual has 3 hectares of land, totalling 45 hectares per group. Because of land scarcity, in each group only four, who are more knowledgeable in farming, engage in agriculture. The other 11 have to work outside the village. . . . At harvest time, however, they must return to participate in harvesting the crop. The 11 individuals who do nonfarm work each pay 150 Rls a month to the four who do the farm work, that is, each of the latter get 11 × 150 Rls a month (Saedloo 1974:25–26).

According to the *Agricultural Census, Phase II, 1974*, table 90 (Plan Organization, Statistical Center 1977), among the holdings of 10 hectares or more, some 65.7 thousand are joint operations, covering a total of 2,062,700 hectares. Of these, some 875,000 hectares could belong to large-scale commercial ventures (Ajami 1981:91), and 369,300 hectares belong to State Farm Corporations and Production Cooperatives (MCRA 1977d:37 and 115), both of which are highly mechanized operations. This leaves 878,400 hectares jointly cultivated by peasant producers. This is a substantial figure but still does not cover an estimated 3.8 million hectares of 10-hectare-and-larger units that could be cultivated only by peasant producers. Some 3 million hectares might fall, therefore, under some sort of farming-out arrangement, without its being reported.

The existence of extensive farming-out arrangements, in the form of *nesfe-kari* or similar agreements, has led many observers to the conclusion that the land reform has not fundamentally altered tenure relations. Mo'meni, for instance, says, "In some places, these [old sharecropping] relations have been transformed into rental agreements. Often the rent is paid in kind which is fundamentally no different from the [ancient] sharecropping system [*mozare'eh*]." He then refers to a number of sharecropping arrangements reported in various publications (Mo'meni 1980:338–339).

Hooglund (1982a:78) also reaches the conclusion that "it is important to understand that the land reform program did not eliminate absentee ownership of agricultural land." But his definition of "absentee ownership" removes all distinction between precapitalist and capitalist "absentee ownership": "The term *absentee* is used in a general sense to refer to all owners who did not personally work their land but either rented it out to tenants or hired wage labor to cultivate it" (Hooglund 1982a:164). Under this definition the Del Monte plantations in California and the *zamindari* system of India would both be characterized as "absentee ownership," even though they differ in every other conceivable characteristic.

The pre–land reform sharecropping system in Iran was quite different from what is called sharecropping at the present time. Currently, there exist various types of sharecropping in rural Iran. The first of these amounts to payment of rents in kind. A second type is based on payment of wages to agricultural laborers in kind. This type of sharecropping is used both by old landlords and by peasant proprietors to pay for seasonal labor. In a third type of sharecropping a number of peasant proprietors work collectively and share the output. As already noted, in these arrangements members of the collective sometimes leave the village for employment elsewhere in order to generate cash earnings for those tending the land. The latter two types of sharecropping are clearly different from the old peasant-landlord agreements. But even the first type of sharecropping, payment of rents in kind, is not identical to what it was before land

reform. Rents-in-kind agreements have now become annually negotiated contracts. The peasants no longer have traditional land-use
rights. Landlords prefer to hire nonlocal migrant peasants in order to
avoid the possibility of future claims to use rights. Often they do not
allow the migrants to build living accommodations, plant trees, or
do anything else of a lasting nature close to farmland. Peasants accept
these sharecropping rental agreements, despite the insecurity inherent in them, because they do not have enough initial cash to pay
rent, and under them they risk less if there is a poor harvest. Landlords agree to this kind of arrangement when they do not want to
bother with the constant supervision that would be necessary if they
were managing production. Under an annually negotiated contract,
all they need do is show up at the time of harvest. Both sides view
such arrangements with suspicion and as a necessary evil. Peasants
would prefer to own the land or pay minimal rents that they could
afford, rents of the same order of magnitude, say, as the land installment payments. Landlords would prefer to receive cash rents, but
very few peasants can afford to pay what landlords demand in cash.

These kinds of agreements cover a great variety of renters and
tenants. In some cases even the more prosperous layers of the village
community lease their land to fellow villagers in exchange either for
cash or a share of the crop.[7] These renters include the old *kadkho-
das*, or village chiefs, oxen holders, and *mirabs*, those in charge of
water distribution, many of whom received land under reform.

One type of sharecropping that grew rapidly during the postreform
period, particularly near urban markets, is that referred to by Mahdavi
as nesfe-kari (Mahdavi 1982). This sharecropping arrangement is carried out by skilled farmers, often from around Yazd, Qom, and
Isfahan, producing for urban markets. It existed on a smaller scale
before the land reform. Salmanzadeh (1980) refers to Isfahani farmers brought to the Dezful area in Khuzistan in 1948 to plant summer vegetables and fruit crops on a half-and-half basis. In his famous
work on the village of Taleb-abad, near Tehran, carried out in the
late 1950s, Safi-nejad reported similar arrangements:

> There is another layer of the population in Taleb-abad and surround-
> ing villages. . . . They are not sharecropping peasants (*ra'yyat*). They
> are known as *Qomi-kar*. In some villages they call them *saifi-kar* [experts
> in summer crops]. *Qomi-karan* are mostly peasants from Qom, known

for their skills in *saifi-kari*. They come to these villages at the start of the planting season in spring and go back to Qom after the summer crop season is finished and everything has been harvested. They only pitch in their labor (and half of the current expenses) and the crop is divided between them and the landlord on a half-and-half basis. (Safi-nejad 1966:123–124)

Safi-nejad also stresses that nesfe-kari is a post-1941 phenomenon (Safi-nejad 196b:255–256).[8]

Nesfe-kari is not a remnant of the old system. On the contrary, it was only after the landlord was free of claims of traditional use rights by local peasants that he was in a position to lease out his land on the basis of this new type of sharecropping. Such sharecropping arrangements are new not only in terms of how they regulate tenure relations but also in terms of the orientation of the producing farmers. Traditional sharecropping peasants primarily had a subsistence orientation. They did not produce cash crops, and they had very little incentive or opportunity to increase either production or productivity. What they marketed from their share of the harvest was often sold to the local shopkeeper, more frequently than not to pay back debts and leave some credit-in-kind for future purchases from the shopkeeper. The nesfe-karan, on the other hand, are specialist farmers, producing vegetables and fruits for the urban market. Because of their direct contact with urban marketing networks, they do have an interest in raising production levels and productivity. This is true despite the high land rent of half their crop. Indeed, because of the high level of entrepreneurship among these farmers, Mahdavi (1982:56) concludes that nesfe-kari arrangements are of a transitional character,

> because after a few years either the landlords and local peasants learn all the production techniques and skill and accumulate enough capital to dismiss the *nesfe-karan* and they themselves continue production on a capitalist basis. Or the *nesfe-karan* buy the land from the landlord and establish themselves as capitalists/managers.

But that either of these events has actually happened with any great frequency is not at all clear. There is as yet too little evidence, and too short a time span — now interrupted by the post-1979 developments — has passed, to judge the empirical validity of Mahdavi's projection. Certainly it is one possible logical development, but many others are equally conceivable. For example, landlords may find that this type of "management" is the most profitable under present circumstances. Local peasants may pick up the skills but not have access to land. The nesfe-karan may accumulate substantial capital, but they might also prefer to move on to paying cash rents rather than sinking their capital into purchase of land.

COMMERCIALIZATION OF AGRICULTURAL PRODUCTION

In chapter 3, I argued that if the rural sector was to be integrated into the national economic development process, it was inevitable that mechanisms would be introduced to guarantee compulsory and permanent participation of peasants in the monetary economy. Without such mechanisms peasants could turn at any time to production for self-consumption and retain their insularity.[9] On the other hand, by increasing the cash needs of farmers, the autarchy of the rural economy would rapidly break down. The peasant then would have to sell his surplus product or labor to meet these new and increased cash needs. This monetary tie would soon begin to direct the fate of the peasantry. In the following paragraphs we will examine how the pattern of production has changed under the impact of the increased commercialization of agriculture.

To satisfy cash needs, several options are open to the peasant. Which of these becomes dominant in a specific country and during a specific period depends on the particular history of that region and time. The options available to the peasant for satisfying his cash needs are: (a) selling his surplus product, (b) selling his surplus time, and (c) renting out part of his land. All peasant households aim to satisfy the totality of their direction consumption and cash needs through the optimum means available given all the limitations any household faces. Typically these include limitations of factors of production, such as land, water, and instruments of labor, including draft animals; limitations of an alternative employment market; and limitations of the market for agricultural produce.

For instance, the choice of renting out part of the land cannot become the general means of satisfying cash needs. To begin with, the produce to be had from the land is normally worth more than the rent that the peasant could obtain from it. Consequently, it is not usually to the advantage of the peasant to lease out land. In some highly exceptional situations this may not be the case, as when the family labor force is too small to cope with cultivation and hiring outside labor is not advantageous, or where proximity to urban centers allows land to be leased to specialist farmers for production of certain fruits and vegetables for the urban market. Second, in a country like Iran most peasant households have holdings barely large enough to satisfy their own needs. From the findings of MCRA surveys, one can arrive at the estimate that in most regions of the country, excluding the rice lands of the north, and given the primitive level of technique, five to ten hectares of land is the necessary minimum for household needs, while 82 percent of all holdings are substantially less than ten hectares. Under these circumstances most peasants are eager to acquire more land rather than rent out their own. The lack of alternative secure employment on a mass scale and the fear of losing the land if they rent it make the peasants prefer leasing in to leasing out. Even when most members of the family find temporary nonagricultural employment, the family feels more secure in leaving the land fallow than in leasing it to others (*Financial Times* [London], July 25, 1977).

The second option, partial wage employment, can and has become important in those areas where proximity to urban industrial centers makes it possible to seek employment outside the peak agricultural season. In such cases, as I will discuss later, agricultural production is left to other members of the family or is carried out through group arrangements with other peasants in exchange for a share of crop or in return for cash payments. By a similar line of argument, the first option, that of selling surplus produce, can become the most important means of satisfying cash requirements only for those peasants who already have sufficient land and sufficient ability to work their holdings.

Breaking down the various sectors of the rural economy by size of landholdings alone is bound to be unsatisfactory. For instance, in the rice-growing areas of Gilan and Mazandaran along the southern belt of the Caspian Sea, a much smaller landholding of two to five hectares is considered a good-sized plot for satisfying the household needs of a peasant family, while the national average is five to ten hectares. Similarly, in a survey of villages near the city of Qazvin — itself an industrial center only 150 kilometers from Tehran and linked to it by a major highway—Mahdavi (1982:67) found that farmers themselves believed that even five hectares of good irrigated land

> could provide them with a comfortable living, if instead of subsistence crops (wheat and barley), they could engage in plantation of more expensive crops such as sugar beet, cotton, summer fruits and vegetables. But so long as the peasants cannot securely obtain their bread [subsistence food]—from the market or the cooperative—they continue to plant subsistence crops.

Even factors other than location and type of crop can significantly affect peasant production. Level of technique, improved irrigation, and other capital inputs are also closely interlinked with the capacity of peasant production to become market oriented. Despite these further complications, however, in an overall evaluation of production patterns we have no choice but to start by making distinctions according to size of landholdings: all agricultural census data are organized in this way, and often no other breakdown is provided. I will attempt to overcome the inadequacies of the existing framework by reference to specific field reports that focus on individual villages and peasant farms.

Therefore, as a first approximation, table 14 has been condensed into the subgroups shown in table 20. The holding sizes in this table are based on the estimated average of five to ten hectares necessary for family subsistence; data variation for groups of under five hectares is not appreciable. Where there are significant variations, I will present finer breakdowns. Furthermore, in all official reports—Iranian government sources, World Bank reports, and ILO reports—farms of ten hectares or more are considered to be "commercially viable holdings"; the smaller holdings in this size bracket consist of peasant family farms, and the larger holdings begin to overlap with capitalist farms.

The various size groups share certain features while differing in others, and therefore I will not discuss each one separately. For instance, there is no major differentiation in crop variation between small and medium groups according to size alone. Both groups share other characteristics as well; for example, both depend on family labor, although the medium-size group hires more seasonal labor, while small groups provide labor for larger farms. What primarily distinguishes the two is that the medium-size group is more market ori-

TABLE 20
Distribution of Holdings, by Type of Farming Group, 1974

Farming Group	Size of Holding (ha.)	Percentage of Holdings	Percentage of Area	Average Plot Size (ha.)
Small Farms	0–5	64.4	14.8	1.5
Overlap	5–10	17.3	18.0	6.9
Commercial Family Farms	10–50	17.3	45.7	17.5
Overlap	50–100	0.66	6.5	65.9
Capitalist Farms and Agribusiness	100 +	0.39	14.9	255.5

Source: Table 14.

ented than the very small farms. Furthermore, discussing each group separately makes it difficult to see the real interrelations that exist among the various groups and bind them together, for instance, the hiring in and hiring out of labor between various groups.

Crop Variation

As noted in chapter 4, Iranian agriculture has not been historically integrated into and affected by the rise of a world market. In this respect, it is unlike the agriculture of many other Third World countries. As a result, agricultural production in Iran continues to be oriented primarily toward food production for internal consumption. Increased production of certain industrial crops, such as sugar beet, cotton, and oil seeds, is for domestic industrial consumption. According to the tables 12 and 93 of the 1974 Agricultural Census Results (Plan Organization, Statistical Center 1977), 83.6 percent of all land under annual crops is allotted to cereals, a marginal decrease from 87.2 percent in 1960. The dominance of cereal production is evident in all size categories (table 21).

Crop variation among farms of less than five hectares is slightly more significant than among those between ten and fifty hectares. In part the difference is a result of the relative weight of small rice plantations: 74.8 percent of the area under rice cultivation is composed of farms under five hectares in size (Plan Organization, Statistical Center 1977: table 188). Still, the same tendency is observed in sugar beet cultivation: 2.1 percent of land in farms under five hectares is allotted to this crop as compared with 1.4 percent in the five-to-ten-hectare category and 1.1 percent in the ten-to-fifty-hectare

TABLE 21

Percentage of Land under Various Annual Crops,
by Type of Farming Group, 1974

Farming Group	Size of Holding (ha.)	Cereals			Total Cereal	Sugar Beet
		Wheat	Barley	Rice		
Small Farms	0–5	52.8	11.6	17.7	82.1	2.1
Overlap	5–10	66.0	16.7	2.1	84.8	1.4
Commercial Family Farms	10–50	68.8	16.5	1.0	86.3	1.1
Overlap	50–100	65.1	13.6	0.6	79.3	2.4
Capitalist Farms and Agribusinesses	100 +	62.2	13.7	0.7	76.6	3.5

Source: Plan Organization, Statistical Center 1977:tables 15, 140, 164, 188, and 204.

Note: No data are available for other crops according to holding size.

TABLE 22

Percentage of Area under Wheat and Barley Cultivation in Various Provinces,
by Type of Farming Group, 1974

Farming Group	Size of Holding (ha.)	Central Province	West Azarbaijan	Khuzis-tan	Khora-san	Isfahan
Small Farms	0–5	75.8	64.2	87.8	73.4	70.6
Overlap	5–10	82.1	77.7	95.2	81.0	77.3
Commercial family farms	10–50	85.5	78.9	94.6	80.6	84.6
Overlap	50–100	75.5	73.5	91.5	75.3	79.6
Capitalist farm & agribusinesses	100 +	75.5	72.0	72.7	69.4	69.7

Source: Plan Organization, Statistical Center 1977:tables 16, 20, 22, 25, 26, 141, 145, 147, 150, 151, 165, 169, 171, 174, and 175.

category. Moreover, if we look at regional breakdowns, we see the same tendency of higher crop variation on farms under five hectares, even in provinces where there is marginal or no rice cultivation (table 22).

Both tables 21 and 22, therefore, indicate similar tendencies in terms of crop variation: higher crop variation for farms under five hectares, higher allocation of land to cereal production for farms between five and ten hectares, and then reversing back to higher crop variation for farms of more than fifty hectares. Field reports of specific villages and regions confirm the same tendency, that is, there is a higher degree of crop variation on very small plots as compared with the medium-size categories. Of course, the grain crop produced on the larger farms of between ten and fifty hectares exceeds the consumption requirements of the peasant household and is in part sold to the market. The higher degree of crop variation on very small farms can be explained in various ways. If the household is oriented to producing for its own consumption, cultivation of various crops can satisfy various consumption needs. On the other hand, in some circumstances, just the opposite may be true: given a minimum level of intensification and proximity to towns, small farmers can obtain higher incomes if they allot their land to cash crops, such as vegetables and fruits.[10]

Marketed Surplus

The 1974 census provides very rough data on marketing. The information is given by the percentage of the number of holdings that market half, more than half, or less than half of their produce. It is categorized twice: according to provinces and according to the size of holdings. There are no cross-references according to holding size in each province. Nor is any information available reflecting crop variation, except that data are provided separately for annual and perennial crops.

According to the 1974 census, for the country as a whole, 51 percent of all holdings reporting annual crops sell no produce to the market, 26.7 percent market less than half their produce, and only 22.3 percent market half or more of their produce (Plan Organization, Statistical Center 1977:table 8).

Marketing trends vary significantly by region. In West Azarbaijan, which has traditionally provided the bulk of the country's dried fruit exports, only 21.9 percent of holdings reporting perennial crops do not sell any produce to market, while 56.8 percent of such holdings market half or more of their produce. Similarly, in Kerman, a region of pistachio and citrus plantations, the corresponding figures are 24.2 percent and 53.0 percent, respectively. Because of the predominance of date palms in Khuzistan, again only 24.4 percent of holdings reporting perennial crops do not sell any produce to the market, while 44 percent market half or more of their produce. At the other extreme, in Hamadan 76.3 percent of holdings reporting perennial crops sell nothing to the market, and only 3.7 percent market half or more of their produce (Plan Organization, Statistical Center 1977:table 8).

Regional variations in sales of annual crops are even more pronounced. In Mazandaran and Gorgan only 19.1 percent of holdings reporting annual crops do not sell to the market, and 50.0 percent market half or more of their produce. This reflects the dominance in this area of Iran of such cash crops as cotton, oil seeds, and rice. In Gilan, where rice and tobacco are cultivated, only 26.3 percent of holdings reporting annual crops do not sell to the market, whereas 49.2 percent market half or more of their produce. On the other hand, in Sistan and Baluchistan, two of the most backward areas of the country, 85.5 percent of holdings reporting annual crops sell nothing to the market, and only 4.4 percent market half or more of their produce (Plan Organization, Statistical Center 1977:table 8).

Marketing trends according to holding size need careful attention and discussion. Here, I will present the data for annual crops only (table 23), since no significant difference appears when one compares these data with those for perennial crops (Plan Organization, Statistical Center 1977:table 9).

The first noticeable correlation is that a higher percentage of sale to the market occurs among the small farms of under five hectares than among holdings of five to ten hectares. As already noted, this is in part because of the predominance of rice fields among small holdings: of all holdings smaller than one hectare and reporting annual crops, 32.3 percent of the land is under rice cultivation. For holdings of one to two hectares reporting annual crops, 34.3 percent is under rice cultivation. For holdings of two to five hectares the figure falls to 11.7 percent; for those of five to ten hectares, it is only 2.1 percent; and for holdings of more than ten hectares the figure finally drops to less than 1 percent (Plan Organization, Statistical Center 1977:tables 15 and 188).

From field reports and individual village studies, it seems possible to ascertain the workings of another factor: for very tiny plots, less than one hectare, there seems to be little point in trying to produce annual crops for the market except on land near the large cities. On somewhat larger plots, an optimum seems to be reachable by concentration on cash crops, while for plots of five to ten hectares — widely agreed to be the size of family plots in most areas of Iran —

TABLE 23
Percentage of Sale of Annual Crops to the Market,
by Size of Holding, 1974

Size of Holding (ha.)	% Not Selling Any Produce	% Selling Less Than Half of Produce	% Selling Half or More of Produce
0–1	55.5	25.9	18.6
1–2	39.5	28.5	32.0
2–5	51.1	26.6	22.3
5–10	59.2	26.5	14.3
10–50	48.4	28.2	23.4
50–100	1.0	1.9	97.1
100 +	3.0	0.2	96.8
All holdings	51.0	26.7	22.3

Source: Plan Organization, Statistical Center 1977: table 9.

self-consumption rather than market production seems to provide a better overall satisfaction of family needs. This trend reverses itself only for plots larger than ten hectares. Not surprisingly, farms of more than fifty hectares produce overwhelmingly for the market. In other words, market orientation is more significant on holdings that are just below and well above what a family needs to be self-sustaining.

As pointed out earlier, the very sharp difference in marketing behavior between farms smaller than fifty hectares and those of fifty hectares or more seems to be a statistical problem, arising from the nature of the ten-to-fifty hectare size category. The majority of holdings in the ten-to-fifty-hectare category fall in the ten-to-twenty hectare group, as comparison with the 1960 data would indicate (see table 14). This phenomenon is also reflected in the average size of seventeen and one-half hectares for plots in this range, of which only ten hectares are under cultivation in annual crops, while more than seven hectares are left fallow or are marginally allocated to perennial crops and fodder (see Plan Organization 1977:table 15). Although farmers working plots greater than ten hectares tend to be more market oriented, there is still a high degree of production for direct consumption in the lower bracket of this group. Only holdings of fifty hectares or more could be said to be wholly oriented to the market. Indeed, it is surprising, at first glance, to find that 1 to 3 percent of farms of fifty hectares and more do not sell to the market at all. This is explicable by the existence of agro-industrial units, whose farming output is used solely for production input.[11]

In terms of overall marketed surplus, the small holdings (less than ten hectares), which account for 82 percent of all cultivated land (see table 20) and produce 41 percent of the gross agriculture output, provide only 5 percent of the marketed output (table 24).[12] The bulk of marketed produce comes from farms of ten hectares and larger.

Unfortunately, a finer breakdown of contributions to marketed output according to farm size does not exist for farms in the greater-than-ten-hectare category. One can broadly delineate three groups. The first of these comprises peasant producers who received large enough tracts of land under the reform program — or who rent extra land on a fifty-fifty arrangement — to enable them to run viable commercial units. These holdings depend primarily on family labor and make incremental small investments in irrigation, improved seeds, and fertilizers. This group, as we will discuss shortly, has succeeded both in expanding its production substantially and in improving its standard of living. A second group consists of the capitalist farms proper, which belong to former landlords who, in many cases even before the advent of land reform, have begun to mechanize their farms and replace sharecroppers with paid workers. The exemption of mechanized farms from land reform gave a further impetus to this development. In more recent years, a significant number of urban investors and industrialists joined this sector of former landlords who have now become gentleman farmers. The final group of commercial agriculturalists is made up of the large agro-industrial complexes, a post-1965 phenomenon.

It is the first two groups of commercial farms — peasant producers and individual capitalist farming enterprises — that Kaneda (1973:24–25) refers to in his ILO report as the "viable" subsector: "(1) 50,000 orchardists farming 200,000 ha. of fruit, (2) 15,000 farmers, each with a holding of 15 ha. or more, (3) 30,000 to 50,000 former village owners who are assumed to have chosen to remain in farming, operating from 600,000 to 1.2 million hectares." A 1975 report prepared by a World Bank mission for the Agricultural Development Bank of Iran refers, in a similar vein, to the commercial sector of Iranian agriculture, representing about 20 percent of the

TABLE 24
Share of Gross and Marketed Output, 1972

Size of Holding (ha.)	% of Farms or Families	% of Land	% Gross Output (value added)	% Marketed Output
300 +	<0.01	2	2	5
10–300	18	63	50	80
0–10	60	35	41	5
Migrant herdsmen and landless peasants	22	0	7	10

Source: Bookers Agricultural and Technical Services Ltd. and Hunting Technical Services Ltd. 1974:vol. 2, annex 5, table 5.4.

farmers and some 70 percent of the land. This report gives somewhat different figures from the Bookers-Hunting report, allocating 77 percent of the marketed surplus to farms of more than ten hectares (Price 1975:14, 22).

As far as the peasant commodity producers are concerned, income growth as high as 300 percent has been reported in the postreform years (Saedloo 1978:116). Some of these peasants were already well-off members of the village community before the reform, but as Kielstra (1975:250) notes, "Before the Landreform, . . . they had few possibilities to invest their money. The only way of investment was to enlarge their flocks. After the Landreform they used their financial reserves to buy a tractor and two pumps and to buy or rent large tracts of land."

Investment in water pumps and tube wells became one of the more prevalent forms of small-scale agricultural capital formation in the postreform period. Along with the price of labor for a peasant and his family, irrigation costs form one of the most substantial current expenditures on peasant-owned farms. One study of the province of Kerman, for instance, indicates irrigation costs ranging from 5.2 percent to 43.1 percent of all current expenditure, with a 25.5 percent average for the province (MCRA 1975e:table 2.4). The qanat, the underground water canal system, has long been an important source of irrigation in Iran. Although water rights were transferred along with land during the reform, the upkeep of qanats required collective decisions and large expenditures on the part of whole villages, and in some cases local cooperatives took over such supervision. Nevertheless, in many places the qanats have fallen into disrepair. Moreover, the more prosperous peasants, using favorable loans from the Agricultural Bank, could afford to sink new wells, which would give them a secure source of water all year round. Former landlords and new capitalist entrepreneurs have also sunk deep wells. Increased reliance on these wells has lowered water tables substantially, making qanat irrigation even less viable and further accelerating the use of tube wells and water pumps. This change became so widespread that a new word was introduced into the Persian agrarian vocabulary: farmers relying on new irrigation methods became known as *tolombe-karan*, that is, pump-operating farmers.

> Tolombe-karan are members of the highest social class [in the village] and cultivate relatively large areas. Family property and additional leased land comprise on the average 15.2 hectares. The tolombe-karan have in general a market orientation and cultivate for the most part sugar-cane and other saleable crops. Their average annual income is estimated at roughly US-Dollars 2,000 per household. The foodstuff consumption per family absorbs only about 44% of their overall production. Thus, a corresponding sum remains to cover the current running and investment costs of their agricultural activity (Ule 1973:114).[13]

Another group that belongs to the category of peasant commodity producers is the large layer of nesfe-karan, referred to earlier. What spurred the growth of these farmers in the postreform period was the availability of land to rent. Agricultural land had become "free" from precapitalist "burdens." Peasants who received land could now rent it out; sharecropping was no longer the sole means of making a living from land. Landlords who kept land through exemptions or by buying the use-right claims of their peasants were no longer subject to such claims, and they were no longer bound to sharecrop their land. They now could rent their holdings out to entrepreneurial farmers.

A further factor that spurred the growth of these farmers was the fast development of urban-industrial centers, which increased the demand for food and industrial crops, as well as for improved and expanded roads and communication networks. The rapid growth of a market-oriented segment of the peasantry was also reflected in both the increasing separation of animal husbandry from crop cultivation and the decreasing importance of traditional handicrafts. The family labor previously allocated to such diverse activities could now be more profitably concentrated on intensive crop production for the market.

Livestock Production and Other Income Sources

Traditionally, peasant family subsistence was supplemented by keeping a few sheep and goats and in some areas by the production of handicrafts. These subsidiary activities partly satisfied home consumption needs and partly provided the family's necessary cash income through the sale of handicrafts and dairy products. More urgent cash needs could be met through the sale of animals. A survey of rural families, carried out in the mid-1960s, shows that in certain regions of the country as much as 30–45 percent of total family income came from livestock production. On the other hand, handicraft production contributed significantly only in areas known for carpet weaving, such as Kashan (Vadi'i 1973:89–90).

Livestock production continues to be an important source of supplementary income for peasant landowners, but since the land reform and the accompanying act that nationalized all forests and pastures, the use of what earlier were considered common pastures has come under the strict supervision of the Forestry Office. Consequently, natural pastures have been leased by the state as large tracts to commercial livestock ventures. The cash rent demanded by the Forestry Office, the minimum area set for such leases, and the bureaucracy involved in acquiring them have made natural pastures less and less accessible to peasant families. As a result, many peasants have sold their livestock and turned to wage labor for supplementary cash income. Reports prepared by the Ministry of Cooperatives and Rural Affairs have noted the sharp decline in animal husbandry:

> In the region covered by Varleh Cooperative, because of good natural pastures, animal husbandry used to be common. Not only did it provide dairy needs of [peasant] families, it was also a source of income both for farming and *khoshneshin* families. In recent years, because of restrictions imposed on the use of such pastures—in order to preserve natural resources—such activities have declined. The questionnaires filled by our sample families indicate that the number of their animals in 1353 [1974] is half that of 1351 [1972]. (MCRA 1975c:54–55)[14]

A *Tehran Economist* article, discussing "rural depopulation," noted with alarm:

> One of the reasons that farmers are abandoning villages and are coming to cities lies in the behavior of the Forestry Office. They [the FO] believe they are implementing the principle of nationalization of forests and pastures, whereas this principle is more sacred than what they understand.
>
> They do not permit the peasants to graze their sheep even in the barren plains. This causes peasants to sell their sheep cheaply to butchers, and since they can no longer make ends meet, they take refuge in the cities. Villages are now inhabited only by old and disabled people who cannot do anything. (*Tehran Economist*, August 27, 1977)

The decline in subsidiary animal husbandry is also reflected in the sharp increase of holdings without any livestock. Although the agricultural censuses of 1960 and 1974 do not provide us with strictly comparable data, the general tendency of decline in livestock production as a joint activity is evident (table 25). In 1960, 49.3 percent of holdings smaller than 1 hectare reported no sheep or goats. By 1974, 70.7 percent of these holdings reported no sheep, and 68.7 percent reported no goats. The figures for holdings of 1–2 hectares are similar. The sharp rise in very large holdings reporting no sheep or goats—for holdings of 100 hectares or larger the increase is from 24 percent in 1960 to some 60 percent in 1974—reflects deepening specialization and separation of farming from livestock production in this category. This is further confirmed by the rise in the average number of sheep per holding to 590.4. Similarly, in 1960, 53.3 percent of holdings under 1 hectare reported no cows or oxen, whereas in 1974, 66.2 percent of such holdings reported none of either. Figures for holdings of 1–2 hectares were 25.3 percent in 1960 and 46.1 percent in 1974. The very large increase in the percentage of holdings reporting no cows or oxen in the group of larger holdings reflects, most probably, the decreasing importance of oxen for plowing purposes, as the use of tractors has become more and more widespread.

While fewer animals are raised on smaller holdings because of restrictions stemming from the nationalization of pasture lands, more of such holdings have to allocate larger tracts of agricultural land to cultivation of fodder plants (table 26). Although the increase is not appreciable in holdings of less than one hectare, where the very small

TABLE 25
Animal Stocks per Holding, by Size of Holding, 1960 and 1974

Size of Holding (ha.)	1960				1974							
	% of Holdings with No Sheep or Goats	Average No. of Sheep and Goats (Holdings Reporting Either)	% of Holdings with No Cows or Oxen	Average No. of Cows and Oxen (Holdings Reporting Either)	% of Holdings with No Sheep	% of Holdings with No Goats	Average No. of Sheep (Holdings Reporting Sheep)	Average No. of Goats (Holdings Reporting Goats)	% of Holdings with No Cows	% of Holdings with No Oxen	Average No. of Cows (Holdings Reporting Cows)	Average No. of Oxen (Holdings Reporting Oxen)
0–1	49.3	14.2	53.3	2.3	70.7	68.7	11.2	7.8	66.2	99.0	2.8	4.3
1–2	52.4	18.1	25.3	2.6	70.2	72.2	12.9	10.2	46.1	98.0	3.0	2.4
2–5	40.1	19.4	17.0	3.1	57.9	60.8	14.3	10.2	41.6	96.7	3.1	2.8
5–10	27.3	23.8	7.4	3.5	44.4	49.6	18.8	10.7	41.0	96.7	3.4	2.9
10–50	21.4	31.0	9.1	5.7	36.6	44.1	29.3	11.4	41.3	96.7	4.1	2.9
50–100	28.6	97.0	7.1	9.9	47.9	59.5	102.5	17.2	53.4	96.9	6.8	5.8
100+	24.4	176.0	14.6	26.1	60.4	67.7	590.4	39.8	65.6	97.9	25.6	13.5

Sources: OAS 1960: tables 117, 118, and 120; Plan Organization, Statistical Center 1977:tables 15, 245, 247, 249, and 251.

TABLE 26
Land under Fodder, by Size of Holding, 1960 and 1974

Size of Holding, (ha.)	% of Holdings with Land under Fodder		Average Size of Land under Fodder (ha.)	
	1960	1974	1960	1974
0–1	12.0	13.1	0.09	0.13
1–2	14.3	23.8	0.16	0.22
2–5	19.1	37.2	0.22	0.34
5–10	30.9	50.4	0.33	0.59
10–50	30.7	57.6	0.65	1.09
50–100	19.0	52.1	1.94	3.66
100 +	14.6	45.8	4.83	14.20

Source: OAS 1960:table 107; Plan Organization, Statistical Center 1977:table 15.

size of the holding prevents such flexibility, among the 1–2-hectare group of holdings 23.8 percent had, on the average, allocated 0.22 hectares to fodder in 1974 as compared with 14.3 percent devoting an average of 0.16 hectares to fodder in 1960. Similar increases can be seen for larger holdings. For very large holdings of more than 50 hectares and particularly for those of more than 100 hectares, the increase in area under fodder cultivation reflects the rise in large-scale combined animal husbandry and dairy production complexes that produce and consume their own fodder.

Livestock production on most peasant-owned farms continues to be mostly for household consumption. In 1974 among holdings of 10 hectares or less, for instance, only between 6 and 11 percent of the household that reported raising sheep or goats—both are more common in Iran than cows—marketed half or more of their produce. The percentage rose to 13.3 percent for 10–50-hectare holdings and to 25.2 percent and 31.6 percent for 50–100-hectare holdings and over 100-hectare holdings, respectively (Plan Organization 1977:table 11).

An additional reason for the general decline of livestock production, as well as for declining handicraft production—although statistical data according to household categories are not available for this—is that more family labor is now put into the intensive cultivation of small holdings. Prior to the land reform, the small farmer knew that if he made an extra effort, most of the income obtained would go to the owners, while the handicrafts were his. In the postreform period, he has both the incentive and the compulsion to put more family labor into his land: he will own the product, he has a smaller holding and a higher cash need, and goods manufactured in urban centers are on balance cheaper than rural handicrafts. Indeed, the only handicraft in Iran that has survived and expanded enormously is carpet making. Here is a typical example:

> He [a farmer in a village near the town of Shahi, owning 1½ ha] has increased the production of wheat for household consumption while using his rice and vegetable production for cash. Vegetables, such as lettuce, tomatoes, and cucumbers have been added to his gardens primarily for cash sales. Time that his wife might once have spent in weaving cloth or reed mats is now spent on the cultivation and sale of vegetables. . . . The Mehrabad family is rather typical of the trend by peasant farmers to devote more time to subsistence-cash farming and less time on other forms of cash acquisition such as hand crafts and trading livestock. The trend away from craft production has been encouraged by the increasing availability of cheap manufactured cloth and plastics . . . In 1972, a weaver received between 130 and 450 rials for a 9 × 12 square feet piece of cloth. A cloth of similar size from the mills of Yazd could be bought for between 50 and 200 rials. (Thompson 1976:239)

Similar accounts are given in MCRA reports (see, for instance, MCRA 1975b)

Instead of crafts and animal husbandry, peasant families with small plots of land have turned increasingly to wage labor to supplement farm income. Seasonal agricultural employment as well as unskilled construction work in urban-industrial centers have provided additional income that sometimes constitutes more than half of a family's net earnings. The United Arab Emirates, and Qatar, Bahrain, and Kuwait have also proved attractive to villagers from certain parts of Iran.

There are no overall statistics on the relative weight of earnings derived from wage labor for various groups of Iran's peasantry. Still, all village reports refer to this phenomenon of combined earnings. They also invariably refer to the small size of landholdings as the reason for these partial migrations. Although there has been some selling off of land to more prosperous peasants by small holders (Moghadem 1977:42–43), the dominant trend is for peasant families to hold onto the land even when the family has given up cultivation for the time being. In some instances the land is left fallow, but more often the land is rented to other peasants or to relatives in return for a share of the crop. Often the family may continue to reside in its village, while male members commute daily or seasonally to employment centers. A few examples will illustrate this newly emerging complex network of social relations.

One excellent study of three villages near Isfahan gives the following picture (Alvandi and Rostami 1979). Of the 210 families, 69 are wholly engaged as workers with no agricultural activities, although they continue to reside in these villages. Another 47 families have holdings of less than 0.9 hectares. Of these, 41 families depend on wage labor in addition to the cultivation of their own land. Of the 80 families who have holdings of between 0.9 and 5 hectares, 32 depend on wage labor in addition to farming their land. Of the rest, 46 families have only one member actively working in agriculture, either because of the small size of the family or because other members are at school. One family rents land from others, and another owns two tractors and earns additional income from hiring them out. Only 11 families have more than 5 hectares of land. Ten of these work solely on their own land. Among the families who are engaged in both wage labor and farming, over 50 percent of cash income comes from wages. The authors of this study conclude that it is the extremely small size of landholdings and not the relatively high urban wages that forces peasant landowners into wage labor; families in the same conditions but with larger holdings employ all their family labor in farming.

Another study, carried out in the province of Hamadan, similarly indicated that peasants who migrated in the postreform years had held, on the average, 2.0 hectares of irrigated land and 1.3 hectares of rain-fed land, while the average holdings of peasants who had stayed in farming was 4.6 hectares of irrigated land and 4.1 hectares of rain-fed land (Ajami 1978:11).

Others report similar conditions. Hooglund (1975:139) found that all peasants who cultivated less than 4.5 hectares, as well as various members of their households, had to seek wage employment — in this case as seasonal agricultural laborers on the lands of larger proprietors. Ashraf reports that in the village of Kafshgar-kola, 80 percent of peasant proprietors have too little land and depend partly on nonfarm income (Ashraf 1973:27). In villages studied by Kielstra

(1975:73) in the southern province of Fars, "migrant labour [to Kuwait and the Gulf states] is now more important as a source of income than agriculture, and amounts to more than half of the total income of the villagers." In a village near Qazvin, income from farming constitutes only 21 percent of the total income of the villagers, while wage labor contributes 34 percent and small businesses 22 percent of total income, with another 23 percent derived from livestock production (Mahdavi 1982:62). Another study of villages near Hamadan reported that out of 501 male heads of families engaged in agriculture, 136 have other jobs as well (MCRA 1974a:table 9). Another regional study, on the province of Yazd, reported that 62 percent of the income of poorer rural families came from nonagricultural sources. In the middle-income category, 54 percent of income came from nonagricultural sources, while for the upper 10 percent of income groups, the percentage of nonagricultural income was 29 percent (MCRA 1975b).[15]

Labor migrations of this type are predominantly seasonal and partial. They are partial in the sense that the peasant household sends one or two young male members to seek urban employment, while the rest of the household continues to work the land. Often the male members return to the village during harvest time, or if they live near industrial centers, they combine agriculture with industrial employment. This phenomenon shows itself both at an aggregate level in population census data, as well as in village reports.

The 1974 Agricultural Census reveals that for all age categories and all holding sizes the female population is less than the male with the following exceptions: the age category 20–39 years for all holdings and also the age category 12–19 years for landed holdings of less than 2 hectares (table 27). For these two categories only, the female population is larger than the male. Part of this difference in the 20–39 year age category is due to compulsory military service for the young males. It is noticeable, however, that the relative difference between females and males even in this age category changes with land size: from 15–18 percent more women in the holdings of less than 10 hectares to 10–13 percent in the holdings larger than 10 hectares. In other words, in the smaller holdings a larger percentage of the young males are absent from the village. This would appear to reflect their greater need to find urban employment. The larger num-

TABLE 27
Ratio of Male to Female Rural Population (Ten Years of Age and Over),
by Size of Holding and Age Group

Size of Holding (ha.)	10–11 Years	12–19 Years	20–39 Years	40–64 Years	65 Years and Older
0[a]	1.17	1.04	0.85	1.26	1.25
0–1	1.35	0.95	0.84	1.17	1.24
1–2	1.29	0.96	0.82	1.29	1.39
2–5	1.19	1.06	0.82	1.28	1.20
5–10	1.25	1.29	0.85	1.26	1.27
10–50	1.32	1.18	0.90	1.20	1.61
50–100	1.08	1.14	0.90	1.23	1.43
100 +	1.01	1.02	0.87	1.33	1.16
All holders	1.26	1.07	0.85	1.24	1.32

Source: Plan Organization, Statistical Center 1977:table 3.
[a]Landless holders engaged in animal husbandry, etc.

ber of females in the 12–19-year age category in the landed holdings below 2 hectares would also seem to reflect this need.

If the family does not have enough working adults to farm its land, the land is often let to other peasants, preferably to close relatives, in exchange for a share of the final crop. In Hamadan, 40 percent of the peasants migrating to cities had sold their land, and 22 percent had their land worked by relatives. Another 13 percent had rental agreements with working peasants, and the remaining 15 percent had made fifty-fifty or similar arrangements (Ajami 1978:12).

In the Baluchi villages of Khash, 34 percent of the peasants had let their land and left for other employment (Azkia, et al. 1976:23–24). According to an MCRA report on migration, in Marun, 29 out of 60 peasants with holdings of less than 3 hectares had let their land on fifty-fifty sharecropping arrangements while working at nearby industrial projects; 64 out of 124 peasants in Gach karan, 143 out of 220 peasants in Fahlian, and 156 out of 237 peasants in Ouch-Tappeh with small holdings made similar arrangements (MCRA 1974c:2–40). In other cases, such agreements have been reported, but in these the crop share going to the nonoperating peasants ranged from one-fifth to two-thirds (MCRA 1974c:41; Kielstra 1975:65).

In Kamround of Ferdows . . . when there is not enough water and less human labor is needed in the *sahra* [the local expression for the work group], two members [out of four] of the *sahra* go to town and after a few months of wage labor in town come back to the village with some savings. They divide equally among all four the total income from farming and that from wage labor in town. (Saedloo 1980:797)

What allows this particular arrangement of satisfying cash and crop needs of the peasantry is, of course, the existence of old working groups, boneh, in Iranian villages.

Peasant Working Groups and Land Fragmentation

As explained in chapter 4, the common practice in Iranian villages was for several peasants to work together throughout each working season and receive their shares of harvest according to preset agreements. The village farmland was not demarcated according to individual use rights, nor even according to each boneh but, rather, according to crops. In other words, certain areas would be allocated to wheat, barley, and so forth, according to the decision of either the landlord or his representative in the village. Within the wheat area, each boneh would be allocated its strip of land to work and harvest. A peasant with land-use rights, a nasaqdar, belonging to boneh A would, therefore, have use rights to a fraction of land planted in wheat worked by boneh A, and to another fraction of land in barley also worked by boneh A, and so on. The land reform provision that each nasaqdar peasant would receive the land to which he held use rights during the year in which the reform was implemented meant that each peasant received many tiny pieces of land. Under the circumstances, the existence of the traditional group working units offered an immediate way of overcoming extreme land fragmentation by allowing peasants to continue working the land in larger plots. Such working units also provided the possibility of the joint cash-and-crop agreements among groups of peasants, discussed above. The whole arrangement is therefore an anomaly resulting from the mesh of traditional arrangements and the inflexibility of the land reform program.

Land fragmentation is a serious problem for peasant families attempting to establish commercially viable units. Unlike nesfe-karan,

TABLE 28
Number of Plots per Holding, by Size of Holding

Size of Holding (ha.)	No. of Plots per Holding	Average Size of Each Plot, (ha.)
Under 1	3.4	0.1
1–2	5.7	0.3
2–5	8.6	0.4
5–10	12.5	0.7
10–50	17.5	1.2
50–100	18.3	4.2
100 and over	14.6	16.6
Country average	8.5	0.8

Source: Plan Organization, Statistical Center 1973:table 5.

who often rent land from large landlords in one plot, the peasant recipients of land under the reform hold their land in many small plots. The 1974 Agricultural Census does not give any information on land fragmentation, but an earlier sample survey gives an indication of this problem (table 28).[16]

No overall survey is available to indicate in what direction and through what arrangements the peasants who received land in such fragments have been trying to overcome this problem. From specific village studies it is clear that a certain amount of land swapping is taking place. In other circumstances the group work units have provided a way of overcoming the fragmentation problem.

Still, there seems to be a tendency toward the gradual dissolution of the group work units wherever the land allotments are large enough to allow individual cultivation. This tendency seems to be more pronounced near large towns where cultivation of summer vegetables and other cash crops, as well as the cultivation of orchards, have provided an incentive for individual peasants to separate their plots (Saedloo 1980:798–800).

Some examples can further clarify this picture. In the village of Talebabad, Safi-nejad found a clear tendency to dissolve the work units. Immediately after the reform the peasants of the village formed themselves into fifteen units, each composed of four households and covering 14 to 16 hectares. Each peasant household had received 3.5–4 hectares. Gradually these units were divided into smaller ones. By 1974 there were 36 individual units, 9 units of two households

TABLE 29
Work Units and Households in Talebabad, 1965–1974

Agricultural Years	No. of Households in Work Units				Total No. of Work Units	Total of House- holds
	4	3	2	1		
1965–66	15	0	0	0	15	60
1966–67	9	0	10	4	23	60
1967–68	5	1	16	5	27	60
1968–69	4	1	18	5	28	60
1969–70	4	1	16	9	30	60
1970–71	4	1	14	13	32	60
1971–72	3	2	14	14	33	60
1972–73	1	2	16	18	37	60
1973–74	0	2	9	36	47	60

Source: Safe-nejad 1974:tables 28–30.

each and 2 units of three households each (table 29). Salmanzadeh reports a similar tendency in villages in the Dezful area of Khuzistan:

> Until 1972–73 Bonvar Hossein farmers were organized in six *bonkus* [the local expression for boneh] (four *jufts* per *bonku*), but thereafter they have organized smaller, two *juft-bonkus* [12 *bonkus*]. *Bonku* membership varied from two to four . . . probably half the membership of the original four *juft-bonku*. Within each *bonku*, farmers with half a *juft* each usually join together and farm their plot as a unit, while a farmer with one *juft* in the same *bonku* would farm independently. In Bonvar Hossein and, most probably, in other villages which have remained traditional, the recent tendency for small *bonkus* is said locally to be because it is "easier to get along with fewer people." There are certainly other factors. Demand for village communal labour has fallen with the introduction of the irrigation scheme and as other changes have occurred in agriculture. Thus the impetus for larger groupings has vanished. (Salmanzadeh 1980:178–179)

According to an MCRA study, on the other hand, each peasant in the village of Husseinabad before the land reform had access to almost twice as much land as afterward. During the reform former landlords remained the owners of 35 hectares of land, while about 45 hectares were sold to sixty families. Their plots ranged from 0.2 to 2.5 hectares each distributed as follows: 26.7 percent between 0.2 and 0.7 hectares, 55 percent between 0.7 and 1.2 hectares, 13.3 percent between 1.2 and 1.6 hectares, and 5 percent between 2.1 and

2.5 hectares. Before the reform each nasaq was composed of ten to thirty pieces. After the reform one of the first things the peasants did was to pool all the land together and reorganize it into four large areas, two of which were allocated to cereal production and the other two to summer crops. There were six work units, called *taq* in this region, composed of seven to twelve farmers each. Each work unit had one area in each of the four plots allocated to it. In fact, then, each holding is composed of only four pieces. The four large areas are mapped so that each *taq* has access to two pieces of cereal land and two pieces of summer crop land, one of each of which is close to a water source (MCRA 1968).

A number of studies carried out by the Ministry of Cooperatives and Rural Affairs report similar regroupments after the land reform. One report states that in the Neishapur area, even in villages where there had been a gradual falling apart of work teams for a number of years, there has been a renewed interest in reviving these units to overcome the problems of fragmentation and the small size of each individual holding (MCRA 1974c:13–14, 38, 107).[17]

Even though the small farmers and the commercial peasant producers differ in their relation to the market, in their dependence on paid employment and other sources of income, and, to a degree, in their individual or group working organization, both groups are deeply integrated into the national market. Moreover, they share one very important characteristic: both depend primarily on family labor in agricultural production.

Family versus Paid Labor in Agricultural Production

According to table 21 of the 1976 National Census (Plan Organization, Statistical Center 1981), out of 2,747,800 rural inhabitants engaged in agriculture, 1,582,000 were "own-account workers," 573,700 were unpaid family workers, 540,800 were paid workers, 26,700 were employers, and 22,700 were state employees. Excluding the latter two categories, this means that out of the total labor force engaged in agricultural production, paid labor constituted 20 percent. This figure is lower, both relatively and absolutely, than the corresponding figure in 1966. In 1966 table 19 of the census results revealed a total of 2,940,100 engaged in agriculture, of which

1,701,100 were own-account workers, 504,600 unpaid family labor, and 684,300 paid workers. Employers counted for 37,800 and there were only 3,400 state employees. Paid labor, consequently, counted for 23.7 percent of the total agricultural labor force in 1966.

This shift in composition of the rural labor force is a direct result of land reform. Once it became evident that agricultural laborers and peasants with no land-use rights were not entitled to receive land, they had little reason to stay in the countryside if instead they could find urban-industrial employment. On the other hand, peasant proprietors had good reason for holding as firmly as possible onto family labor. The breakdown of landholdings according to their size and the form of labor clearly indicates the predominance of family labor in all holdings of up to 50 hectares (see table 19).

There is a very small percentage of farms under 50 hectares on which most or all farm labor is done by paid workers: 4.2 to 7.3 percent. Most probably such farms, particularly the smaller ones, are orchards or other perennial crop cultivations which often depend on employed labor, regardless of their size. The fact that only 7.3 percent of holdings within the 10–50-hectare size predominantly use employed labor can be explained by our previous observation that the majority of such farms are within a 10–20 hectare range. In other words, they are family-size plots. What is more problematic in the 1974 census data is the very large percentage of holdings above 50 hectares that depend solely or mostly on family labor: 63.2 percent among 50–100 hectare holdings, and 36.1 percent among holdings of 100 hectares and more. This, we have argued, could make sense only if such holdings are rented out by farmer families as smaller sublet holdings.

Of course, there is no uniformity on the village scale. According to all reports, larger producers often employ members of households with small holdings, or the landless khoshneshins, on a seasonal basis, especially for certain crops and jobs that require intensive seasonal labor (for example, cotton picking), while the poorer households have little or no land on which all members can work, and so they release paid labor to larger holdings as well as to capitalist units. Okazaki (1969:274–275) gives a vivid picture of this differentiation between villagers among the employers of agricultural labor and the employees in a northeastern village:

These eight households [employing nondomestic wage labor and in possession of tobacco and cotton lands in excess of 3 hectares] are, furthermore, responsible for the hiring of most of the seasonal labor employed in the village for cotton and tobacco growing: fourteen out of the eighteen cotton share-cropping families in the village are employed by them, and the entire force of fifteen female laborers engaged on a seasonal basis to work the tobacco crops is in the employ of these eight large planters, hired to supplement a limited domestic female labor force of some fifteen women available to these planters. In addition to the seasonal labor force enumerated above, these same eight households employ a sizable number of day-laborers during the busy season. . . . Whatever the particular form it takes, however, it is clear that wage-compensated, non-domestic labor is absolutely essential to the cotton and tobacco economy of the larger-scale peasants of Shirang-sofla. . . . The situation of the small peasants is quite the reverse. None of the six households in the group 18–23 are able to hire any wage labor at all; quite the contrary, with the single exception of household 20 (a widow), each of the households in this category serve as providers of labor.

Most peasant producers seem to prefer paying wages in kind, that is, either as a share of the harvest or as a fixed amount at the end of harvest. If the laborer participates in most of the agricultural work throughout the season, his share may be as high as one-third of his output (Azkia et al. 1976). Even when hiring agricultural machinery, producers prefer to pay in kind:

For ploughing, the rental of the tractor was paid in cash, but the rental fees of the combine, the thresher and milling machines were all paid as a share of crop, even in areas where commercial agriculture was widespread. For threshing the rate was 5 per cent . . . , for harvesting wheat and barley by a combine, depending on output per hectare and the state of the land, it varied between one-twelfth and one-eighth of the harvest. (Fallah 1982:118)

It must be noted that the preference for payment in kind is also reflected in the peasants' attitude toward the cooperatives. The most common complaint against the co-op is that peasants cannot pay in kind for goods or for credit at the time of harvest. So they continue to turn to local shopkeepers and moneylenders even though in purely monetary terms dealings with them are far less advantageous to the peasants.

This preference for minimizing household monetary needs probably stems to some extent from the lack of easy credit, but more important, it results from the insecurity that peasants feel about prices, a factor out of their control that has traditionally been loaded against them. Most frequently it has been either the landlord or his manager, in prereform times, or the local shopkeeper and middlemen buying the harvest who traditionally have held the strong hand in fixing prices.

Of course, closely related to the question of paid versus family labor is the extent of mechanization in Iranian agriculture. Not only do small and medium-size landholders try to minimize paid, and particularly cash paid, labor, they also have little reason to replace family labor with machines. The primary reason for both phenomena is that the family can find very little alternative employment. The price of its labor is zero, as far as the household is concerned, so it might as well be engaged on the family farm as an alternative to paying for someone else's labor or investing in machines.

For example, according to a Plan Organization study, nonmechanized irrigated wheat and barley cultivation takes 47 to 56 man-days per hectare. Using tractors for plowing reduces this figure to 30 to 37 man-days per hectare, while complete mechanization reduces it to only 19 days per hectare (Saedloo 1974:37–52). For machinery to make any economic sense to the peasant, he should be able to cover the costs through alternative employment of family labor released from agricultural work, to increase output per hectare sufficiently to make up for additional costs, or to reduce overall costs in other ways.[18] This is why, for instance, peasants use tractors but do not invest in threshers and harvesters. The use of tractors saves on the cost of draft animals, and, as we have seen, the upkeep and hire of livestock became more costly in the aftermath of the nationalization of pastures, as actual crop land had to be allocated to fodder. Even villagers whose traditional occupation was to keep oxen to be rented out for farm work (gavbands) increasingly sold their animals and bought tractors. In this case, mechanization made real economic sense in the given social setting and was not an abstraction built purely on the economy of labor time. Labor-days saved through use of threshers and harvesters earned no other cash and did not reduce costs. They represented a net loss which was by no means compensated for by the extra "leisure" time of the family's women and children. Here is one example from a village in Fars:

> Since the past few years a combine that does the harvesting and thresh-ing all at once can be hired from an entrepreneur in Lar. But the rent for the combine is rather high (200 Rials for each 50 *man* harvested that is worth 1200 Rials in the case of wheat and 800 Rials in the case of barley) and there is no profitable alternative employment for the labour saved by using a combine, therefore most groups prefer to do the harvesting by hand, especially in years when the harvest is not exceptionally good. (Kielstra 1975:64)

So long as there is no alternative secure employment available for the mass of the rural population, the solution of other subsidiary problems — for example, land fragmentation, credit, services, and so on — will not substantially change agricultural technique except where it leads to real savings in costs or to significant increases in output. Pure labor-saving considerations are not a factor.[19] This is why among all agricultural machinery, the use of the tractor is the change most welcomed by peasants, as already indicated. In 1960 only 4 percent of landholdings were fully mechanized and another 6 percent partly mechanized. Seventy-five percent used animal power exclusively. By 1974, 44 percent of all holdings used tractors for plowing. Even in the very small holdings, tractors have made their way (table 30).

Putting tractors aside, labor-saving machinery is used by large capitalist farms to reduce wage costs. But even here, because there is a mass of rural labor available at very low wages, mechanization is slow in coming. The fast growth in the use of tractors and tillers in contrast to the slow growth of other labor-saving machinery is reflected in the total number of sales per year by the Agricultural Machinery Development Organization (table 31).

Unlike the use of machinery, however, chemical fertilizers — which do not save labor but do increase output and, in fact, increase the demand for labor — have widespread use in all farm groups of what-ever size. Indeed, in Iran, as our data show, smaller farmers tend to use a relatively greater quantity of fertilizer, since it is one of the very few ways of increasing output. Total consumption of chemical fertilizers in Iran rose from fairly insignificant amounts in the 1950s to about 100,000 tons by the mid-1960s and to more than 600,000 tons by the mid-1970s, with fairly widespread use by all farming

TABLE 30
Percentage of Holdings and Area Using Tractors,
by Type of Farming Group, 1974

Farming Group	Size of Holding (ha.)	% of Holdings Using Tractors	% of Area Plowed by Tractors
Small farmers	0–5	29.3	33.0
Overlap	5–10	63.9	48.4
Commercial family farms	10–50	73.6	56.1
Overlap	50–100	91.4	73.0
Capitalist enterprises	100 +	96.3	82.9
Country average		43.6	56.3

Source: Plan Organization, Statistical Center 1977:tables 15, and 260.

groups. The last column in table 32 shows that small and medium-size farms use an even greater quantity of chemical fertilizer per hectare than very large enterprises.

Problems of Large-Scale Capitalist Farming in Iran

Penetration of capitalist production into agriculture faces particular problems distinct from those of other industries. For instance, the period of rotation of capital in agriculture is generally much longer than in industry. The reason for this is not only because land rent or purchase price requires a substantial portion of investment but also because there are built-in limitations to reducing the cycle of production through technological innovations. Generally, the result in agriculture is a lower annual rate of profit than in other industries. Similarly, various parts of the production process cannot be made to proceed simultaneously throughout the year by introducing new technical divisions and reorganizing labor.

More important, the nature of agricultural production poses structural problems for the constitution and reconstitution of the labor force. Part of the labor force is needed only seasonally. No capitalist will pay workers year round to be able to employ them only during part of the year. Also, unlike children of workers in towns, who tend to be the next generation of industrial workers, children of agricultural workers tend to migrate to urban centers. Capitalists in agriculture have to rely on peasant households releasing labor, seasonally as

TABLE 31

Agricultural Machinery Sold through the Agricultural Machinery Development Organization, 1967–1977

Year	Tractors	Tillers	Disc Harrows	Trailers	Seed Broadcasters	Fertilizer Broadcasters	Sprayers	Weeders
1967–1971	13,070	0	2,068	254	25	149	628	—
1972	5,787	1,166	911	661	31	90	1,155	4
1973	4,781	719	1,258	820	36	67	154	1
1974	7,561	3,525	1,829	321	62	130	248	3
1975	9,038	4,293	1,603	2,001	238	90	1,401	—
1976	7,458	4,803	1,088	1,677	25	43	308	—
1977	11,650	4,015	1,731	2,947	31	63	—	—

Source: Plan Organization, Statistical Center, *Statistical Yearbook of Iran* for 1967–1977, (Tehran).

TABLE 32
Consumption of Chemical Fertilizers, by Size of Farm, 1974

Farming Group	Size of Holding (ha.)	No. of Farms Using Chemical Fertilizers (thousands)	% of Farms Using Chemical Fertilizers[a]	Estimated Amount Used (kg per cultivated ha.)[b]
Small farms	0–5	585.2	45.1	451.3
Overlap	5–10	121.6	37.5	274.4
Commercial peasant farms	10–50	102.2	31.3	400.7
Overlap	50–100	7.0	51.5	239.6
Capitalist enterprises	100 +	5.4	64.8	212.6
Country average		821.4	41.7	344.5

Source: Plan Organization, Statistical Center 1977:tables 39, and 257.
[a]Calculated as percentage of all holdings reporting irrigated cultivation.
[b]No data are available giving the area in which fertilizers are used. Estimates have been made on the assumption that in each size group the same percentage of irrigated land under cultivation is fertilized as the percentage of the number of such holdings.

well as generationally, to provide them with workers. The very success of capitalist penetration of agriculture, however, erodes the peasant household that provides the agricultural labor force. Often capitalists have to create new peasants by giving land to agricultural workers.

Furthermore, the means of production in industry can be multiplied at will, whereas in agriculture the chief means of production, the soil, cannot be enlarged or extended merely with more capital. In industry, accumulation of capital can proceed independently of the concentration of capital; often it precedes the latter. A large quantity of capital may be formed or a large enterprise may be set up without necessarily forcing smaller enterprises out of business. In any case, the loss of small businesses occurs, in general, as a consequence and not as a precondition of the formation of large enterprises. On the contrary, in agriculture, as Kautsky (1970:216–218) has argued, where the land is held in small units, the most important factor of production, the land itself, can be acquired and consolidated only if many small proprietors are driven off first. That is, the disappearance of small producers is a precondition for the formation of large enterprise.

Moreover, in agriculture the advantages of large-scale production compared with that of smaller units are not as sharp and clear-cut as in industry. Enlargement of an industrial plant goes hand in hand with a growing concentration of production that entails such advantages as economies of scale, easier surveillance, and so forth. In agriculture the advantages are partially counteracted by the necessity of the vast geographical extension of production, making, for instance, supervision more difficult. On top of this, at least for the first generation of large capitalist farms, the "labor problem" poses a special difficulty: managers often have to depend for agricultural labor on the very same peasant whom they have expelled from the land. This problem hardly ever arises in industry for two reasons. First, the bankruptcy of small producers occurs after the establishment of large-scale manufacturing, as already pointed out. Second, because most workers come from the countryside, they are former peasants rather than former craftsmen. Former peasants, working as day laborers on land they still consider theirs, have many more reasons to disrupt production.[20]

Some of these problems were evident in Iranian agriculture. For instance, new forms of sharecropping as well as piece payments were used on capitalist farms to keep agricultural workers on the land: "Some of the landlords have set up mechanized agricultural and dairy farms on land they kept after the land reform. . . . They hire local villagers on a full-time or seasonal basis. . . . Sometimes, to keep rural workers happy, the landlord allows them to cultivate a small piece of land on a sharecropping basis" (Alvandi and Rostami 1979:34). Azkia et al. (1976:45–46) also report both sharecropping, in the form of payment of wages as a portion of what each worker harvests in one day, and piece work, in the form of cash wages in proportion to individual output per day, in the cotton fields of Gorgan.

Mahdavi (1982) reports similar piece-work arrangements on capitalist farms near Qazvin. Salmanzadeh (1980:33) reports a complicated arrangement worked out in one case on a sugar cane farm: "The amount harvested by each group [of cutters, team leader (*sohani*) and water man (*saqa*)] was recorded daily and each group member, including the *sohani* and the *saqa*, were paid every 15 days according to the formula: P = T (T + 26), where P is the payment in rials, T is the average amount of harvest per head (tonnage) and

26 is a fixed coefficient." He further notes that in 1973–1974 these payments amounted to about 231 rials (about $3) per day, 50 to 100 rials higher than the average wage paid to workers in the nearby agribusiness.[21]

For seasonal labor, women have also been employed during peak seasons (Gupta 1973:5).[22] But the major obstacle to the penetration of capitalist agriculture was the existence of a relatively large population of both subsistence peasants and petty commodity producers. Despite the rural-urban migrations of the 1960s and 1970s, the absolute number of rural households continued to increase. To make large tracts of land available for large-scale capitalist farms, clearing peasants off the land continues to be the only time-honored "solution." But under conditions of slow growth in industrial employment, any such large-scale "clearing-off" operations are extremely dangerous politically. Unlike the classical development of capitalism, the creation of "free laborers" in agriculture does not occur hand in hand with the creation of the demand for labor. The Iranian government, despite its eagerness to support and encourage development of capitalist agriculture, had to remain cautious on this ground.

Clearing-off operations were carried out selectively and intermittently. Pilot operations were carried out in Khuzistan beginning in the mid-1960s. As many as 5,317 landed families and 3,064 khoshneshin families were moved from the area covered by the irrigation canals of Dez Dam to make room for some six agribusinesses, covering 68,000 hectares (ADBI 1978:7–8). Only a small fraction of the families formerly working on this land were reemployed as day laborers on these complexes.[23] By the mid-1970s, some 300,000 hectares of land covered by irrigation canals from various dams were under lease to agribusiness (Ajami 1981:91).

The major push toward large-scale "land clearance" came with the increase in oil revenues and the review of all development plans in 1974–1975. In June 1975 the government passed legislation concerning the development of a total of 1.8 million hectares of land (irrigated cultivations covered a total of 6.1 million hectares in 1974) with irrigation networks of major high dams in twenty regions, called Agricultural Development Poles. Within each such region the government would prepare plans and build irrigation networks down to the tertiary canals and supervise the consolidation of all landholdings contained within the region. Minimum farm size permitted within the boundaries of a pole was set at 20 hectares for irrigated land and 50 hectares for mechanized farms. Smaller units would have to join to form a unit either on a private basis or under the supervision of the Ministry of Agriculture. Within each pole the Ministry of Agriculture would set the minimum level of investment required. The ministry would also initiate the formation of production cooperatives among peasants who were beneficiaries of land reform to help with initial capital investment. Those who failed to come up with the necessary capital or who were unwilling to participate in larger units were required to sell their land to the ministry. The ministry would combine such land to make large units for rental to companies or persons whose projects had been ratified.

If we remember that 82 percent of all landholdings in Iran, involving 2 million families, were under 10 hectares and a substantial portion of the 17 percent of holdings between 10 and 50 hectares was under 20 hectares, the massive scale of this projected development becomes evident. Not surprisingly, the government implemented the project with caution.[24] By 1978 only one Agricultural Development Pole, covering some 14,000 hectares around Mahabad, had been developed.

Aside from the problem of the physical presence of peasants on the land, which blocks the free entry of new capitalist enterprises into agriculture, the large peasant population poses a problem even for those former landlords with access to large land tracts who kept their land after the reform and who were, therefore, in a position to move to capitalist farming. From the point of view of both subsistence farmers and commodity producers, access to land is simply a means to make a living. As long as intensive cultivation of small plots covers the cost of production and family subsistence, the peasant clings to his land. Alternatively, this means that peasant producers can afford to pay much higher rents than capitalist farmers. The latter expect, in addition to current expenditure and rent, a minimum rate of return on capital.[25] Witness the widespread sharecropping practice of fifty-fifty rent agreements in Iran. For a capitalist to pay the equivalent of half his output as rent would leave very little, if any, margin for profit. A peasant, however, is not concerned with making a notional profit but with making a living. He is prepared to work the land as long as the yield, after deduction of actual disbursements, is positive and enables him to eke out his subsistence (Chayanov 1966). Similarly, a landlord would do better, under these circumstances, to rent out such land to peasant producers and invest the rental income in industry and construction, rather than reinvest it in agricultural production. Investment in agriculture becomes viable only if capitalist enterprises can jump over the rent barrier and raise output per hectare to a point substantially higher than what the peasant producer can achieve.

For these reasons, capitalist production in agriculture often starts from those branches of agriculture that are not highly dependent on large areas of land, such as poultry and livestock production and related industries. For instance, in 1969, 22 percent of capital investment in projects approved by the Agricultural Development Bank of Iran (ADBI) was for livestock production projects, 58 percent was for poultry production, and 13 percent was for development of orchards. By 1975, however, 45 percent of capital in projects approved by the ADBI belonged to agro-industrial companies, 9 percent to agriculturally related industries, 11 percent to agricultural services companies, and another 11 percent to distribution and marketing companies.

The substantial movement of capital into agriculture came during 1971–1972. Before the 1970s the government's chief priorities were industry and infrastructure. From the early 1970s more funds were allocated to agriculture, in particular after the sudden increase in oil revenues in 1974. Without substantial government subsidies, the initial costs of investment in agriculture would have been too high to attract private enterprise. A high degree of mechanization was indispensable for such projects if output was to increase and labor and supervision costs were to be minimized. In addition, integrated agro-industrial projects were favored because they were more likely to make successful overall returns on capital. But such projects required even higher outlays of initial capital.

By 1974 the government had set up favorable new terms to encourage the growth of agro-industrial projects: it undertook to pay for 85 percent of all preparatory expenditure of such projects, and for 50 percent of all expenditure related to construction of irrigation canals, land leveling, and preparation; it further provided for another 25 percent of such expenditures in the form of loans. It agreed to pay loans up to 60 percent of total investment in poultry and livestock production and in forestry projects and to pay for all transportation expenses of imported cattle and poultry from ports to project sites. The capital of the Agricultural Development Bank of Iran was increased from 5,000 million to 10,000 million rials. The maximum ceiling for individual loans was increased from 2.5 million to 5 million rials, and interest rates were reduced from 7 to 6 percent. Agricultural land covered by high dam irrigation networks were leased on a thirty-year basis at very low rent — the *Tehran Economist* called this a give-away. Agro-industrial projects were granted a ten-year tax holiday and could import all necessary machinery duty-free.

Several government institutions, ADBI, the Ministry of Agriculture and Natural Resources, and the Industrial and Mining Development Bank of Iran, sometimes in association with private investors, were in charge of larger projects that required direct state investment, at least in the initial phases. By July 1977 the government felt fairly confident that many of these companies were on solid ground, and thirty-four units were offered for sale to the private sector.

In the meantime, many Iranian capitalists who had made their initial wealth in the new industries during the 1960s were now looking for new channels of investment. A new breed of agricultural capitalists began to develop, not from among the old landlords investing in several hundred hectares of land saved from land reform, but out of a new generation of urban industrialists moving into large agricultural projects of several thousands of hectares of land and millions of rials of capital each. The Iranian men of wealth had come more than a full circle: from wealth accumulated in the bazaar during the nineteenth century to landed aristocracy; from landed wealth to nouveau riche captains of industry during the 1960s; and now back once again to the land but as modern capitalists of the late 1970s.

The turn of capital to agriculture in the 1970s is quite evident from figure 1, which illustrates the formation of gross domestic fixed capital in agriculture. The number and total capital of projects approved by the ADBI show a similar tendency (table 33). A survey of agricultural companies registered during the 1970s reveals an increase in the number as well as in the capital of new projects, even though by 1975–1976 a higher proportion was taken up by the expansion of

Figure 1. Formation of Fixed Gross Domestic Capital in Agriculture
(constant prices)

Capital (billions of rials)

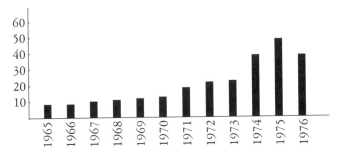

Source: Central Bank of Iran, *Annual Reports* for 1965–1976.

TABLE 33

Projects Approved by the Agricultural Development Bank of Iran, 1968–1977

Year	No. of Projects	Loan and Capital Investment by the Bank (billions of Rls)	Total Capital of the Project (billions of Rls)
1968	4	0.1	0.2
1969	16	0.3	0.9
1970	39	0.8	2.2
1971	56	1.1	2.7
1972	182	1.7	5.8
1973	310	2.6	5.7
1974	530	15.7	30.8
1975	684	41.8	101.4
1976	580	21.1	53.1
1977	601	32.9	66.7

Source: Central Bank of Iran, *Annual Reports for 1968–1977 (Tehran)*.

existing projects and there was a leveling off of new ventures (table 34 and figure 2).[26]

The highly concentrated and compartmentalized structure of capital in agriculture, with few agribusinesses capitalized at over 1 billion rials and many smaller units capitalized at under 100 million rials, reflects the two different directions from which capital was moving into agriculture. The small firms often belonged to former landlords who had chosen to stay in agriculture in the 1960s and were able to invest in several hundred hectares of land. To this group a

TABLE 34
Number and Capital of Registered Agricultural Companies, 1972–1977 (billions of rials)

Year	No. of New Firms	Registered Capital	Capital Increase of Existing Firms	Total New Capital in Agriculture
1972	23	1.65[a]	0.07	1.72
1973	35	4.80[b]	1.44	6.24
1974	76	6.02[c]	0.62	6.64
1975	254	4.24[d]	2.34[f]	6.58
1976	310	8.46[e]	7.22[g]	15.68
1977	185	2.41	7.93[h]	10.34

Source: See footnote 26, this chapter.

[a]Two firms capitalized at Rls 0.5 billion each.

[b]One firm capitalized at Rls 1.5 billion; one at Rls 0.75 billion; and two firms at Rls 0.5 billion each.

[c]One firm capitalized at Rls 2.0 billion; one at Rls 0.6 billion; ten firms at Rls 100–500 million.

[d]Two firms capitalized at Rls 0.6 billion each.

[e]One firm capitalized at Rls 1.1 billion; four firms at Rls 0.5 billion each.

[f]One firm's capital increased from Rls 0.25 billion to 1.0 billion; one from Rls 0.02 billion to 0.75 billion; one from Rls 0.5 billion to 0.8 billion.

[g]One firm's capital increased from Rls 0.8 billion to 5.0 billion; one from Rls 0.7 billion to 1.0 billion; one from Rls 0.5 billion to 1.6 billion.

[h]One firm's capital increased from Rls 5.0 billion to 7.0 billion; one from Rls 0.5 billion to 2.0 billion.

Figure 2. Number and Registered Capital of Agricultural Firms

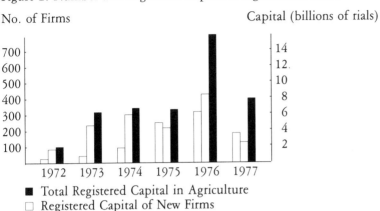

No. of Firms   Capital (billions of rials)

■ Total Registered Capital in Agriculture
☐ Registered Capital of New Firms
☐ Number of New Firms

Source: See footnote 26, this chapter.

new segment of successful farmers was gradually being added: well-to-do peasants with substantial holdings of 20 hectares or more and specialist farmers renting land to produce fruits and vegetables for the urban markets.

The very large ventures constituted the movement of large urban capital into agriculture. The money came both from international investors and from Iranians already known for their hold on certain industries. Chief among the latter group was the shah's private bank, Bank Omran; many members of the Pahlavi and Diba families; and famous owners of manufacturing industries, such as Tavakoli, Khorram, Agah, Yeganegi, Kazerouni, Barkhordar, Farmanfarmaian, Garami, Shoraka, Mahdavi, Hedayat, Bagherzadeh, and Fallah. One banker and his family, Yazdani, owned several agribusinesses with a total registered capital of 5 billion rials. During the last years of the old regime, he bought many of the cotton-ginning plants and sugar refineries that the government offered for sale to the private sector. Another group, Bagherzadeh and partners, had a virtual monopoly over the poultry and egg market in all major towns. Similar tendencies were developing in the dairy industries.[27]

The success of capitalist ventures in agriculture was only slightly marred by the fiasco of international agribusiness in Khuzistan. The

Khuzistan projects involved major international investors, such as Transworld Agricultural Development Corporation, Dow Chemical, Shell International Petroleum Company, Mitchel Cotts Group, the Chase Manhattan Bank, the Hawaiian Agronomics Company, and Mitsui (of Japan), along with Iranian private investors and the government, primarily through the Agricultural Development Bank of Iran. Although these investors were allocated 68,000 hectares of the best agricultural lands in Khuzistan, covered by the irrigation networks of the Dez high dam, and enjoyed vast financial assistance — the ADBI paid 50 percent of all initial costs of land preparation, they could import all machinery without paying duties, and they enjoyed the ten-year tax holidays of foreign investors — none of the Khuzistan projects became profitable ventures. Because the yields were invariably much lower and the costs much higher than predicted, the investors quickly accumulated vast financial losses. Under these circumstances they refused to place any further deposits for current expenditure, and repeated loans by the ADBI could not salvage their operations. By 1976 they had accumulated losses greater than their initial capital, without even taking into account their debts to the ADBI and other institutions. Finally the ADBI had to step in and take charge of all these ventures. A report prepared by the bank in 1977, and updated in 1978, recommended that the land be turned over to smaller ventures — in plots ranging from 100 to 500 hectares each — modeled after successful locally run enterprises owned by Iranian capitalists (ADBI 1978). Table 35 summarizes the situation for the four largest companies.

The ADBI report on these corporations noted a number of factors it held responsible for the failure (ADBI 1978:65–69). Some involved technical and managerial problems. The report noted that the size of operations was larger than those projected as optimum by the U.S. Department of Agriculture for similar ventures in the United States. All ventures were managed by foreign managerial companies whose previous experiences, the report argued, did not correspond to Iranian conditions. It further charged that the foreign staff were primarily interested in drawing large salaries, with no concern for the actual outcome of the operations. Other problems cited were the inability to import machinery and parts on schedule because of port

TABLE 35
Summary of Information on Khuzistan Agribusinesses, 1977

Name of Company	No. of Ha. Allocated (thousands)	No. of Ha. Leveled by 1977 (thousands)	No. of Ha. under Cultivation[a] (thousands)	Current Expenditure per Ha. (thousands of Rls)	Income per Ha. (thousands of Rls)	Accumulated Loss by 1977 (mils. of Rls)	Paid-in Capital (mils. of Rls)	Debt to the ADBI (mils. of Rls)	Debt to Other Sources (mils. of Rls)
Iran-California	10.6	4.7	6.3	48.1	31.2	308	230	555	131
Iran-America	20.2	5.5	9.0	n.a.	10.2[b]	198[b]	458	528	263
Iran-Shellcott	15.7	5.6	5.5	65.1	29.3	998	600	621	453
Iran-International	16.7	6.0	5.0	96.0	65.0	527	1,200	552[c]	500
Total	63.2	21.8	25.8	—	—	—	2,488	2,256	1,347

Source: ADBI 1978:40.
[a] Includes 4,300 ha. of unleveled land, rented by companies to *saff-karan* (specialists in summer crops); does not include another 6,000 ha. of unleveled land rented by companies to local peasants.
[b] 1976 figures; 1977 figures not available.
[c] Includes a 228 million rial loan from the National Bank of Iran.

backlogs and customs delays and the difficulties of repairing equipment due to the lack of spare parts, skilled workmen, and adequate facilities.

As far as human problems were concerned, the bank report noted several. For example, "the purchase of land from peasants and their resettlement produced ill-effects. These peasants had to work as day laborers on their own land which had been transferred to these companies. Naturally, on top of numerous social problems, their lack of interest has caused low productivity" (ADBI 1978:41).[28] On the managerial level, the bank noted that management firms were paid for all their costs, regardless of performance, leaving no incentive for them to minimize costs and produce profits (ADBI 1978:44). The investors were more concerned with immediate returns on capital, and when the ventures did not show any profits within the first two or three years, they refused to make any further capital payments, thereby compounding the financial problems. The report drew a contrast between these failures and the success of commercial farms owned and locally managed by Iranian capitalists in Gorgan, Fars, and other provinces. On this basis, it recommended takeover of the failing concerns by the government, which would turn them over on favorable terms, in 100–500-hectare plots, to what it termed "family concerns." This terminology referred to the fact that the successful commercial ventures were owned and managed by family investment groups. There was not time enough for these recommendations to be implemented before the 1979 revolution. In its aftermath, the lands were taken over by local peasant families and agricultural workers and reverted to small family plots.

The ADBI report sums up the dominant thinking in agricultural policy just prior to the 1979 revolution. From the late 1960s to the mid-1970s, such policy emphasized large agribusiness. The Agricultural Development Pole legislation was originally intended to eradicate subsistence agriculture and to replace it with operations of the Khuzistan type. The failure of Khuzistan projects produced a change in government orientation, away from large agribusiness and toward capitalist enterprises of up to 500 hectares. Larger operations that were seen as nationally important but unprofitable in the short term were to be the direct concern of the government until they reached profit-generating stages, at which time they would be turned over to the private sector.

Changes in Production and Productivity

During the two decades prior to the change in the regime, Iranian agriculture saw substantial growth in production of certain commercial crops, while production of grains grew very slowly, despite a continuing predominance of grain production and a growth in the areas allocated to its cultivation. The average annual rate of growth in agriculture for the 1960s and early 1970s was estimated by official government sources (Central Bank annual reports) at between 3 and 4 percent. Other sources (such as the ILO) give lower figures of about 2.5 percent (Kaneda 1973:1; Aresvik 1976:53; *Financial Times*, October 21, 1976). With a growth in demand for food estimated at about 12.5 percent annually, Iran not only changed from a net exporter of agricultural produce to a net importer by 1968; its import bills rapidly mounted from 5 billion rials in 1970 to 20 billion rials in 1972 to 76 billion rials in 1974 and to more than 130 billion rials in 1975.[29] These huge imports were conveniently financed by the rising oil revenues. It was much more "efficient" for the government to import food than to plan for basic solutions to a backward agricultural sector. In short, oil revenues became the curse of Iranian agriculture.

Cropping patterns did not change radically. Grains continued to be the major crop, with increases in production resulting from increased hectarage rather than from increases in output per hectare. This was probably due to the fact that the Green Revolution never arrived in Iran. As late as 1975 the World Bank report on Iranian agriculture noted, "at present, good quality seeds of assured pedigree and high germination rates are difficult to find in Iran and there is a pressing need to develop a seed industry of high integrity monitored by officials of exemplary honesty and incorruptibility" (Price 1975:18). For certain industrial crops, such as sugar beets, cotton, and oil seeds, direct contracts between farmers and industrial consumers involved the provision of improved seeds by the industrial concerns as part of the collaboration and their advance to the farmers. For basic grains, however, the major channel was the local cooperatives. Improved seeds

TABLE 36
Output, Area, and Yields for Grains and Pulses

Crop	Year	Tonnage of Output (thousands)	No. of Ha. (thousands)	Tonnage of yield/per ha.
Wheat	1960	2,924	4,012	0.73
	1967	3,853	4,340	0.89
	1968	3,861	4,804	0.80
	1974	2,886	5,973	0.48
	1975	4,366	5,565	0.78
Barley	1960	809	1,193	0.68
	1967	582	761	0.76
	1968	962	1,057	0.91
	1974	751	1,404	0.53
	1975	1,019	1,439	0.71
Rice	1960	709	329	2.12
	1967	1,083	261	4.15
	1968	1,172	318	3.69
	1974	826	353	2.34
	1975	1,023	400	2.55
Pulses	1960	73	132	0.55
	1967	83	184	0.45
	1968	101	160	0.63
	1974	186	479	0.39
	1975	148	328	0.44

Sources: The statistics for 1960 and 1974 are from the Agricultural Census (OAS 1960; Plan Organization, Statistical Center 1977), those for other years are from Central Bank of Iran *Annual Reports* for 1967, 1968, 1975. The census data tend to be more accurate and less exaggerated.

provided through cooperatives were not the Mexican variety of wheat and other internationally developed high-yield varieties (HYVs). They were developed by the Institute for Improvement and Provision of Seeds within the Ministry of Agriculture and were called "improved local seeds." In any event, the scale of this operation was marginal. In 1974, for instance, the cooperatives provided some 50,000 tons of "improved local grain seeds" out of a total of 787,000 tons of seeds consumed. The slow growth of output and stagnant yields of basic grains and pulses is evident from table 36.

The very low output and yield figures for 1974 partially result from the fact that most grain cultivation is not irrigated but rain fed, and 1974 happened to be a particularly dry year. Even without the 1974 figures, however, the comparison between 1960 and 1975 does

TABLE 37
Output, Area, and Yields for Commercial Crops

Crop	Year	Tonnage of Output (thousands)	No. of Ha. (thousands)	Tonnage of yield/per ha.
Sugar beet	1960	707	47	15.04
	1967	2,830	128	22.11
	1968	3,412	146	23.37
	1974	3,749	159	23.58
	1975	4,494	177	25.39
Cotton	1960	328	319	1.03
	1967	378	300	1.26
	1968	545	338	1.61
	1974	648	381	1.70
	1975	436	283	1.54
Oil seeds	1960	8	52	0.15
	1967	6	16	0.37
	1968	9	20	0.45
	1974	71	115	0.62
	1975	107	143	0.75

Sources: The statistics for 1960 and 1974 are from the Agricultural Census (OAS 1960; Plan Organization, Statistical Center 1977), those for other years are from Central Bank of Iran, *Annual Reports* for 1967, 1968, 1975. The census data tend to be more accurate and less exaggerated.

not indicate any substantial growth in yields. They fare particularly badly in comparison with other Near Eastern countries, with average yields in 1972–1974 of 1.1 ton per hectare for wheat, 1.0 ton per hectare for barley, and 3.7 tons per hectare for rice (Aresvik 1976:50).[30]

The only crops that have shown a consistent rise in output and yield are those cash crops with an industrial market, that is, sugar beets, oil seeds, and cotton (table 37). Productivity per unit area varies greatly between different types of farms. Unfortunately, the national statistics give productivity figures for only four crops, and those are given according to farm sizes. The figures show a definite tendency for higher productivity per unit area in the very small farms, decreasing for the larger farms of up to 50 hectares and increasing once again for the very large farms, except for those producing rice (table 38).

Productivity figures according to farm size alone are not very useful, however. More detailed area studies show that mechanized farms are generally not less productive than smaller peasant holdings. Ajami's

TABLE 38
Agricultural Yields, by Size of Farm, 1974

Size of Farm (ha.)	Wheat (Kg/ha.)	Barley (Kg/ha.)	Rice (Kg/ha.)	Sugar beet (Kg/ha.)
0–1	1,594	1,434	2,719	31,372
1–2	973	995	2,466	19,104
2–5	659	611	2,291	22,530
5–10	480	460	2,301	22,243
10–50	346	385	1,909	21,470
50–100	530	574	2,703	24,884
100 +	690	1,073	1,746	26,704
Average	483	535	2,337	23,704

Source: Plan Organization, Statistical Center 1977: tables 140, 164, 188, and 204.

TABLE 39
Output of Various Type of Farms in Sheshdangi, Fars, 1966

Crop	Mechanized Farm (9,640/rl/ha. constant capital investment), 500 ha., 1 Owner	Exempted Land (practically no investment except for a tractor), 218 Ha., 1 Owner	Tenant Farmers (7,360/rl/ha. constant capital investment), 340 Ha., 13 Owners	Peasant Owners (3,800/rl/ha. constant capital investment), 157 Ha., 34 Families
Wheat	2,234	1,438	2,233	1,625
Barley	2,154	1,280	1,295	1,474
Sugar beet	28,500	0[a]	27,500	21,330
Melons	12,576	0[b]	16,000	0[b]

Source: Ajami 1973:63–87.
[a]No sugar beet output, due to lack of sufficient irrigation.
[b]No land under melons.

study of one village in Fars is quite indicative (table 39). Another study of commercial agriculture in Iran categorizes various farm holdings, all of them above 10 hectares, according to size of holding as well as other factors, such as presence of irrigation. In this case, there is no uniform correlation between large mechanized capitalist farms, small family farms, and output figures (Qahreman 1982:137–142; see table 40).[31]

Monetization of Rural Consumption

There is no doubt that in the 1960s, and still more so through the 1970s, the level of income and cash expenditures of the rural population rose steadily. Two factors, however, overshadowed this rise: a

TABLE 40
Yields of Various Crops for Several Groups of Commercial Farms, 1975

	Group 1	Group 2	Group 3	Group 4	Group 5
No. of ha. irrigated	200 +	100–200	40–100	20–40	10–20
No. of ha. rain-fed	500 +	250–500	100–250	50–100	25–50
Average tonnage of yield per ha.					
irrigated wheat	3.2	2.1	2.0	1.9	1.9
cotton	1.7	1.8	1.8	1.8	2.1
alfalfa	7.9	5.7	8.3	5.2	8.5
sugar beet	26.9	14.1	25.5	19.2	23.5
rice	4.0	4.3	4.2	3.5	7.0

Source: Qahreman 1982: tables 1 and 5.

high degree of internal differentiation within rural areas and an even higher degree of differentiation between rural and urban areas. Ajami (1981:94) estimates that while in 1957 the ratio of urban to rural average per capita expenditure was about 2.1, by 1977 this ratio had reached 5.2. Kaneda (1973:2) gives somewhat different figures for the per capita income ratio of urban to rural areas, changing from 4.6 in 1959 to 5.7 in 1969. He also calculated that the share of Tehran in the distribution of "disposable income" would grow from 24 percent of total in 1965 to 33 percent in 1980 and that of other urban centers from 33 percent to 36 percent, while the share of rural areas would decline from 42 percent to 30 percent from 1965 to 1980 (Kaneda 1973:11). Kaneda's calculations were based on pre-1973 tendencies. In actual fact, the post–oil-boom tendencies created even sharper differentiation: the actual figures for the 1975 share of Tehran in overall consumer expenditure rose to 40 percent and that of other urban centers to 36 percent, while the share for rural areas declined to 24 percent.

These considerations aside, the rise in average rural family expenditures is perceptible. Starting in 1964, the Plan Organization carried out regular surveys of family expenditures for both rural and urban areas. Data prior to the 1960s are not available, except for occasional surveys. One source quotes a monthly rural per capita income of 140 to 500 rials, or roughly $2 to $7, for the late 1950s (Bowen-Jones 1968:369). Another refers to expenditures of 250 rials a month, both in cash and self-consumption, on food, tobacco, cloth-

TABLE 41
Household Expenditure in Rural Iran, 1964-1977

Year	Monthly Household Expenditures, Current Prices	Total Expenditure on Food (includes tobacco)	Value of Food Items Not Bought (Self-Consumption)	% of Food Expenditure to Total	% Self-Consumption to Total Food Bill	Consumer Price Index for Urban Areas	Monthly Household Expenditure, Adjusted
1964	3,479	2,461	1,164	71	47	64	5,444
1966	3,988	2,492	845	60	35	65	6,173
1968	4,005	2,581	1,015	64	39	66	6,059
1970	4,178	2,791	1,010	67	36	69	6,022
1972	4,940	3,237	1,412	66	44	78	6,341
1974	11,044	6,073	2,940	55	48	100	11,044
1976	12,678	6,504	2,844	51	44	128	9,897
1977	17,267	8,504	3,401	49	40	160	10,778

Source: Plan Organization Of Iran, Statistical Center, *Household Budget Statistics, Rural Areas,* 1964-1977 (Tehran). Central Bank of Iran, *Annual Reports, Various Years* for 1964-1977 (Tehran).

ing, and fuel for 1962 (Mo'meni 1980:61). The data from 1964 onward are problematic. Various years give different information and classifications that are not readily compatible. Nonetheless, the figures for the total average household expenditure give a rough picture (table 41).

The first point that is clear from table 41 is that to speak of the absolute and growing impoverishment of the peasantry, as some commentators have, is groundless. The monthly household expenditure figures, at current prices, show a steady rise. Unfortunately, no consumer price index is available for rural areas. The Central Bank reports give only urban price index figures. But it is certain that the rate of inflation is much higher in the urban areas. For instance, rent for houses in cities is much higher and shot up rapidly, especially in the 1970s. In the rural areas, few households pay any rent. Similarly, the "basket of goods and services" selected by the Central Bank to calculate price indexes includes many items that are simply not available in the rural areas. Such items often have a higher inflation rate than tobacco and basic food items, many of which had prices fixed by the government. Still, even if we use the urban price index, which is highly exaggerated relative to rural figures, to adjust the expenditure levels into current prices, there is still a real and substantial rise in monthly household expenditures of about 100 percent from 1964 to 1977. This rise is confirmed by many village field reports (Azkia 1969:89; Salmanzadeh 1980:158-172).

Second, a decreasing percentage of household expenditure is allocated to food, 71 percent in 1964, 49 percent in 1976. This is the case even though food still takes up half the household budget, and the figure is definitely much higher for lower-income groups in the villages and for remote villages far away from urban centers. The percentage of self-consumed — that is, home produced and home consumed — food to total food expenditure, however, has decreased only slowly, from 47 percent in 1964 to 40-44 percent in 1976-1977. That would indicate that increased cash incomes are spent on nonfood consumer items and services. Again, village field reports confirm this overall picture (MCRA 1975d:95; 1975e:70-74; 1976a:45). It is important to point out that MCRA reports point to a high degree of regional differentiation. In some areas self-consumption ratios to the total food bill are as high as 80 percent. There are also some variations according to expenditure groups. Estimates of these variations, shown in appendix C, confirm that:

1. For higher expenditure groups, a smaller part of expenditure consists of food. Moreover, this portion has rapidly decreased over the recent past, from about 60 percent in 1965 to about 20 percent in 1976. For lower-expenditure groups, it has remained about 70 percent of total expenditure. The average is about 40 percent (table 41).

2. The ratio of self-consumption food items to the total expenditure on food does not differ appreciably in different expenditure groups, nor has it decreased substantially over the past decades.

3. The higher-expenditure groups account for an increasing percentage of total rural expenditures, although accurate comparison is difficult because of the nature of the data.

Among the nonfood expenditure items, an increasing portion is spent on household goods and services (table 42). The 1976 Household Budget Statistics (Rural Areas) showed that 52 percent of all households had radios (usually transistor radios), 15 percent had gas cookers, 11 percent had tape recorders, 10 percent had bicycles, 7 percent had motorcycles, and 8 percent had refrigerators.[32] This information indicates that although more than half the rural population had enough extra income to buy a transistor radio, few had enough to purchase any other, more expensive consumer items.[33] Again, in villages closer to the urban-industrial centers, there was a higher level of expenditure for consumer items. Mahdavi (1982:63) reports that in a village in the Qazvin area, out of 120 households, "over fifty have televisions; some seventy families have Land Rovers; and two have cars. Many children have bicycles. Six families have tractors; nine have pickup vans; one has a truck; and two have combines." Mahdavi also reports that most houses had refrigerators, electric irons, sewing machines, and other such items.

Not all villages, however, were located near important industrial centers, such as Qazvin, or close enough to the Tehran market for their sales of agricultural products to prosper in this way. Moreover, the increase in incomes was extremely uneven. In the village Mahdavi reported on, the annual per capita income of peasants increased nineteenfold, from 3,800 rials in 1954 to 70,000 rials in 1980, while

TABLE 42

Percentage of Expenditure in Each Major Nonfood Category, 1965–1976

Item	1965	1967	1969	1971	1973	1975	1976
Clothes and shoes	29	30	24	24	26	24	23
Housing	10	9	13	12	11	12	12
Water, lighting, and fuel	20	20	19	15	12	7	7
Household goods and services	11	16	15	15	17	21	19
Health and medical care	12	12	16	10	12	8	7
Transportation and communications	6	5	6	6	7	6	12

Source: Plan Organization of Iran, Statistical Center, *Household Budget Statistics — Rural Areas*, for years given (Tehran).

TABLE 43

Per Capita Annual Rural Agricultural Income, 1972

Income Group	% of Rural Population	Mean Income (U.S. $)
$0–$100 (with 0–3 ha.)	46.7	70
$100–$199 (with 3–10 ha.)	32.9	131
$200–$399 (with 10–50 ha.)	19.2	302
$400 (with 50 + ha.)	1.2	1,000

Source: World Bank 1974: 20.

the annual per capita income of a former landlord, who had become a capitalist farmer, increased ninetyfold, from 170,000 rials to 15 million rials (Mahdavi 1982:65). The disparities also existed among various layers of villagers. In the village reported on by Kielstra (1975:245), family incomes of the three richest families grew 2.5 times over about a decade, while the family income of small cultivators grew 1.5 times and that of laborers changed little.

Although no national surveys exist on income differentials in rural areas, the consumer expenditure figures (see table in appendix C) according to various expenditure categories show increasing differentiation between groups. Clearly the income distribution could be even more skewed were we to take into account the higher rates of saving and production expenditure for higher-income groups. One

World Bank survey for 1972 gave the income distribution shown in table 43. The regional reports of the Ministry of Cooperatives and Rural Affairs show similar income distribution patterns.[34] It is clear that the improvement in the living conditions of the lower-income groups did no more than alleviate the previous grossly inadequate standards of living, and most of the new income was spent on food consumption and on only a very few consumer items, such as transistor radios.

Summary

Iranian rural society was dramatically affected, beginning in the early 1960s, by the totality of changes that were introduced into it. Land reform, in particular, produced irreversible changes in landowner-ship and tenure relations — changes that in turn have generated long-term modifications in the social structure and in the economic orga-nization of villages.

Roughly half the agricultural land came under the direct terms of the land reform programs, enabling about a third of rural house-holds to purchase some land, thereby doubling at a stroke the num-ber of small owner-cultivators. By the same token, some 1 million heads of households, one-third of all the rural families, fell outside the benefits of land redistribution, and their traditional ties to rural society were qualitatively modified: previously they could with some justification maintain the hope that someday they might acquire land-use rights and become nasaqdar villagers. Now this avenue was apparently closed to them forever.

Tenure relations were also drastically changed, even on land that was exempt and remained in the hands of its original owners. Tradi-tional sharecropping was replaced on small holdings by cultivation by the owners and on the larger tracts by more mechanized cultiva-tion and employment of paid laborers. To the extent that sharecrop-ping remains, it is either a form of rental payment in kind, as in cases where peasants temporarily abandon cultivation for urban employ-ment while renting out their land to other villagers for a share of the crop, or it is a form of payment of wages in kind that ensures the self-interest of agricultural workers and reduces the necessity of direct supervision. A third type of sharecropping occurs in agreements made between specialist farmers and landlords. These agreements are more like joint investment projects in which the two sides share equally in current expenditure and final output, with the landlord providing the land and the farmers providing the labor. It is evident that these relations are all very different from traditional sharecropping. These agreements are not automatically renewed by the force of custom and tradition. Rather they are of a more contractual nature and are renegotiated annually. In fact, they all represent various transitional forms of the rural economy as it is integrated increasingly into an expanding monetary economy. They are not a stifling block to that expansion, caused by unyielding traditions of backwardness in the countryside. Indeed, a significant characteristic of these changes is that they are a creative and resourceful adaptation to the changing circumstances by the rural population.

On the smaller farms, the peasants' survival began to rely on a new combination of activities: partial self-subsistence cultivation, partial production for sale, and an important contribution — especially on the very small farms of under 5 hectares — of income from wages. This wage income derives either from local agricultural labor on larger neighboring farms or — and often this is more important — from the urban employment of some household members for at least part of the year. This development alone has had considerable and novel implications for the whole rural-urban dichotomy in latter-day Iran.

The middle-size farms, particularly near large urban centers, enjoyed notable growth in their production and general prosperity. They provided the towns with fruits and vegetables. They also provided local factories with inputs such as sugar beets, oil seeds, and cotton. Both on the small and middle-size farms, family labor provided the bulk of agricultural labor. Aside from the use of tractors, some smaller capital investments on these farm groups were made for fertilizers and improved irrigation. Large capitalist farms saw a surge of growth both in their numbers and in the amount of capital invested during the 1970s. The most profitable of these ventures ranged in size from 100 to 500 hectares, but the experiment with very large agribusiness enterprises of several thousand hectares proved to be a financial, social, and political fiasco.

Although the growth of monetary relations in the rural areas and the commercialization of agricultural production provided a larger internal market for consumer goods as well as some production inputs,

TABLE 44
The Place of Agriculture in Iranian Economy, 1968–1976

	1968	1969	1970	1971	1972	1973	1974	1975	1976
Rural population (millions)	16.7	—	16.3	16.5	16.9	—	—	—	17.9
as % of total population	60.6	—	58.4	58.2	57.2	—	—	—	53.0
Agricultural Labor force (millions)	3.4	—	3.2	3.4	3.7	—	—	—	3.0
Agricultural labor force as % of total labor force	47.2	—	45.1	47.2	48.7	—	—	—	34.1
Agriculture's contribution to GDP, (%)	27.2	24.0	20.5	17.4	16.5	12.1	9.4	9.4	9.4
Total government revenues (millions of $)	1,698.7	1,906.7	2,285.3	3,452.0	4,028.0	6,197.3	18,592.0	21,094.7	23,252.0
Oil revenues included in total revenues (millions of $)	824.0	934.7	1,117.3	2,074.7	2,380.0	4,149.3	16,069.3	16,624.0	17,720.0
Development expenditure on agriculture (millions of $)	97.3	93.3	121.3	121.3	206.7	170.7	410.7	483.0	457.3
Agricultural development expenditure as % of total development expenditure	9.1	7.4	8.2	7.9	10.9	7.9	9.0	6.9	5.4
Agriculture credit allocated to the private sector (millions of $)	252.0	270.7	245.3	232.0	385.3	496.0	834.7	1,253.3	1,748.0
Agriculture credit as % of total private sector credit	11.5	10.3	8.1	6.3	8.0	7.6	9.1	8.8	8.9
Agricultural import bill (millions of $)	48.0	37.3	68.0	170.7	205.3	358.7	1,104.0	1,726.7	1,320.0

Sources: Central Bank of Iran, *Annual Reports* for 1968–1976 (Tehran); Plan Organization of Iran, Statistical Center, *Statistical Yearbook of Iran* 1968–1976 (Tehran).
Note: Dashes indicate reliable data not available; $ figures are calculated on the basis of the official exchange rate over this period, 1 U.S. $ = 75 rials.

overall the agricultural sector became increasingly marginal. The existence of a huge rentier oil income for the state made it possible for Iran to plan industrialization without depending on major surplus accumulations or savings in the agricultural sector. Moreover, as we have already pointed out, the oil revenues easily subsidized the necessary import of agricultural products. This meant that Iran, unlike many other Third World countries, could plan industrialization and to a great extent neglect the agricultural sector. By 1976, although 53.0 percent of the population lived in the rural areas and 34.1 percent of the labor force was engaged in agriculture, only 5.4 percent of development expenditure was allocated to agriculture (table 44).

Although the oil revenues could cover Iran's rising food import bill, the neglect of agriculture produced problems at several levels, such as the small size of the rural consumer market and the continued existence of a large subsistence sector. As the ILO report noted:

> Stagnating rural incomes and low urban subsistence wages have limited the market for industrial goods to the urban middle and upper classes. The size of the domestic market is small by comparison with the optimum production of most intermediate and capital goods, in relation to which most of future industrial expansion has to take place (ILO 1973b:52).

The low income of the majority of the rural population was not only a problem of the internal market, limiting industrial growth, it also reflected the low productivity of labor in agriculture and a growing gap between agricultural production and the national demand for agricultural produce.

During the post-1974 boom, fed by oil revenues, the capitalist sector in agriculture grew with the encouragement and financial support of the government. In the absence of any drastic increase in industrial employment, however, the impact of this accelerated growth in rural Iran exacerbated many of the existing problems. Much of the sudden rise in urban employment was due to a boom in construction; thus the employment it generated was seasonal, unskilled, and temporary. Most of the people who came from the villages in search of such employment left their families to continue steady-state subsistence farming on their small plots as an alternative to selling out. While this situation created localized problems, both in time and place, of labor shortages in agriculture, it cannot be said to have resulted in the "depopulation" of the countryside. Nor did it provide a reason for the more prosperous peasants to mechanize their production; it was not their sons who were going off to unskilled employment in the cities. They benefited to some extent from the growing demand for agricultural products in the cities. But since the government was oriented toward the establishment of Agricultural Development Poles, which jeopardized the fate of all farms of under 20 hectares, even the more prosperous farmers lived in an atmosphere of uncertainty, which was bound to affect adversely their long-term investments on the land. The government plans themselves faced problems of their own: with the slow growth of industrial employment and the explosion of shantytowns in all major cities, it was too risky for the government to undertake enclosure moves of the nineteenth-century type in order to prepare the ground for the Agricultural Development Poles. Agriculture was in a new quandary by 1979, when the government was removed by revolution and the entire constitution of the state was irreversibly changed.

7

Cooperatives and Corporations

In the agricultural sector, state intervention cannot end with implementation of land reform on the assumption that spontaneous development of "market forces" will take their "natural course." For instance, the channeling of agricultural surplus to industry cannot be left to the invisible workings of "terms of trade" between agriculture and industry. Agricultural production and sales often do not fall within any national trade grid that would allow for such spontaneous movements. It is up to the state to develop market networks to ensure the flow of agricultural commodities on a national scale once the old networks dominated by traditional landlords have been broken up. Prior to land reform, landlords sold the bulk of their share of the harvest to urban markets. In the aftermath of reform, it is the responsibility of the state to devise methods by which the agricultural surplus can continue to make its way to urban-industrial markets.

Similarly, increased consumption of various manufactured products by the rural population need not be left to the initiative of traditional wandering rural salesmen. Government-sponsored consumer cooperatives can be instrumental in introducing new goods and services into the countryside.

In the case of Iran, government intervention to integrate the rural sector into a national network of trade took three major forms. First, at the level of exchange, where the growth of a national market for both agricultural and manufactured goods was sought, the government intervened through the establishment of an extensive network of rural cooperative (co-op) societies. Second, at the level of production, farm corporations and production cooperatives were intended by the government to set the pace and pattern for increasing production and productivity. Third, the government provided credit both for production and consumption, and the agricultural co-op societies were to become the major creditor for the majority of peasants, while the Agricultural Development Bank of Iran was oriented toward large-scale capitalist farming.

The central importance of establishing such co-ops and credit institutions was foreseen from the very beginning of all land distribution programs in Iran. In an early document, "General Frame of Reference within Which Planning Details for Rural Development in Iran May Proceed," Paul Maris projected, as one of the "immediate objectives," the sponsorship of "the development of farmers cooperative organizations and credit societies and the creation of institutions through which the credit needs of small farmers may be adequately met." Maris projected four categories of credit: "a. Production or short-term credit; b. Durable goods or intermediate credit; c. Permanent investment or long-term credit; d. Cooperative credit."[1] As V. Webster Johnson of the Near East Foundation later pointed out, provision of rural credit became a central concern of all rural development programs as

> a practical means to introduce more capital into agriculture. Excessive charges by the money-lenders reduce the farmer's incentive for saving and thrift, and restrict funds for new production investments. Cooperatives provide a means of servicing economically the credit needs and other services of small farmers. They are a means of mobilizing existing capital in villages and there is today in Iran considerable unused or poorly used capital. (Johnson 1960:320)

More specifically, Johnson argued that "without additional capital on reasonable terms, it is not possible for them [the new landowning peasants] to increase the use of fertilizers and improved seeds; adopt more modern farm tools and machines, and better livestock production practices; develop and acquire ownership of land; improve rural living conditions; and market effectively farm products by farmers cooperative organizations."[2] From the outset, therefore, membership in the local cooperative society was a precondition for a peasant to become a land reform beneficiary. The first such co-op was set up in the Varamin area near Tehran in conjunction with the Crown

Land Distribution Program under the auspices of Point Four and the Near East Foundation (NEF).

This co-op, covering twelve villages, was established as a multi-purpose society. It extended production loans to members, not in cash, but in the form of cotton seeds, pesticides, and fertilizers. The NEF and the Point Four technical staff were also prepared to help supervise production and marketing. In exchange for production credit, the farmer was obligated to sell to the co-op at least enough of each cotton harvest to repay the loan. Some farmers opted to sell the entire harvest to the co-op, while others sold their surplus to local tradesmen or took it to town themselves. The co-op had agreed to deliver raw cotton to the local government-owned Jitu ginning factory. This proved to be a relatively successful operation, at least in its early years. It was on the basis of this success that the government decided to expand on it by setting up Rural Development Blocks in various regions of the country. Several factors, however, worked against easy extrapolation from the situation in Varamin. First, Varamin was a relatively prosperous rural area. Because of its proximity to Tehran, farmers had already had experience with cash crops and marketing. Attempts to work out similar production credit contracts with farmers in other parts of Iran proved to be successful only in regions growing similar cash crops (for example, cotton, oil seed and sugar beets), but such efforts failed to produce results when subsistence crops (for example, wheat and barley) were involved. Second, Varamin was a showcase from the very outset. Much financial and technical assistance was provided in this area both by Point Four and by the Near East Foundation. Such assistance for some 50,000 villages, beyond the 12 villages in Varamin, would require vast expenditures of state and international capital, not to mention the impossibility of providing the necessary trained personnel on the same scale as provided in Varamin. Third, and possibly most important of all, given the availability of foreign exchange from the country's growing oil revenues, it became progressively easier for the government to import necessary agricultural goods than to increase internal production and marketing. The incentive for setting up cooperatives as vehicles for increasing production and establishing well-functioning market channels became weaker and weaker, while Iran's agricultural import bill grew at a staggering pace. In other words, as we have already argued, as producers of agricultural surplus, peasants were not a crucial linch-pin in Iran's "primitive accumulation." This in turn undermined the potential of peasants to become a mass consumer market for the products of the new urban industries. The integration of the Iranian peasantry within the national market economy remained tenuous.

RURAL COOPERATIVE SOCIETIES

The big effort to establish an extensive network of co-ops began with the launching of the land reform program in the early 1960s. By the early 1970s there were some 8,400 rural co-ops with about 2 million members. In 1973 these were reorganized into larger units with a consequent reduction in the number of co-ops to 2,717. By 1976, according to the latest available statistics from the old regime, there were 2,886 co-ops with about 2.9 million members, covering nearly 46,000 villages (table 45). That is, almost all Iranian villages, esti-mated at about 50,000, and all farming families, estimated at between 2.5 and 3 million, were at least formally in a rural co-op. The ini-tiative for setting up a society was almost always taken by the Min-istry of Cooperatives and Rural Affairs. A survey of co-ops in 1975 showed that only in 5 percent of them had the villagers taken the initiative (Plan Organization 1975:16).

Originally, the membership of cooperatives was limited to peas-ant landholders and livestock breeders. This eliminated all khoshneshins from membership, which added to their already disad-vantaged position relative to all other villagers. Although this restric-tion was removed in the early 1970s, the 1975 survey indicates that only 29 percent of rural co-ops had khoshneshin members, and these members made up only 4 percent of the total membership of all co-ops (Plan Organization 1975:27). Once the membership require-ments and restrictions were removed, the primary incentive to buy co-op shares became the borrowing provision that set the maximum loan that a co-op could extend to any member at ten times the amount of shares held by that person.

The major activities of all rural co-ops were projected as:

1. Acceptance of members' savings on behalf of the Agricultural Coop-erative Bank of Iran;

TABLE 45
Number and Capital of Rural Cooperatives, 1963–1976

Year	No. of Co-ops	No. of Members (thousands of persons)	Capital (billions of rls)
1963	2,722	542	0.4
1965	5,518	764	0.7
1967	8,236	1,087	1.3
1969	8,102	1,400	2.0
1971	8,450[a]	1,854	2.8
1973	2,717	2,263	3.9
1975	2,858	2,685	5.7
1976	2,886[a]	2,868	7.0

Source: Central Bank of Iran, *Annual Reports* for 1963–1976 (Tehran).
[a]Figures for 1963–1971 cover about 27,000 villages; those for 1973–1976 cover about 46,000 villages.

2. Provision of all items of consumption for personal, family and work purposes, including such items as animal feeds;

3. Collection, storage and marketing of the products of the members;

4. Provision of services to improve personal life or to satisfy production needs, such as provision of agricultural machinery and tools and the organization of their joint use, provision of means of transport for members, provision of housing, drinking water, health and education facilities, electricity and telephone, vaccination of animals, and so forth;

5. Provision of credit and loans as needed by members.[3]

Although the co-ops were thus ambitiously defined as multipurpose societies, in actual fact the main activity of most co-ops remained limited to provision of credit and a small number of consumer goods, such as fuel, tea, and sugar (MCRA 1976a). According to the 1975 survey, while 93 percent of the co-ops had some consumer sales activity and 90 percent extended loans to members, only 23 percent were active in providing agricultural machinery and other inputs, and 21 percent had programs to buy the surplus product of peasants (Plan Organization 1975:110). On the national scale, 5,742 co-op shops had annual sales figures of 4,000 million rials, while only 500 co-ops reported buying surplus wheat harvest (*Tehran Economist*, March 20, 1976).

All surveys of rural co-ops share Ajami's conclusion: "Most of the cooperative societies are small units without adequate financial

TABLE 46
Distribution of Cooperative Shares, by Membership Category,
1975 (in percent)

Membership Category	No. of Shares					Total
	1–9	10–29	30–59	60–99	100 and over	
Co-op officials	9	15	13	19	44	100
Landholders	36	24	17	13	10	100
Khoshneshins	93	7	0	0	0	100

Source: Plan Organization 1975:table 14.

resources and qualified personnel. They have, therefore, not been able to expand their activities beyond granting small, short term loans. Their functions in the field of supplying new agricultural inputs and marketing have been very limited" (Ajami 1976a:201). According to the 1975 survey of the Plan Organization, 52 percent of the co-ops had capital of less than 1,250,000 rials (about U.S. $16,500), and another 36 percent had capital of between 1.25 and 2.5 million rials. The same survey indicated that 86 percent of the co-op managers considered the present capital and credit extended to co-ops inadequate (Plan Organization 1975:33 and 107).

Distribution of shares held by members reflected their relative financial well-being, since more prosperous peasants could afford to buy more shares. Moreover, the more prosperous peasants consistently took up managerial and official posts at the co-ops. As managers and officials they were in a position to influence decisions regarding the granting of loans and the buying of new shares. The 1975 survey of the Plan Organization showed that 44 percent of co-op officials had more than 100 shares each, and only 10 percent of ordinary landholding members had more than 100 shares each (table 46). The average number of shares held by co-op officials was 143, while landholding members had 26 shares on the average, and khoshneshin members had only 6 shares (see table 47).

Furthermore, co-op regulations tended to accentuate these differentiations: at the time of loan payments, fixed at a maximum of ten times each member's share, 5 percent of the loan would be automatically deducted and paid toward purchase of new shares by that member (MCRA 1976a:77). One study of co-ops in the Saqqiz region showed that within the seven years 1963–1970, while the average

TABLE 47
Number of Cooperative Shares Held
by Various Membership Categories, 1975

Membership Category	No. of Members	Total Shares	Average No. of Shares per Person
Co-op officials	202	28,942	143
Landholders	34,881	891,060	26
Khoshneshins	1,364	8,320	6

Source: Plan Organization 1975:table 15.

minimum number of shares per member declined from 7.2 to 5.9 shares, the average maximum number of shares per person increased from 66.4 to 125.9 shares (MCRA 1976a:78). Even among co-op officials a "rank-related" hierarchy is evident.

The same MCRA study also indicated a very high degree of kinship interrelatedness among co-op officials. The 1975 survey of the Plan Organization showed similar patterns. The survey concluded:

> The majority of rural social and economic organizations are managed by a handful of people. It is clear from their family origins that there is a high degree of kinship connection amongst them. We can thus conclude that although co-op officials are elected by the rural community, the election procedures and criteria do not make it evident to all members that they could stand as candidates for co-op official elections (Plan Organization 1975:15).

Co-ops as Credit Institutions

During the 1960s and 1970s, a three-tier system of agricultural credit developed in Iran. On top there was the Agricultural Development Fund of Iran, established in 1968, which later, in 1973, changed its name to the Agricultural Development Bank of Iran. The fund was established with the specific aim of encouraging "private investments in agriculture and livestock husbandry, and promoting the commercialization of agricultural concerns." The fund started with a capital of 1 billion rials, and by 1975 the bank's capital had been increased to over 10 billion rials. It extended credit to, and participated in joint investments with, large agro-industrial companies. Its minimum loan was originally set at 5 million rials, but this was later

TABLE 48
Cooperative Shares Held, Loans Received, and Land
Held by Cooperative Officials According to Rank

Official Post	Average No. of Shares		Average Loan Received (rls)		Average Amount of Land Held (ha.)[a]	
	1963	1970	1963	1970	Irrigated	Rainfed
Managing directors	33.5	79.5	1,333	14,167	11.0	33.4
Chairmen of boards	22.0	62.7	7,091	12,818	6.4	13.1
Board members	29.2	62.0	7,693	11,617	5.0	15.8
Alternate board members	21.8	57.0	6,770	11,080	4.5	10.2
Inspectors	18.0	51.0	6,611	10,736	4.1	8.8

Source: MCRA 1976:table 3.
[a]1970 only.

reduced to 1 million rials. Nonetheless, it continued to cater only to large investors. Between 1968 and 1976, it extended a total credit of more than 85,000 million rials, and its average loan amounted to 35.5 million rials (see table 49).

For smaller agricultural investments, the Agricultural Cooperative Bank (ACB), whose capital in 1975 was 29 million rials—that is, less than the average ADBI loan—provided credit. The maximum loan ceiling of the ACB, 500,000 rials, created a rather large gap between it and the original minimum loan of ADBI (5 million rials). The difference was only partially bridged by the reduction of ADBI's minimum loan to 1 million rials.

The ACB extended credit both to individuals and to rural cooperative societies. Credit to individuals was to cover both current production expenditures and long-term investments. In practice, most of the credit was used for current expenditures and consumption, and as a result, the bank allocated its funds more and more through a scheme of "supervised loans" (table 50). Nonetheless, "current expenditure" loans continued to constitute more than half the credit extended in 1976.

The rural cooperative societies provided small loans to members for one year. The ACB provided credit to the rural co-ops at 4 percent interest; the co-ops charged their members 6 percent. The loans were small, up to ten times the member's share, with a fixed maximum at the beginning of 20,000 rials, raised to 30,000 rials in 1973,

TABLE 49
Loans Extended by ADFI/ADBI, 1968–1976 (millions of rials)

Year	No. of Projects	Amount of Loan or Shares Held by ADBI	Average Loan per Project
1968	4	52	17.0
1969	16	320	20.0
1970	39	836	21.4
1971	56	1,107	19.8
1972	182	1,745	9.6
1973	310	2,650	8.5
1974	530	15,660	29.5
1975	682	41,795	61.3
1976	580	21,083	36.4

Source: Central Bank of Iran, *Annual Reports* for 1968–1976 (Tehran).

TABLE 50
Individual Loans Extended by the Agricultural Credit Bank
of Iran, 1963–1976

Year	No. of Loans Extended (thousands)	Average Amount of Loan (thousands of Rls)	% of Loans Supervised
1963	320	11	0
1965	548	10	0
1967	327	16	0
1970	212	42	3
1972	263	55	16
1976	—	—	23

Source: Central Bank of Iran, *Annual Reports* for 1963–1976 (Tehran).
Note: Dashes indicate data not available.

and were designed to help farmers with their current production and consumption expenditures. The loans were extended once a year on a collective return guarantee. That is, no new loan would be extended to any farmer until everyone had paid back his previous year's loans. In practice, this forced farmers in trouble to borrow from traditional usurers in order to pay back their co-op.

Provision of small loans seems, in fact, to have become the most common activity of co-ops. Many MCRA reports indicated that peasants basically considered the local co-op to be a bank branch (table 51). Despite the rapidly increasing number and amount of co-op

TABLE 51

Loans Extended by Cooperatives to Members, 1963–1976

No. and Average Amount of Loan	1963	1964	1965	1966	1967	1968	1969	1970	1971	1972	1973	1974	1975	1976
No. of loans (thousands)	151	329	391	559	673	738	844	902	876	1,165	1,176	1,363	1,000	1,400
Average amount of loan (thousands of rials)	3.3	4.4	4.8	5.4	6.1	6.8	6.8	7.0	7.8	8.6	10.5	14.5	15.4	20.0

Source: Central Bank of Iran, *Annual Reports* for 1963–1976 (Tehran).

TABLE 52
Use of Loans from ACB and Rural Cooperatives
as Reported by Various Sources

Source of Information	% Used for Consumption	% Used for Production	% Used for Production & Consumption	% Used for Other Purposes
Azkia 1969:108	66.7	2.1	—	32.2
Nik-kholq 1971:59	87.8	11.8	—	0.4
Plan Organiza- tion 1975:70	46	37	—	17
MCRA 1975d:200	16–46	7–29	30–73	—
MCRA 1976a:55	17–31	4–33	63–73	—
Khosravi 1976:157	55.3	33.5	—	11.2

Note: Dashes indicate data not reported.

loans, the traditional lending sources remained strong, indicating the inadequacy of the co-op's financial backup, and most loans were spent on consumer needs.

Although all ACB loans were supposed to go toward production costs, and many rural co-op loans were called production loans, in actuality various MCRA regional reports and other field reports indicate that only about a third of all loans were actually spent for production purposes (table 52). In part this was because the amount of loans available from co-ops and the ACB was so small. The average size of a loan from co-ops has been estimated at about 6,000 rials a year per member, which is equivalent to the average expenditure required to produce 1 hectare of dry-farmed winter wheat (Plan Organization 1975:61). Moreover, according to the same survey, 31 percent of loans were below 3,000 rials and 43 percent between 3 to 5 thousand rials (Plan Organization 1975:66). Although the maximum loan was raised to 30,000 rials in 1973, the 1975 survey shows that only 3 percent of co-op members received the maximum loan (Plan Organization 1975:68).

The ACB offered larger loans to individuals, but to get a bank loan required several trips to town, much unfamiliar paperwork, and

TABLE 53
Source of Rural Credit, excluding ADBI projects,
as Reported by Various Sources (in percent)

Source of Information	Rural Co-ops	ACB & other banks & institutions	Noninstitutional Sources
Price 1975:17, Table 7	23.8	18.4	57.7
MCRA 1976a:54–58	28.3	30.1	41.6
MCRA 1976b:14	33.0	27.0	40.0
MCRA 1976c:8	10–28	16–40	31–68
MCRA 1975d:108	39.4	22.3	38.3
MCRA 1975e:92	38.7	27.5	33.1
Azkia 1969:106	34.9	9.3	55.7
Bergmann 1975:66	14.6	6.8	75.9

giving the land deeds to the bank as security—something most new proprietors were unwilling to do. The 1975 survey of the Plan Organization showed that 70 percent of the peasants thought the influence of traditional moneylenders and traders had not decreased, because co-op loans were insufficient, co-op shops were poorly stocked, and peasants often needed quick, small loans. This was another problem with co-op loans. They were extended only once a year and had to be repaid all at once. Most MCRA reports indicated that peasants complained that they could not borrow money throughout the year, nor could they pay back in installments (Plan Organization 1975:53, 116; MCRA 1975d:188; 1976a:62; Ashraf 1973:21–22). As a result of these problems, despite the increased loans from the co-ops, peasants continued to depend largely on the traditional moneylenders, local shopkeepers, and traders, who continued to provide, on the average, half the credit needs of the rural population (table 53). Even commercial farmers depended for a substantial part of their credit, 23 to 33 percent, on noninstitutional sources (Qahreman 1982:143–144). The rate of interest charged by these sources was very high—rates as high as 68 percent have been officially recorded (Plan Organization 1975:69; MCRA 1975d:105; 1976b:d; 1976c:table 11).[4]

Such dependence on traditional sources of credit also constituted a primary reason for the continuation of such practices as *salaf-khari*, that is, the preharvest sale of crops to local traders and shopkeepers at prices highly disadvantageous to the peasants—30 to 60 percent less than the prices during the harvest season (MCRA 1976c:23). Peasants also complained that while local shopkeepers and traders could be paid back in kind at the time of harvest, the co-ops could only be paid back in cash.

Co-ops as Consumer Shops

Aside from lending money, the next most common activity of the co-ops was to market a number of basic consumer items, with paraffin, tea, and sugar in the forefront. By 1976 there were 5,742 co-op shops in rural Iran. On an aggregate level, the co-ops provided a very small fraction of the total consumer expenditures of rural families. Their total sales in 1975 came to some 4 billion rials (*Tehran Economist*, March 20, 1976). When averaged over a total co-op membership of 2,685,000, such sales amount to less than 1,500 rials per rural family and constitute 1.9 percent of the total 1976 cash expenditure of an average rural family. The 1975 survey by the Plan Organization also indicated that, with the exception of tea and sugar, the primary source of consumer products continued to be traditional shops (table 54).

Still, it would be misleading to dismiss the significance of co-op shops on these grounds alone. A centralized network of 6,000 shops represented the beginnings of a potentially important commercial network that could have growing influence on the consumption patterns of the rural population. The rapid change in type of fuel, from dung and wood to paraffin, is a prime example of such influence. By the mid-1970s, paraffin constituted more than half the fuel requirements of rural households (MCRA 1975d:85; 1976a:50). Similarly, increasing utilization of certain production inputs, such as chemical fertilizers, improved varieties of seeds, pesticides, and so forth, were influenced by the increased availability of these items through the co-op shops (table 55).[5] The co-ops had also begun providing some agricultural equipment for common use through rentals, although this remained a very marginal activity.

The most common complaints about co-op shops were that they stocked very few of the daily needs of peasants and that they engaged only in cash transactions. Many studies indicated that more than two-thirds of members would have preferred to have credit accounts,

TABLE 54
Source of Basic Requirements of Cooperative Members (in percent)

	Co-op	Open Market
Sugar and tea	47	53
Other subsistence needs	14	86
Clothing	3	97
Seeds, fertilizers, other farming needs	36	64
Other needs	16	86

Source: Plan Organization 1975:table 21.

TABLE 55
Production Inputs Marketed by Cooperatives (tons)

Year	Chemical fertilizer	Seeds	Pesticides
1970	59,000	410	—
1974	169,000	5,000	—
1975	173,000	16,000	582
1976	170,000	20,000	840

Source: Central Bank of Iran, *Annual Reports* for 1970–1976 (Tehran).
Note: Dashes indicate data not available.

to be paid back in kind at harvest time—the common practice with local shopkeepers and an option the co-ops would not accept.[6]

Co-ops as Marketing Agents

The least-developed area of the co-ops' activities remained the purchase and marketing of surplus agricultural produce. It has been estimated that less than 1 percent of all marketed agricultural produce was purchased and sold through the co-ops. What produce the co-ops did market was sold primarily to state institutions such as the army.[7] Still, by the mid-1970s, the marketing activity of the co-ops had begun to increase. In 1970, co-ops had purchased produce worth 642 million rials; by 1975 and 1976 this expenditure had increased to 7,954 million rials and 5,340 million rials, respectively (Central Bank of Iran *Annual Reports* for 1975 and 1976).

According to the 1975 survey by the Plan Organization, 79 percent of the co-ops showed no marketing activity. What is significant,

TABLE 56
Sale of Produce by Peasants to Cooperatives

Source of Information	% of Peasants Who Have Ever Sold Produce to the Co-op	% of Peasants Willing to Sell Produce to the Co-op	% of Peasants Willing to Receive Credit in Exchange for Farming Surplus
MCRA 1975d	14.4	74.5	—
MCRA 1975e	2.3	70.3	69.7
MCRA 1976a	29.0	96.0	90.0

Note: Dash indicates no data given.

however, is that a large majority of peasants wanted the co-ops to buy their surplus or extend consumer credit to them in exchange for their surplus (Plan Organization 1975:53 and 85). A number of MCRA reports confirm the results of the Plan Organization survey (table 56).

There were also occasional newspaper reports that farmers had requested the local co-op to buy their crops but were refused on various administrative grounds, such as "the purchase order has not arrived yet from the central authorities," and so forth (*Tehran Economist*, October 23, 1978). Such bureaucratic bungling could only deepen the mistrust of peasants toward the authorities, since most had to sell off their harvests immediately and could not wait for "purchase orders" to arrive.

It would be misleading to think that bureaucratic bungling was the primary reason for the failure of co-ops to develop into marketing agents of agricultural surplus. The basic reason for this failure was the government's fundamental economic "autonomy" from an agricultural surplus that it did not really need in order to finance its own activities. Not only did it not depend on such surplus for accumulation and investment in other sectors of the economy, but the flow of oil revenues made it possible for the government to import food. The government found it easier to cover the urban food demand through increased imports rather than through long-term planning and the arduous establishment of marketing networks that would channel the agricultural surplus from millions of production points toward urban markets.

FARMING CORPORATIONS AND
PRODUCTION COOPERATIVES

Rural cooperative societies were, in the first instance, instruments of the state intended to provide credit. Only secondarily were they marketing agencies and outlets for consumer products. Direct state intervention in peasant production took the form of what were known as farming corporations and production cooperatives.

The primary goal of this form of intervention was to increase production and control the choice of crops on a national scale. In the years following the implementation of land reform, the government, as well as the peasants, faced unpredictable market fluctuations. Many peasants who had just received land turned to cultivation of specialized cash crops—for example, melons, sugar beets, and cotton—on lands traditionally allocated to grains. If cotton prices were up one year, peasants turned to cotton, only to face the possibility of a slump the following year. As early as the summer of 1966 it was reported that the government felt it necessary to increase its control over agriculture through the creation of large-scale farming units (*Economist Intelligence Unit* [*Iran*] 3, 1966).

The original legislation forming farm corporations was passed in February of 1968. According to this legislation, if the majority of peasants in a given area agreed, the Ministry of Cooperatives and Rural Affairs—which was then called the Ministry of Land Reform—would establish a farm corporation in that area. All peasants would give up their land titles to the government, and in exchange for their land, evaluated by the government along with the evaluation of so-called production investments, such as deepwells, and agricultural machinery, they would receive proportional shares in the corporation. A board of directors, elected annually by the shareholders and including one government representative, would make all the farming decisions. The shareholders would have the option of working as laborers for the company, or they could seek employment elsewhere. The ministry would supply the corporation with skilled personnel, agricultural engineers, veterinarians, accountants, and so forth, whose salaries would be paid by the government during the initial period. In addition, the government would pay the cost of necessary infrastructural investments on the land (for example, the cost of building irrigation canals and the like) and would extend loans at a 1 percent rate of interest for other expenses. At the end of each agricultural year, accountants would calculate the income generated and the costs incurred and would deduct a certain percentage for amortization of capital, another 15 percent for corporation deposits and savings, 5 percent for health insurance, and 2 percent for new buildings and houses. Furthermore, the board of directors could vote to allocate certain sums for the next year's expenditures, for debt servicing, and for bonuses to be paid to the managing directors. The remaining profits would be divided according to the number of shares held by shareholders.

Peasants who had recently become owners were not impressed and did not volunteer for such projects. They treated them with deep suspicion, and typically they felt that exchanging their land titles for shares would turn them into *ra'iyat-e dowlati*, "state serfs" (Azkia 1969:72).

In the absence of peasant initiative and voluntary consent, officials required peasants to sign consent forms. Charges of coercion were common. According to one source, "one observer of long experience in the land reform field, after interviewing farmers in 8 villages included under three different farm corporations, stated he had found not one farmer who favored them, but only feelings of resentment, frustration and helplessness in their unsuccessful opposition" (Platt 1970:80).

A new bill in October 1968 solved the government's problem: formation of farm corporations no longer depended on the consent of the majority of peasants in a given area but solely on the judgment of the ministry (Ashraf 1973:12). Coercion had become legal. During the following decade some ninety farm corporations were formed, affecting nearly 34,000 peasants and some 300,000 hectares of land (table 57).

Government reports on the workings of farm corporations invariably painted a rosy picture. Increases in cultivated area, production, and yield were upheld as measures of success. Indeed, there were considerable increases in production and yield for most crops. Those crops that needed more human attention and labor, however, such as rice and summer vegetable cash crops, saw a decline in yield, most likely because of peasant dissatisfaction with the corporations (MCRA

TABLE 57
Farm Corporations of Iran

Year	No. of Corporations Formed	No. of Villages and Farms Affected	No. of Shareholders	Total No. of Shares	Total Population of the Area of Farm Corporations	Shareholding Population	Total Land of Corporations (ha.)
1968	14	84	4,820	207,650	43,552	24,749	58,857
1969	5	31	1,586	74,529	15,419	9,911	21,015
1971	8	58	2,874	126,128	24,345	15,482	24,518
1972	16	168	6,433	303,258	55,317	33,436	70,558
1973	22	205	7,902	313,187	63,820	44,127	64,874
1975	20	229	8,787	345,648	86,171	49,682	67,340
1976	4	38	1,261	49,478	11,046	8,045	11,572
Total	89	813	33,663	1,419,883	229,670	185,435	318,734

Source: Ministry of Cooperatives and Rural Affairs, *MCRA Activities in Establishment and Management of Farm Corporations and Rural Production Cooperatives through March 20, 1977* (Tehran).

1977d:38–40). The government also pointed to increases in the overall income of peasants (MCRA 1977d:93–94). Other semiofficial sources, however, were critical of the project on financial grounds. The increases, they pointed out, were gained at the cost of huge government expenditure. The *Tehran Economist* noted that without enormous subsidies, grants, and low-interest loans, every single one of these corporations would show large losses:

> The balance sheets of cooperatives and farming corporations often do not show how government money is spent. On the contrary, they attempt to give positive balance sheets. But it is unthinkable that such balance sheets would be acceptable to financial and economic authorities. Undoubtedly we all support the existence of agricultural cooperatives and farming corporations, and for our part we hope that these two types of ventures will solve many of our agricultural problems. But at the same time we cannot, as in the past, accept that thousands of millions of rials be spent on these institutions and in certain cases, instead of an increase in production and a reduction of costs, very little produce be delivered to our economy at high prices. (*Tehran Economist*, June 19, 1976)

For instance, in 1971, farm corporations showed a sum total of 185.2 million rials profit (541 rials per share). In the same year, government grants to the corporations amounted to 342.5 million rials, and low-interest loans accounted for a further 105.9 million rials. Without these grants and loans, the corporations would have shown a net loss of 263.3 million rials (Plan Organization, Statistical Center, *Statistical Yearbook* for 1972, p. 314). The MCRA reports on individual corporations confirmed this overall picture (table 58). Not every project, however, even in a capitalist society, need be profitable. The problem with the corporations was that they were not only a financial liability but a social and political disaster.

Peasants who had just received land were deeply mistrustful of losing their titles and receiving shares in corporations instead. They resented becoming workers for a state corporation just at a time when they felt relieved of the burden of being subservient to the landlords. This feeling was especially deep in villages where old landlords had held large plots of land and would, as a consequence, become the largest shareholders in the new corporations. The corporations were seen by peasants as new mechanisms through which the old landlords would control village life once again.

TABLE 58
Changes in Annual Income of Peasants in Corporation Areas (in rials)

Name of Corporation	Average Annual Peasant Income Prior to Formation of the Corporation	Average Annual Peasant Income after the Formation of the Corporation	Government Grants Included in Annual Peasant Income
Firouzabad	27,186	69,116	56,426
Kazeroun	23,260	27,826	14,006
Afzar	20,056	25,395	37,737
Qir	17,116	33,414	26,319

Source: MCRA 1975a:5–13.

In the Dargazin Corporation, for instance, the smallest share-holder held 1.6 shares, while the two largest—both former land-lords—held 1,118 and 618 shares. In the first year of the corporation's work, the net profit per share was 134 rials (less than US $2.00) per share.[8] This meant an annual profit of $2.86 for one shareholder and $1,997.49 and $1,104.16 for the largest shareholders. The peasants felt that government grants and loans were being channeled to those who were already prosperous, while their recent hopes for improving their lives through owning their own plots of land had been thwarted. Increasingly, they had to seek alternative employment to make a living. Of course, the sharp differentiations among shareholders only reflected inequalities that already existed. But the peasants felt that while earlier they had been able to improve their subsistence through hard work, there now was no reason to work on the land, where the bulk of the benefits would accrue mainly to large shareholders.

One study showed that among shareholders with fewer than fifteen shares, a total of 150 days out of 300 were spent working outside the corporation, while shareholders with forty shares or more worked 43 days for the corporation and 22 days outside; members of their households put in a total of 223 days for the corporation and 27 days in other employment (Hajebi et al. 1971:36). Similar results were reported by another study: shareholders with thirty or more shares worked 127 days for the corporation out of a total of 151 working days. Those with fewer than fifteen shares worked 95 days for the corporation out of 174 working days (Nik-kholq 1971:26).

TABLE 59
Perceptions of Who Benefits Most from Farm Corporations

| | Shareholders' Perceptions | |
Amount of Shares Held	Those Who Have More Shares Benefit Most (%)	Those Who Work Hardest Benefit Most (%)
Less than 15 shares	53.3	13.3
15–30 shares	33.3	8.4
30 shares & more	19.0	33.4

Source: Nik-kholq 1971:252.

Only about a third of the income of shareholders with fewer than fifteen shares came from profits and sharecropping for the corporation, while more than two-thirds of the income of those with thirty or more shares came from the corporation (Nik-kholq 1971:41–53; Hajebi et al. 1971:20–32). In a classic case of inverted existential rationalism, the latter naturally felt that those who worked more benefited more from the corporation (table 59).

The small shareholders also lost on traditional sources of credit. Without access to land, and dependent mostly on insecure outside employment of one sort or another, small shareholders were refused credit by local shopkeepers. One study shows that prior to the formation of the corporation, the average annual credit received from local shopkeepers was 11,350 rials, while in the following years it was only 2,307 rials (Nik-kholq 1971:53). The reduction in credit had an immediate adverse effect on the living standards of this group of peasants: the annual average consumer expenditure per household decreased from 89,815 rials to 63,999 rials (Nik-kholq 1971:66–67).

It should, therefore, not come as a surprise that when asked how they felt their social status had changed after the establishment of the corporation, more than two-thirds of the shareholders indicated that they felt a diminution in their social standing and honor (Nik-kholq 1971:246). More than 50 percent said that if the corporation were dissolved, their living standard would improve (Nik-kholq 1971:251). In a different corporation, 70 percent of the peasants continued "to pay visits" to their land, and 57 percent preferred to work on "their" plot when work teams were organized (Azkia 1969:74).

Such deep underlying resentment inevitably resulted in indifferent work practices. This problem was so severe that after the first year all corporations reverted to traditional working methods. Instead of working on large-scale plots as laborers, peasants were organized into traditional work teams, or bonehs, and worked on a sharecropping or piecework basis:

> The managements in all four farm corporations studied in Khuzistan were fully aware of this indifferent attitude held by the majority of the peasant shareholders and as a result had organized the cultivation of some crops on a modified sharecropping basis — the corporation provides the seeds, land, water and machinery and the peasants provide the labour. The harvest is then divided according to a mutually agreed rate. The adoption of this centuries-old practice has contributed towards the "financial success" of these farm corporations (Salmanzadeh 1980:234).

More important, the government was forced to de-emphasize farm corporations in favor of a new type of intervention: the production cooperative. Article 1 of the law concerning the establishment of production cooperatives, passed in 1971, stressed that the Ministry of Land Reform should act "with due consideration to the principle of the peasant's individual ownership and all the rights derived from that ownership" (MCRA 1977d:105). The production cooperatives were different from the corporations in that they did not take full control of the land. They extended government credit and loans for mechanization and improved agriculture to work teams organized on the traditional basis. Where such work teams did not exist, the production cooperatives required their formation. Government direct control took the form of making the decision about crop selection.[9] More area was allocated to such crops as sunflower seeds, sugar beets, and opium. Between 1972 and 1976, thirty-five production cooperatives were established affecting just under 10,000 peasants and some 50,000 hectares of land (table 60).

The most telling evidence of the failure of all these initiatives taken by the state — both the corporations and the production cooperatives — were the actions of peasants after the overthrow of the regime in 1979: all such corporations and production cooperatives were dissolved. Peasants took over corporation lands, and private individual cultivation replaced all previous arrangements. This is in sharp con-

TABLE 60
Production Cooperatives, 1972–1976

Year	No. of Co-ops Formed	No. of Villages & Farms Affected	Total Agricultural Land of Co-ops (ha.)	No. of Peasant Owners Involved
1972	6	34	6,628	1,299
1973	8	53	12,662	1,886
1974	10	58	10,381	2,971
1975	10	50	18,337	3,223
1976	1	14	2,600	321
Total	35	214	50,572	9,700

Source: Ministry of Cooperatives and Rural Affairs, *MCRA Activities in Establishment and Management of Farm Corporations and Rural Production Cooperatives through March 20, 1977* (Tehran).

trast to the peasants' attitude toward the cooperative societies. After the change of regime in 1979, peasants demanded the extension and expansion, and not the dissolution, of cooperative societies and their consumer, credit, and marketing functions. We will discuss these paradoxes in the next chapter.

8

The Changing Sociology and Politics of the Peasantry

During the mass urban upheavals of 1977–1979, which led to the overthrow of the Pahlavi dynasty and the establishment of the Islamic Republic in Iran, a striking new feature of Iranian politics was very often reported and commented upon: villagers were actively participating in what were essentially urban demonstrations (Hooglund 1980, 1982b; Hegland 1982).

Moreover, since the establishment of the new regime, there have been both important regional peasant movements, such as the one in Turkoman-Sahra, and many local developments and political activities in almost all villages throughout the country (Hooglund 1980; Hegland 1980. The unprecedented scale of peasant activity, demanding various changes, has forced agrarian issues to remain in the political foreground for the first time in modern Iranian history. The new Islamic Republic could not possibly ignore the villagers. It has tried its hand at the redistribution of land through reform and at military suppression, for example, in Turkoman-Sahra and Kurdistan. It has also attempted to co-opt local peasant militants into Islamic organizations. At the same time, the new Islamic Republic has tried to control and intimidate rural areas through the dispatch into the countryside of zealous supporters under the banner of Jahad-e Sazendegi, the Battle for Reconstruction. Jahad-e Sazendegi has also been instrumental in improvements in village life through the building of roads, public baths, mosques, and schools and through the provision of more sanitary drinking water, electrification, and so forth. The government has continued to debate, amend, implement, and suspend various legislations on land reform (Ashraf 1982). It has still not decided on a final bill for comprehensive rural policy. Meanwhile, in all villages, peasants have taken over farming corporations as well as lands belonging to former landlords and capitalists who have fled the country. Peasants who had recently been expelled from their land have returned and have taken back their old plots, and they have consistently pressed the central government to deal with their grievances and demands (Hegland 1980). All these developments are new and significant for Iran.

They are significant because, on the whole, Iranian history, unlike that of many other Asian countries, has been marked by an absence of peasant rebellions and movements. With the exception of the movement in Gilan (1917–1921), even during periods of revolutionary mass activities in Iran, there has been little participation from the countryside. During the Constitutional Movement (1906–1911), there were only three recorded peasant uprisings, in Rasht, Talesh, and Yazd. All three were protests against heavy taxation. During the post–World War II period, aside from peasant participation in the movement in Azarbaijan, there were recorded reports of only twenty-two incidents of peasant protests (Abrahamian and Kazemi 1978).

In attempting to explain this feature of the Iranian peasantry, two diametrically opposed explanations have been offered. One explanation attributes the problem to the absence of a revolutionary policy toward the peasantry by any of the country's political parties. The second explanation adopts an objectivist viewpoint and roots the lack of earlier peasant uprisings in the particularities of the Iranian economy and land relations. Paradoxically, both of these explanations gained currency under the influence of the Chinese revolution, in view of the role of the Chinese peasantry and the Chinese Communist party in that revolution. The Chinese experience had an enormous impact on Iranian intellectuals, political activists, and historians during the late 1950s and the 1960s.

The success of the Chinese Communist party in leading peasant uprisings toward a complete takeover of state power and the subsequent initial gains of the revolution for the rural masses convinced many Iranian oppositionists that the earlier defeat of the Iranian revolution, in particular the defeat of all revolutionary and reform movements during the 1941–1953 period, derived from both a failure to understand the revolutionary potential of the peasantry and the absence of any radical agrarian program. This conviction was particularly strong among those currents who broke away from the Tudeh party, the Iranian Communist party, under the influence of the Chinese Communist party.[1] The Vietnamese experience added further conviction to this belief. Such militant oppositionists went so far as to propose a line of action for Iran which was almost a replica of the Chinese experience. They advocated going to the countryside to organize the peasant masses into a people's army which could surround the cities from the countryside. Ironically, all this talk of a peasant revolution and the formation of people's armies was proceeding just when the Iranian land reform had begun in earnest during the early 1960s. That is, these ideas were propagated during a period marked both by very high expectations and by confusion among the peasants. It also was a moment of tremendous expansion by the forces of the state into every corner of the Iranian countryside.

On the other end of the spectrum, the writings of Mao on the character of the Chinese peasantry inspired a whole series of written works on the conditions under which peasant upheavals occur historically. These works speculated about which specific layers among the peasantry play the leading role, which specific issues peasants organize around, and which specific forms of struggle are most conducive to success. To summarize a very long and rich debate on these issues:

1. The conditions that cause peasant uprisings and make it possible for the peasantry to organize to fight back are provided by a weak central state and its endemic fiscal crises that lead to higher taxation of peasants, as well as to increased fluctuations and insecurities of the market for agricultural products within the context of a generally unstable market economy.

2. In the initial stages of the struggle, the "middle peasants," that is, those working the land with their families, play a leading role in initiating and organizing all peasants to fight back, because the middle peasants enjoy a certain degree of autonomy with respect to the big landlords, while the poorest layers within the villages are highly dependent on them. These poorer layers, it was argued, join the struggle after it gains a certain momentum and credibility, while the middle peasants, being more severely affected by the crisis and having a

certain independence, both economically and politically, from the big landlords, play the decisive and leading role in organizing.

3. The issues most important to these struggles are those of access to land, lower taxation, and better marketing, pricing, and credit conditions. Therefore, the struggle is not directed against the "rich peasants" as much as against the big landlords and against the state itself.

4. Because of the nature of agricultural production and the dependence of peasants on the land and their year-round work on the land, the most suitable form of struggle, lending itself to continual production on the land, is rural guerrilla warfare.[2]

Using this model, some writers on the Iranian peasantry have argued that the lack of these preconditions explains the nonrevolutionary character of the peasantry of modern Iran. The monopoly of land ownership in Iran, either by the state or by a few big landlords, and the predominantly sharecropping relations of production gave rise, according to this viewpoint, to a highly constrained and locked-in rural population, dependent either on the state or on the landlord. The middle or independent peasantry that was crucial in the Chinese and Vietnamese experiences simply did not exist in Iran. Furthermore, the integration of Iran within the world market did not take the form of penetration of market relations into the countryside. The Iranian countryside had remained more or less isolated from the national market and was, therefore, relatively immune to its fluctuations. As a consequence of these two factors, even though there had been a series of weak central governments in modern Iran, Iranian history had not witnessed the classical pattern of peasant uprisings typical of other Asian countries (Abrahamian and Kazemi 1978).

It is not my purpose here to accept, criticize, or refute the historical validity of this thesis with regard to its applicability or lack of such to Iran before land reform was initiated. Rather, I will try to show that these observations, whether or not they accurately interpret past Iranian history, have now been completely superseded by developments within the Iranian economy and social structure, largely introduced by land reform and its effects over the past two decades.

The social consequences of land reform were reflected politically in two major ways. First, during the period leading to the change of regime in February 1979, it was the mass of urban dwellers, people of recent rural origin, and the commuting youth of the villages who took part in the urban mass demonstrations, while villagers often kept a skeptical distance. Second, following the collapse of the old regime, peasants burst onto the scene of social struggle within their villages, presenting their own demands and exercising their own forms of activity.

By the 1970s the Iranian rural scene was no longer that of an isolated economy. The land reform program and the general economic and social changes in the country had indissolubly linked the Iranian village to the urban centers. A number of urban manufactured goods now made their way regularly to the village. Some of them, such as the moped and the bicycle, made market towns more accessible to rural dwellers. Others, such as transistor radios, cassette players, and television sets—no matter what one may think of the quality of the programs broadcast—opened fresh links and associations between the world of the villager and the world of urban life. Banks, cooperatives, and other state institutions, the literacy corps, health workers, and so forth, all provided new forms of urban intervention within the villages, as did to an even greater extent the agroindustrial complexes and the nearby factories.

A large mass of villagers—those without land or with only a little land—engaged in periodic inter-rural and rural-urban migrations on a scale previously unprecedented in Iran. Zaboli villagers from the far southeast of the country were working on the modern farms of Gorgan and Mazandraan eight hundred miles away. Older migrant workers who had gained new skills were moving even farther to Azarbaijan in northwest Iran, where new agro-industrial complexes were competing for skilled agricultural workers, such as combine operators and the like. Skilled Isfahani and Yazdi farmers could be found in Mashad, Azarbaijan, Khuzistan, and Fars, literally in all four corners of the country.

The most important links integrating rural Iran into urban life, socially, economically, and later politically, were the millions of transient immigrants. They were transient or temporary, in the sense that they still often retained land and had family and close kin in their original villages and continued to return to their home base, if not as daily commuters, then on weekly or monthly visits or, at the least, seasonally.[3] As I have argued in previous chapters, this particular pattern of partial migration was a result of the industrial employment structure that emerged in the 1960s and 1970s. The limitations and fluctuations of urban industrial employment made it very precarious for villagers to leave the land altogether and en masse. In addition, the level of urban wages was not sufficient to feed an entire household. Consequently, one or two young male members of the household would go to seek urban employment while the rest of the household continued to work the land. Often the male members returned to the village during harvest time, or if they lived near industrial centers, they combined agriculture with industrial employment on a regular basis.

Such semimigration had a double effect. On the one hand, it allowed the level of urban wages to remain low, since these wages did not have to provide for a worker's entire family. It also increased the degree of "toleration" of rural poverty by relieving the peasant household of some of its members, who might in addition possibly send some money or "gifts" home. On the other hand, however, it broke down the traditional isolation of the villages from urban life.

It was this layer of the population that was instrumental in making the political upheavals of 1977–1979 a countrywide affair. Iranian villages were no longer isolated small dots on a huge map. The movement of millions of people had connected these villagers up into a network of political turmoil. As Eric Hooglund points out,

> [M]igration did not mean an "uprooting." Quite to the contrary, after settling in towns, most migrants maintained regular contacts with relatives in their natal villages. This continued association of migrants and villagers served as an important means through which information about the city was disseminated in the villages. (Hooglund 1982a:147)

This situation was new to Iran, although not new elsewhere. A rather similar layer of first-generation worker-peasants had taken political ideas into the Russian countryside at the turn of the century. But whereas they had brought Social Democratic and Social Revolutionary politics, their Iranian counterparts now were bringing home Islamic politics. Rude's discussion of "popular ideology" is very pertinent:

Popular ideology in this period [of transition from preindustrial to industrial society] is not a purely internal affair and the sole property of a single class or group: that in itself distinguishes it from ideology as "class consciousness". . . . It is most often a mixture, a fusion of two elements of which only one is the peculiar property of the "popular" classes and the other is superimposed by a process of transmission and adoption from outside. Of these, the first is what I call the "inherent," traditional element . . . the second element is the stock of ideas and beliefs that are "derived" or borrowed from others. . . .

So two things are important to note: one is that there is no such thing as a *tabula rasa*, or an empty tablet in the place of a mind on which new ideas may be grafted where there were no ideas before . . . ; and the second is that there is also no such thing as an automatic progression from "simple" to more sophisticated ideas. (Rude 1980:28)

He further elaborates what he means by "inherent" ideas and their political limitations:

By "inherent" beliefs I mean, for one thing, the peasant's belief in his right to land. . . . Analogous to the peasant's belief in the common justice of being allowed unfettered possession of his land is the belief of the small consumer, whether a villager or townsman, in his right to buy bread at a "just" price, as determined by experience and custom, or the worker's claim to a "just" wage.

But how far can this "inherent" ideology by itself carry the protesters? Into strikes, food riots, peasant rebellions (with or without success); and even into a state of awareness of the need for radical change . . . ; but evidently it cannot bring them all the way to revolution. (Rude 1980:30–32)

It is here that the influence of urban-national politics on the shaping of political ideas in rural areas becomes particularly decisive:

[P]opular achievements, whether in "pre-industrial" England or elsewhere, could not advance far beyond this point [of strikes, riots, or rebellions] without the native "plebian culture" or "inherent" ideology becoming supplemented by that "derived" element of which I spoke before: the political, philosophical or religious ideas that, at varying stages of sophistication, became absorbed in the more specifically popular culture. . . .

[I]t must be emphasized, whether the resultant mixture took on a militant and revolutionary or a conservative and counter-revolutionary form depended less on the nature of the recipients or of the "inherent" beliefs from which they started than on the nature of the "derived" beliefs compounded by the circumstances then prevailing and what E. P. Thompson has called "the sharp jostle of experience." What I am arguing is that there are three factors and not only two to be taken account of: the "inherent" element . . . ; the "derived" or outside, element, which could only be effectively absorbed if the ground was already prepared; and the circumstances and experience which, in the final analysis, determined the nature of the final mixture. (Rude 1980:33–35)

The "sharp jostle of experience" in Iran took the form of the integration of village life into urban experience, rather than formation of rural organizations and peasant movements. The millions of young villagers who migrated back and forth carried with them more than new urban material needs and goods. As new political currents and movements were taking shape in the towns during the 1970s, this layer of the population brought these ideas back into the villages. Moreover, the movement against the shah and the demonstrations of 1978–1979 were not confined to one or two major cities; they occurred on a forty-day religious cycle in practically all cities and major towns. This made urban politics ever more accessible to villagers, who could now join in and follow national developments. As the opposition movement against the shah became increasingly hegemonized by the clergy and their ideas for an Islamic government, these "derived" ideas molded, in a very particular and quite unique direction, the "inherent" system of values among villagers seeking a better life. "The commuters brought new interpretations of religion to their villages. . . . This politicization of religion was eagerly accepted by village youth. In this process, they acquired a new interest in religious personalities and practices" (Hooglund 1982a:145). Visits to villages became occasions to pass on information about the latest political developments and to organize support for the movement.

Prior to the overthrow of the old regime, this was the primary form of rural engagement in national politics. The participation of villagers in political activity was limited mostly to the younger ones who had become "urban commuters." Moreover, this participation took the form of engagement in urban affairs, with the focus being on central government or national affairs, rather than on local or rural problems. It was only after February 1979 that villagers began to engage in political activities related to the villages specifically and to raise their own local demands and expectations for the new order. These demands themselves were clearly linked to the changes that had occurred in the Iranian countryside since the early 1960s.[4]

To begin with, the demand for land was raised in all the cases reported in the press. This is not surprising in view of the fact that a large proportion of Iranian peasants had very small holdings. This demand was not directed toward a "landlord class," however, since large landlords no longer existed, nor were the landlords, perceived by peasants as a separate coherent class, dominating the affairs of the countryside. Particularly in the first year, peasants demanded and, in most instances, simply took over land from any person or institution whom they saw in possession of what they felt "justly" — to use Rude's expression — belonged to them. These included some large landlords, who continued to hold land after the reform of the 1960s, particularly when such persons had left the country, the agribusinesses, the state farm corporations, the production cooperatives, and the large and sometimes even the medium-size holdings where there were local disputes among the richer and poorer or landless villagers.[5] In practically all such cases of direct expropriation, the land was divided by the villagers themselves and cultivated as individual holdings. In subsequent years, from 1980 to the present time, the government has tried to introduce "order" into the countryside by stopping and reversing all expropriations, pending the new land reform legislation. It is not clear, however, how successful such attempts have been.

Furthermore, it is significant that the demand for land was not the only or even the most universal cry of the peasantry. Other problems, all consequences of the previous period of change, and in some cases extensions of the previous reforms, were raised. Chief among them have been:

1. Cancellation of all standing land payments due to the central government
2. Cancellation of all debts to banks and extension of long-term, interest-free loans
3. A system of guaranteed purchase of agricultural produce by the government
4. Provision of fertilizers, pesticides, and machinery at prices that peasants can afford

5. Cancellation of water dues and charges for grazing animals on nationalized pastures and of charges for use of forest timber
6. Expansion of the facilities of the local cooperative shops to deal with more local needs

Even more interesting, and completely new, is the range of original demands that have clearly reflected newly felt needs arising from extensive urban contact. These have included:

1. Electrification of villages
2. Provision of drinking water
3. Provision of health clinics and doctors
4. Provision of schools and teachers
5. Improvement of roads

In several instances there have been demands for the establishment of "seasonal factories" to deal with seasonal unemployment and to provide additional income.

In other words the integration of the rural areas into the national economy brought with it increased social and economic expectations and political involvement and awareness among peasants on a level unprecedented in modern Iranian history. That this national dimension of rural politics has been molded and dominated by Islamic concepts is not the issue of our discussion here. The facts of economic integration and the movement of masses of rural inhabitants in and out of the cities created a new type of rural person, quite different from the prereform Iranian peasant, whose life experience and horizons of expectation were largely limited to his village and the question of land. The peasant now has completely new needs and expectations of social welfare, needs that were unthinkable thirty years before the revolution. He has seen that what happens in the politics of the city also concerns him; this in itself has been a revolutionary transformation. The peasant's participation has not taken the form of some brand of rural politics or guerrilla warfare; it has taken the form of trying to get his demands heard and fought for within the national urban political framework of change that has taken place. The peasant has quickly become a new type of citizen in a far more closely integrated nation-state.[6] This change is an irreversible legacy of the Iranian land reform of 1960–1972.

Appendixes

APPENDIX A
CONTRIBUTION OF LAND PAYMENTS
TO CAPITAL FORMATION

The Iranian Land Reform Law of 1962 provided for cash payment to owners of one-tenth — and later of one-fifteenth — of the evaluated land price at the time of its appropriation by the state, and the balance in nine — and later in fourteen — equal annual installments through nonnegotiable government bonds bearing 6 percent interest on the outstanding balance (1962 Land Reform Act, article 11). The land was then sold to peasants at a price 10 percent higher than the purchase price, to cover administrative charges, and paid in fifteen annual installments (1962 Land Reform Act, article 15). The compensation bonds could be used by former landlords for payment of taxes, purchase of new lands for development, and purchase of shares in the Government Factories Corporation. They could also be discounted by banks against credit for "productive investment," which was defined as investment in industry, mines, and agriculture (cabinet decree, February 17, 1962).[1]

A similar procedure was adopted during the third phase of the reform in 1968, requiring the sale of land to tenants. During the second stage of the reform, the lease option was chosen by the majority of landlords. If peasants were not able to pay their installments, the government would reimburse the landlord with bonds which could be used as credit to establish industries, to invest in government projects, or to buy fallow or undeveloped land. In January

TABLE A-1
Gross Domestic Fixed Capital Formation

Year	Billions of Rials[a]
1962	49
1963	53
1964	62
1965	78
1966	87
1967	113
1968	130
1969	132
1970	140
1971	179
1972	212

Source: Central Bank of Iran, *Annual Reports* for 1963–1972. Figures are rough, as the data from the *Annual Reports* differ from those of Central Bank of Iran, *National Income of Iran 1959–1971* (Tehran, 1973).
[a]Constant 1959 prices.

1975 the Agricultural Cooperative Bank offered to discount these bonds at 9 1/2 to 10 percent interest.

Still, it must be emphasized that the actual contribution to capital formation by both types of payments—from peasants to the state, and from the state to the landlords—was not significant. To begin with, article 8 of a cabinet decree, issued on February 10, 1962, permitted the Agricultural Bank of Iran to cash land bonds prior to their date of maturity. The interest paid on such bonds was to be determined by the bank's board of directors (Ministry of Agriculture 1962:254). In effect, this nullified all institutionalized attempts to force productive investment of the land bonds. Moreover, the price paid in cash by the government to the landlords for the first installment totaled 3.1 billion rials (approximately U.S. $41 million). The total land price and interest payments under the first phase of land reform through 1972 was 11.6 billion rials (U.S. $155 million). Comparing these figures with those of gross domestic fixed capital formation during this period from 1962 to 1972 shows the relatively small orders of magnitude involved—something less than 1 percent (table A-1).

Moreover, not only were very few of the bonds received by the landlords exchanged for Government Factories Corporation shares, but also a still smaller fraction were discounted at the 4 percent special rate arranged by the State Agricultural Bank against loans for approved new investments than were discounted by speculation through private channels at rates as high as 30 to 50 percent.[2] According to Platt (1970:98), through 1965, $4.36 million were discounted by the Agricultural Bank at 4 percent against credit for investment; $21.36 million were discounted speculatively, and there were no bonds at all converted to Government Corporation Shares. Large sums of money left the country for investment abroad (Denman 1973:268).

This picture was modified only marginally in later years, when government-owned factories were offered for sale to the public and proved to be profitable ventures. From March 1965 until March 1971, a total of 543 million rials (U.S. $7.2 million) had been exchanged for shares in government-owned factories. This constitutes about 8 percent of the total face value of the bonds issued during the first phase of land reform. Another 433 million rials (U.S. $5.7 million) had been used to pay taxes (Zandjani 1973:168–170).

APPENDIX B
THE POSITION OF THE CLERGY
IN THE 1962 LAND REFORM

It has become an accepted fact — one that is all too obvious and as if naturally given — that the opposition movement among a section of the Iranian clergy during 1962–1963, which culminated in the mass protests of June 1963 and their bloody repression by the army, was directed against the 1962 land reform.[1] From this point of view, many analysts have argued that the clergy saw the land reform as a threat to the religiously endowed (waqf) lands as well as to the clergy's landowning kinsmen. The actual record does not support such a straightforward and singleminded interpretation. Although some ayatollahs had opposed land reform, this was not the central issue of the 1962–1963 confrontations. The first demonstrations and petitions of the clergy began almost a year after the land redistribution started, and they were directed, not against the land reform, but against the new local election bill the cabinet had passed on October 7, 1962.

At a much earlier time, when the original land reform bill was being discussed by the parliament in February 1960, Ayatollah Borujerdi had written a letter to Ja'far Behbehani, his nephew and a member of parliament, complaining that the bill was ill-advised and contrary to the *shari'a* (religious law) (Akhavi 1980:91). Several *ulama* (members of the clergy) agitated against the 1962 land reform on the grounds that the government should have solicited their opinion on such an important matter. Once the Additional Articles of January 17, 1963, were announced, requiring charitable waqf lands to be leased on ninety-nine-year terms to the peasants cultivating them, certain members of the clergy posed strong opposition (Lambton 1969:105–108). Nonetheless, the majority of the clergy, and particularly the more political and activist circles around Khomeini, did not oppose land reform as such.

Indeed, just these elements of the clergy were wary of the possible success of the government's contention that the opposition was instigated by the landlords, and so they went out of their way to deny any such connections. In a statement issued a day after Khomeini's arrest on June 5, 1963, Shari'atmadari reiterated this theme:

> The shi'i ulama have no connections with big landlords and they do not oppose peasants' ownership of land. Contrary to deceitful government propaganda, the interests of the ulama will not be threatened by such ownership; they will be better served. The ulama are more linked to the peasants than to landlords. Our protest against the government concerns the application and implementation of the [reform] law in which, we say, legal and religious conditions must be observed. In any case, our struggles do not principally relate to this [land reform] issue. (Davani n.d.:vol. 4, p. 105)

Even on the issue of waqf land, the clerics rejected the government accusations:

> The present ruling elite . . . says that the clergy is against land distribution, because of their hold on awqaf [endowment land]. This is ridiculous. All the awqaf is held by the government. . . . The awqaf of Qa'inat, with its enormous revenues, is held by Mr. 'Alam [then the prime minister]. The big awqaf dedicated to Imam Reza's shrine [in Khorasan province] is all in the hands of the government. Go and contact any of the theological students in Qum and inspect all the books of revenues for the seminaries and see if a penny from the awqaf shows

up there. . . . Go and investigate if a penny from a big or feudal landlord has reached Qum. (Davani n.d.:vol. 4, p. 139)

There was no ambiguity, however, about the clerical opposition
to the local election bill, which they opposed on three grounds: first,
it removed being a Muslim as a requirement for electors and candidates in these elections; second, in the swearing-in ceremony the
Qur'an was replaced by any "holy book"; third, it allowed women
both to vote and stand as candidates in these elections.[2] The first two
of these changes would allow the followers of minority religions to
hold elected offices. In some of the clergy's earlier statements, the
issue of the women's vote was considered to be less important. The
first protest telegrams sent to 'Alam by Ayatollahs Zanjani, Damad,
Amoli, Ha'iri, and Khomeini did not even mention the women's
vote (Davani n.d.:vol. 3, pp. 31–32, 40, 96). Davani, himself a clerical participant, recalls the clerical perception of the issue in this
way:

> The issue of women's vote was but an excuse. The main aim [of the
> government] was to eliminate the condition of Islam from the require-
> ments of the electors and the candidates so that the road would be
> opened up for other sects, for Jews, Christians, Zoroasterians, and espe-
> cially for the astray sect of the Baha'is, those dangerous agents of for-
> eigners in Iran. To facilitate this, they removed the Quran from the
> swearing-in ceremony and replaced it with "holy book," so that such
> sects and even members of the Baha'i political party, who call their
> forged creed a "religion" and consider their book of superstitions a
> "holy book," could be elected to the provincial councils of the Islamic
> country of Iran, and could take the fate of Muslims into their hands,
> by intervening in all public affairs and thus gaining vast prerogatives
> over the affairs of Iranian people. (Davani n.d.:vol. 3, p. 29)

It is indicative of the outlook of many of the clergy that the
election bill, more than the land reform, should have been the cat-
alyst for the emergence of their organized opposition to the shah.
From the clerical viewpoint, the changes that the shah had embarked
on constituted the final stage in the undermining of the traditional
Islamic society first initiated in the mid-nineteenth century by reform-
ist ministers such as Amir Kabir, continued by the constitutionalist
movement, and greatly accelerated by the explicitly anticlerical policies of Reza Shah. The links between the controversy over the elec-

tion law, the defense of Islam per se, and the overall historical process of social change were explained by the oppositionists at Qum. For example, in one of his telegrams to the prime minister, Khomeini vividly sketched out what were to become his familiar motifs of foreign conspiracy and internal decadence:

> It is incumbent upon me, according to my religious duties, to warn the Iranian people and the Muslims of the world that Islam and the Qur'an are in danger; that the independence of the country and its economy are about to be taken over by Zionists, who in Iran appear as the party of Baha'is, and if this deadly silence of Muslims continues, these elements will soon take over the entire economy of the country and drive it to complete bankruptcy. Iranian television is a Jewish spy base, the government sees this and approves of it (Ruhani 1977:177–178)[3]

When the shah put his six-point program to a vote on January 26, 1963, it included land reform, the women's vote, nationalization of forests and pastures, and a workers' profit-sharing scheme. The clergy interpreted this program as a rejection of their demand for greater influence in the government and as a further attempt to curb the clergy's social influence and political role. They called for a boycott of the referendum. It must be emphasized, however, that no single plank in the program was the sole cause of the clerical boycott. Rather, the clergy voiced their fears of the project as a whole. In their eyes, the shah's program was a final assault on Islam. The clergy saw it as the rejection of the clerical demand to reverse the course of the previous decades and to move in an Islamic direction. The existential tone of the declarations of the time make this evident, as this statement by Khomeini demonstrates:

> People who are responsible to the law and to the nation have fooled His Majesty into doing this job for them. If they want to do something for the good of the people, why do they not turn to the program of Islam and Islamic experts, so that all classes will enjoy a comfortable life, and so that all will be happy in this and the other world? Why are they instituting cooperative funds that are robbing the fruits of the peasants' labor? With the establishment of these cooperatives, the Iranian home market will be lost, and both merchants and farmers ruined, while other classes will suffer a similar fate. . . . The clergy registers the danger for the Qur'an and our religion. It seems that this compulsory referendum aims to lay the basis for the removal of the clauses [in the constitution] linked to religion. The Islamic ulama had previously felt

the same danger to Islam, the Qur'an, and the country when the government took measures to change the local elections. Now it seems that the enemies of Islam are trying to achieve the same thing through fooling a bunch of naive people. (Davani n.d.:vol. 3, pp. 205–206)

The postrevolutionary practice of the clergy in power, since February of 1979, vindicates this evaluation: the clergy has done much to Islamicize both Iranian society and the state, including the place of women in society and politics. The clergy has not reversed the land reform. On the contrary, the politically dominant faction within the ruling bloc has been trying to pass a land reform legislation through the Majlis that would sanction land takeovers by peasants since 1979 and would deal with lands exempted from the shah's earlier reform measures. Only on the issue of the waqf lands, for obvious religious reasons and not because of financial considerations, has there been discussion of declaring any previous land reform transactions void.

APPENDIX C
CONSUMPTION EXPENDITURE OF RURAL HOUSEHOLDS

Table C-1 has been constructed on the basis of annual surveys published by the Plan Organization on consumptive expenditure of rural households. The data for all selected years have been reduced to six expenditure categories, because for the period 1966–1970 the six categories comprised the extent of the published data. Other years included a wider classification, ranging from nine to twelve groups. The expenditure groups are defined differently from year to year, and in the absence of accurate information on rural consumer price indexes, it is not possible to make accurate comparisons. The reduction of other years to six expenditure groups is, therefore, partly arbitrary, although a general measure of changing expenditure patterns has been taken into account.

TABLE C-1
Differentiation of Rural Households on the Basis of
Annual Consumption Expenditure, by Expenditure Group

Year	Expenditure Group (thousands of Rls)	% of Households	% of Total Rural Expenditure	% of Food & Tobacco in Total Household Expenditure	% of Self-consumption in Food & Tobacco Expenditure
1965	Under 30	33	20	60	44
	30–50	37	31	73	47
	50–75	18	24	69	46
	75–100	7	14	62	52
	100–150	2	5	72	40
	150 and over	2	6	56	45
1967	Under 30	34	13	71	27
	30–60	39	31	69	30
	60–90	15	20	64	34
	90–120	6	12	59	37
	120–240	6	18	52	36
	240 and over	0.9	6	40	35
1969	Under 30	38	16	73	35
	30–60	40	35	73	37
	60–90	13	19	68	39
	90–120	5	10	63	36
	120–240	4	13	54	37
	240 and over	0.7	6	38	24
1972	Under 36	35	15	74	46
	36–60	32	25	73	44
	60–120	25	34	66	43
	120–180	5	12	58	43
	180–360	2	11	39	43
	360 and over	0.3	3	32	46
1973	Under 36	27	10	74	48
	36–60	29	19	72	41
	60–120	31	35	66	40
	120–180	8	16	55	39
	180–360	4	14	45	39
	360 and over	1	8	28	39
1976	Under 60	23	6	67	51
	60–120	33	18	67	47
	120–240	30	32	61	42
	240–600	12	26	48	41
	600–1200	1.5	8	23	38
	1200 and over	0.6	10	6	37

Source: Plan Organization of Iran, Statistical Center, *Household Budget Statistics — Rural Areas* for 1965–1976 (Tehran).

Notes

CHAPTER 1

1. Details of these bills will be discussed in chapter 5.
2. See chapter 5 for details.
3. See chapter 6 for details.
4. See Lambton 1969:37–40. The full texts of these decrees appear as appendixes in the Persian translation of Lambton's book *Landlord and Peasant in Persia* 1953. See also Hooglund 1982a:44.
5. Quoted in Mo'meni 1980:104, which see for further discussion of the Tudeh party's agrarian program. All translations from Persian sources are mine.
6. See Mohammadi 1973:5 and 56–57.
7. See "The Imperialist Agricultural Policy in Iran" and "Agriculture as a Means of Expansionism," *Tufan* (Tempest) 3, no. 112, December 1976, and no. 116, April 1977. The quotation is from no. 116. I do not mean to deny that the U.S. government has repeatedly used grain deliveries as a means of exerting political pressure on other governments. See, in this respect, George 1976:chapter 8. It is the conscious preplanned link of causality established between land reform, ruin of agriculture, and food-as-weapon that is incredible.
8. "Let Us Spread the Anti-Feudal Movement," *Setarey-e Sorkh* (Red Star) 1, no. 5, September 1970.
9. It is all the more surprising that Kazemi sees forestalling a revolution in the countryside as a political aim of the land reform since he is the coauthor of another essay analyzing the causes of the absence of peasant movements in modern Iranian history. See Abrahamian and Kazemi 1978.
10. See Shaji'i 1965.
11. See Eckstein et al. 1978:7–8.
12. See Walinsky 1977:132, 133.
13. See ibid., p. 130.
14. See ibid., p. 384.
15. See ibid., pp. 384–386.
16. See Alavi 1975; Foster-Carter 1978; Harriss 1980; and Wolpe 1980.
17. See Shanin 1972 and Tuma 1965.

CHAPTER 2

1. The Fedayeen, for instance, argue, "In our opinion, there is no need to prove that imperialist domination and feudal domination are fundamentally and from a broad historical perspective in conflict with one another. As Marx noted, world capitalism, wherever it goes, to varying degrees, destroys the existing relations and tries to swallow within its international order the societies that it dominates. We think that the coexistence between imperialism and feudalism is a temporary tactical coexistence and inevitably the feudal order would gradually disappear in the

international capitalist system" (SCFK 1973a:153–154). The Mojahedin express similar views (SMKI 1972).

2. "In the colony, although surplus value is realized, it is not accumulated locally within the colonial economy. By virtue of colonial exploitation it is drained out of the colony and leads to capital accumulation and rise in the organic composition of capital not in the colony but in the imperialist metropolis" (Alavi 1980:394). On the impact of colonial economy on the agricultural sector, see Szentes 1976:248.

3. In this sense I believe that Alavi's 1975 analysis, emphasizing the change between colonial and postcolonial economies, is more accurate:

> The indigenous capitalist development has promoted the manufacture of a wide range of commodities, especially consumption goods, in India. That has altered, though partially, the pattern of generalized commodity production, that is now internalized to a greater degree so that the internal disarticulation of the Indian economy is, to that extent, ameliorated. The external dependence is increasing in the field of capital goods and research intensive technology, and not with regard to industrial commodities in general as before.

> Secondly, as a consequence of the indigenous capitalist development, an increasing proportion of surplus value is appropriated internally, by the indigenous capitalist class. By that token, the deformed pattern of extended reproduction, via the metropolitan bourgeoisie and metropolitan capital accumulation, is partially modified; the process of extended reproduction is more internalized. These structural differences distance the *post-colonial mode of production* from the colonial mode. . . . The distinction between "colonial" and "post-colonial" status is not established at the political level alone. In India, it might be argued, there is by and large, some degree of correspondence in the time between the transition from the colonial to the post-colonial mode of production and the achievement of political independence. (Alavi 1975:192–193)

4. See also Frankel 1943.

5. On these points, see Mandel 1975.

6. See also Petras and La Porte 1971:11–26 for a brief review of some of this literature.

7. This was an improvement over the nineteenth-century arguments. The reader familiar with the literature on southern Africa may recall that colonizers there perceived the lack of enthusiasm on the part of the local population to earn more money as innate laziness.

8. For a review presentation of this vast literature, see Elkan 1973, especially chapters 1 and 2.

9. Three decades later, the Brandt Commission report (1980:232) observed the same pattern: "For reasons which are partly historical, partly based on the self-interest of donors and partly due to an inadequate understanding of the role of external resources in helping development, most of the official finance which developing countries get is earmarked for the purchase of capital goods from outside. In the initial stages aid was no more than an extension of credits which industrialized countries were providing to promote the export of their capital goods."

10. See Johnston and Mellor 1961 and Dorner 1972:16–17.

11. Indeed, it has been correctly observed that these models were more accurate descriptions for developments in countries that had cut themselves off from the circuit of international capital accumulation, at least for an important initial period

of industrialization, such as Japan and, in a different context, the Soviet Union. See Wilber 1969.

12. The same document continues to emphasize other important roles of the agricultural sector in these terms: "(h) Helping in the diffusion of wealth, which alone can provide a mass market for industry, not to speak of an adequate effective market for agricultural products. The greater part of the population in most developing regions is still agricultural, so that without prosperity here, the whole process of economic development is thwarted. (i) Providing a market for "producer goods" industries, that is, farm machinery and equipment, fertilizers, chemicals for control of pests and diseases" (FAO 1969:11).

13. World Bank, *Agriculture: Sector Working Paper*, June 1972. Reprinted in Wilber 1973:164–172.

14. *Questions and Answers: World Bank and International Development Assistance*, quoted in George 1976:253.

15. For the text of McNamara's speech, see McNamara 1981, particularly 141–152. See also Lele 1975:82.

16. See Bennholdt-Thomsen 1980a:16 for a table of World Bank credits by region and type of investment for the period 1969–1977.

17. For further discussion, see Shanin 1980 and Bennholdt-Thomsen 1980a and b. An important question is whether this structural problem of industrialization in backward countries is (a) an internal distortion, as Warren (1980:10) believes and (b) a transitory problem related to early stages of industrialization. As to the first question, Szentes gives an opposite evaluation, both in terms of the history of industrialization of these countries as well as current policy and the tendencies of movement of international capital. See Szentes 1976, particularly pages 175–177 and 232–240. Moreover, at the current level of integration of Third World economies into the world economy, the old internal-external division seems rather dubious. See also Bernstein 1982.

As to the second point, although a few of the Third World countries, notably Brazil and India, have moved toward development of a producer-goods sector, the tendency is very weak and far from general. It is difficult to see, at the current level of technology (and its monopoly development) and economies of scale, how a different type of capitalist industrialization would emerge in the Third World. If the constraint of profitability were removed, however, the picture could change drastically.

CHAPTER 3

1. For a synthesis of recent analyses of the process of integration of precapitalist rural economies into capitalism, see Bernstein 1977. This article is included in Harriss 1982, which has a good selection of articles covering this topic.

2. For a very early and perceptive Marxist critique of colonial land policies in terms of their destruction of natural economies and their effect on the indigenous population, see Luxemberg 1968:chapter 27, "The Struggle against Natural Economy." For a lucid discussion of proletarianization of the peasantry in southern Africa, see Bundy 1972 and Arrighi 1973. For the relationship between recent land reforms and the destruction of natural economy and industrialization see Zaldivar 1974 and Bradby 1980.

3. For an evaluation of tenure changes resulting from land reform in a number of countries, see Jacoby 1971; Laporte et al. 1971; Byres 1974; Abdel-Fadil 1975;

World Bank 1975; S. Eckstein et al. 1978; Theobald and Jaward 1982. The case of Iran will be dealt with in Chapter 4.

4. By 1969 it was estimated that the shantytown population in Latin America was growing at about 15 percent per year, compared with a 5 percent growth in the overall urban population. See Dorner 1972:92.

5. See Walinsky 1977:360. See also World Bank 1975:72.

6. Abdel-Fadil has made similar observations in the case of the Egyptian agrarian reforms:

> Whether the cultivator is an owner of land or leases it from the owners, he has no choice but to deal with the village cooperative, the only source available for credit, seeds, fertilizers and pesticides. . . . The cooperativization package has effectively become a means of taxing agriculture indirectly, by permitting the procurement and marketing of the main cash crops at *tax-element-inclusive prices*. If one adopts Sanghivi's distinction between the *optional* and *obligatory* surplus, it may be argued that the cooperativization policy has succeeded in increasing the size of the "obligatory surplus" necessary to pay back the peasants' input loans in kind and to meet other financial obligations due to the state (i.e., land tax). Thus cooperativization can be seen as a clever institutional arrangement by which the state was able to increase its inflow of *grain* and the major *export crops* in order to expand urban employment and maximize the country's foreign exchange earnings (1975:119–120).

See also Tuma 1965:181–182.

CHAPTER 4

1. Ann K. S. Lambton's book (1953) remains a classic reference on this subject. Hooglund (1982a:chapters 1 and 2) provides a good general picture of agrarian society in Iran in this period. More specialized writings will be referred to for additional information throughout this chapter.

2. No'mani (1980) discusses these various categories at length and gives figures for the relative size of land held under each category up to the end of the Safavid period (seventeenth century). See his pages 145–236.

3. It is difficult to see why many historians from the Iranian left have referred to the abolition of toyul by the first Majlis as an "anti-feudal measure." All the measure did was to consolidate private ownership of land relative to the state's previously unfettered right to take such lands back. See, for instance, Ahmad Qasemi, *Shish sal inqilab-e Mashrute-ye Iran* (Six years of the Iranian constitutional revolution n.p., n.d., p. 11).

4. Keddie (1960:10) also refers to these laws, but she cites a thirty-year possession period. The Civil Code of 1928 also recognized de facto possession as proof of ownership.

5. The small percentage of Crown villages is due to the fact that from the early 1950s the shah began a program of the sale of the Crown lands. Percentages refer to number of villages in each category, rather than hectarage. No cadastral surveys have ever been carried out in Iran.

6. Recently, Mo'meni (1980:54–56) proposed that the traditionally accepted view that the landlord-peasant share depended on how the respective inputs were worked out was false and that the peasant's share depended on the necessary subsistence level of consumption. For a concise and convincing rebuttal of this argu-

ment, see Minoo Alvandi, "On the Division of Crop According to the Five Factors of Production," (in Persian), in Agah 1982: 401–417.

7. See Safinejad 1974:50–60, 99–115, and 163–168.

8. For development of modern agriculture in these two provinces, see Okazaki 1968 and Salmanzadeh 1980.

9. Here is how one researcher explains the reasons for high concentration on subsistence crops:

> Field patterns are strikingly homogeneous in the various alluvial fan settlements of the Kuhi Jupar. Whether the village is owned by a single absentee owner or by a number of peasant proprietors, village fields are divided into communal wheat fields, double-cropped vegetable land, and walled orchards. In each village these three types of cultivated land have the same relative position. Peasants favor a combination of fields and crops that will minimize the risk of crop failure and fulfill a variety of family needs. They will work a one-crop field if paid a cash wage but even then they are reluctant, because this forces them to deal extensively in the city marketplace and convert coins into the family food supply. The landlord is equally reluctant to replace sharecropping agreements with cash wages, fearing peasant idleness and theft. Both of these attitudes reinforce traditional cropping practices and retard consolidation of fields in larger, more economic units.

> At Muhiabad, for instance, the landlord attempted to introduce sugar beets as a cash summer replacement crop when opium was outlawed in Iran. Sugar beets were foreign to the household economy; the peasants had to decrease their cultivation of food crops on a market venture and become involved in transactions with the newly constructed sugar beet mill at Bardsir (or Mashiz) some forty miles southwest of Kirman City. The sharecroppers of Muhiabad, therefore, refused to work the sugar beet fields on a sharecropping basis and would work only for cash. The landlord did not wish to assume the entire financial risk of crop failure; thus sugar beets were not cultivated on the large scale originally planned (English 1966:59–60).

10. According to the FAO *Production Yearbook* for 1960, Japan registered yields of 2.54 tons per hectare and 2.75 tons per hectare for wheat and barley, respectively.

CHAPTER 5

1. For a summary of major points of these reports see Ray 1951.

2. R. K. Ramazani (1982:4) dates this orientation to Reza Shah, once he was under the threat of Anglo-Soviet occupation, and to Mohammad Reza Shah as early as October 1941. His arguments in support of such an early shift are not convincing. It seems more likely that the shift came after recognition of the role Americans played in pressuring the Soviet Union to withdraw its troops from northern Iran in 1946.

3. See, for instance, Memorandum of Conversation [with Hussein Ala, Iranian ambassador in Washington], by the Assistant Chief of the Division of Greek, Turkish, and Iranian Affairs (Dunn), September 30, 1948, in USDS 1977:182–184.

4. See, for instance, telegram from Secretary of State Acheson to the embassy in Iran, June 23, 1950 (USDS 1978:562–563), and "Regional Policy Statement: Greece, Turkey and Iran," December 28, 1950 (USDS 1978:254–270).

5. For more detail see Lambton 1969:50–55.

6. The peasant emphasis of the State Department press release proved to be somewhat misdirected. First, over one-third of the Crown lands, particularly in the fertile provinces of Mazandaran and Gorgan, were sold to capitalist entrepreneurs, including other members of the Pahlavi family. Second, the Rural Development Bank remained the private bank of the shah, and over the next two decades it became one of the largest private investors in Iran. The sale of Crown lands was suspended under the government of Mosaddeq, as part of a number of unresolved political disputes between Mosaddeq and the shah. It was continued after Mosaddeq's overthrow in August 1953. By 1961, 517 whole villages, whose total agricultural land amounted to some 200,000 hectares, had been sold to 42,000 buyers (*Tehran Economist* November 16, 1979). The remainder of the Pahlavi estates from 1961 onward were sold under the comprehensive land reform program. For details see Zandjani 1973:26–37.

7. For a comprehensive source on Paul Maris's work in Iran, the interested reader is referred to "The Paul Maris Reader: A collection of His Writings and Related Papers on Rural Development and Land Reform in Iran, 1952–1954," report no. 003604, Ford Foundation Archives. New York; hereafter referred to as "The Paul Maris Reader." In at least one report, Paul Maris is referred to as "one of the principal drafters" of the shah's land distribution program (Memorandum of conversation, October 29, 1953, p. 1, box 9 Iran—Rural Village Development, A976 to 55-77), Rural Credit Program file, Ford Foundation Archives, New York. As a measure of Maris's influence, we can point out the close correspondence between his recommendations and proposals all through the period of 1952–1954 and what was, in fact, carried out by the Iranian government. For instance, Maris insisted in many of his writings that no peasant should be sold less land than the minimum on which a peasant family could support itself. Therefore, he opposed proposals according to which peasants would be sold only the plots they currently cultivated. Instead he favored the transfer and resettlement of the "surplus families" to other areas or other employment ("Principles to Be Observed in Obtaining Objectives," c. 1953, in "The Paul Maris Reader," p. 30). This recommendation was ultimately carried out, and the Crown lands were sold by hectarage subdivisions. For example, ten-hectare lots were sold in the Gorgan area, and eight-hectare lots were sold in Varamin. The later land reform legislation of 1962 opted for the alternative of selling to peasants whatever land they happened to be cultivating at the time.

Another curious measure of Maris's influence is reflected in his authorship, in 1954, of at least two of the four lectures proposed to be given by Asadollah Alam, a close friend and confidant of the shah and the head of the Crown Lands Organization (Amlak). The lecture series was entitled "Agrarian Reform—Its World-Wide and Domestic Implications" and was to be delivered at Tehran University to an audience of members of the Majlis, high government officials, and the faculty and students of the university. See letter from Paul V. Maris to Robert E. Culbertson, April 13, 1954, in "The Paul Maris Reader," p. 214. The English draft of lectures 1 and 4 are in "Alam Speeches" box 9 (Iran—Rural Village Development A976 to 55-77), Ford Foundation Archives, New York. We can understand this incident as an example of the subservience of the Iranian government to the dictates of the U.S. government and American private interests. Alternatively, and I think more accurately, we can see it as an example of the utter political and bureaucratic poverty of a ruling elite that did not even have its own speechwriters.

8. "The Paul Maris Reader," p. 497, Ford Foundation Archives, New York.

9. Ibid., p. 55.

10. Ibid., p. 118.

11. See memorandum to Mr. Kingsley from Harvey Hall, December 18, 1963, PA 55-185, sec. 4, Ford Foundation Archives, New York. For the only other source that has made extensive use of this survey, see Keddie 1980:175–185.

12. See, for instance, "General Frame of Reference within Which Planning Details for Rural Development in Iran May Proceed," December 7, 1953, in "The Paul Maris Reader," pp. 46–54, Ford Foundation Archives, New York.

13. V. Webster Johnson, "Rural Credit in Iran," draft report, July 12, 1956, pp. 1–3, box 9 (Iran—Rural Village Development A976 to 55-77), Agricultural Credit Seminar (November 6–10, 1956) file, Ford Foundation Archives, New York.

14. For more information on the Rural Development Seminar, see the following items in "The Paul Maris Reader": "Rural Development Seminar on Land Reform," April 27, 1954 (pp. 258–259); "Questions for Rural Development Seminar" (pp. 279–281); "Rural Development Seminar on 'What level of living can two men and two oxen support'" (pp. 315–316); "Rural Development Seminar Emphasizes Importance of Rural Credit" (pp. 321–324); "Five Months Discussions in Rural Development" (résumé prepared by Paul Maris for presentation by Asadollah Alam); pp. 325–339; "Rural Development Seminar on the Public Domain" (with copy of bill relating thereto; pp. 448–461); "Rural Development Seminar, Again on Public Domain" (pp. 480–482).

15. The question of sale of land in the public domain was raised in 1949 by Arsanjani, who later became minister of agriculture and was in charge of the 1962 land reform, in a proposal to General Razmara, the prime minister at the time. In the spring of 1950 a bill was submitted to the Majlis concerning the sales, but in the ensuing political crisis over the oil nationalization issue, the assassination of Razmara, and Mosaddeq's premiership, the bill lay dormant (Lambton 1969:50). In 1955 the Majlis finally ratified a new bill on the basis of the proposal drafted by the Rural Development Seminar. The sales started in 1959, and "by 1963, when the transfer of the state land came under the comprehensive Land Reform Law, some 157 villages had been transferred to 8,366 tenants" (Ajami 1976a:192). For further details see Zandjani 1973:38–49.

16. See Kenneth R. Iverson, "Report on Iran," report no. 7, August 24, 1953, box 11 (Iran—Village Development Continued, Public Administration 58–79 to 59-195A, and Economic and Social Research 55-173 to 60-367A), Iran—Program Development and Background 1953–1954 file; Ford Foundation Archives, New York.

17. Memorandum of conversation, October 29, 1953, box 9 (Iran—Rural Village Development A976 to 55-77), Rural Credit Program file, Ford Foundation Archives, New York.

18. Ibid., pp. 2–3.

19. Kenneth R. Iverson, "Report on Iran," November 18, 1953, p. 5, box 11 (Iran—Village Development Continued, Public Administration 58–79 to 59-195A, and Economic and Social Research 55-173 to 60-367A), Iran—Program Development and Background 1953–1954 file, Ford Foundation Archives, New York.

20. "Principles to Be Observed in Obtaining Objectives," c. 1953, in "The Paul Maris Reader," p. 30, Ford Foundation Archives, New York.

21. For the text of the original draft as well as the final legislation, see *Tehran Economist*, May 4, 1960.

22. See USNSC 1961b. Also see "Political Characteristics of the Iranian Urban Middle Class and Implications for U.S. Policy," March 20, 1961, National Security Files, box 115, Iran—3/21/61–3/31/61 file, John F. Kennedy Presidential Library, Boston, Mass.

23. See the two papers cited in the preceding note.

24. Amini himself denies strongly that either his appointment or the land reform program was carried out under American pressure. See Iranian Oral History, Center for Middle Eastern Studies, Harvard University, Ali Amini interviewed by Habib Ladjevardi, December 4, 1981, Paris. According to Hooglund (1982a:47–48), Amini was the American choice for premier, and this view was communicated to the shah by the U.S. ambassador. His source of information is William G. Miller, a former political officer at the U.S. embassy in Tehran.

25. Lambton (1953:264) noted that the fortunes of landlords no longer compared well with those of contractors and merchants.

26. See also Zandjani 1973:157–158.

27. See, for instance, "Statement Read before Council of Ministers on October 3, 1958, by Mr. Salman Asadi, Chairman of the Foreign Transactions Co.," *Program Area One, Near East and Africa, Iran Office—Rural Village Development, box 12, A-289, Plan Organization file, Ford Foundation Archives, New York.*

28. See Ahmadi 1962:vol. 1, pp. 107–108, 118; vol. 2, pp. 63, 71.

29. For other lengthy interviews by Arsanjani, expanding on similar themes, see Ministry of Agriculture 1962:216–228 and 243–250.

30. For more discussion of the frequently repeated, but little substantiated, opposition of the clergy to land reform, see appendix B.

31. See Arsalan Khal'atbari's series of articles in the *Tehran Economist*, May 20, 1961–June 10, 1961; October 21, 1961–November 18, 1961.

32. The essay was serialized in the *Tehran Economist* from September 2, 1961, to October 7, 1961. This journal is the source for all references to the essay.

33. In all the literature on the Iranian land reform, Arsanjani is credited with this "practical innovative" idea, but Mahdavi's essay seems to be the first written presentation of it. Private interviews with other people who were involved with the work of this legislation indicate that an agricultural engineer, Mr. Khalkhali, with extensive field knowledge of Iranian villages, first made this proposal. Khalkhali later headed the implementation of land reform for the first few years.

34. All legislation related to land reform is reprinted in a collection published by the Royal Inspectorate (in Persian); see Kamangar 1974. I have used this book throughout as reference to various legislation, except where otherwise specified.

CHAPTER 6

1. Tehran University publications are listed under their authors' names: Azkia 1969; Hajebi et al. 1971; Nik-kholq 1971; Azkia et al. 1976. Some of the information has also been extracted from SCFK 1973b.

2. For further general discussion of this point, see Halliday 1979:chapter 6, "Oil and Industrialization."

3. Ajami (1981:91) estimates that such "very large holdings" cover about 815,000 hectares.

4. The actual picture is somewhat more complicated. A small fraction of the khoshneshin who were oxen-holders did receive land. For a full discussion, see Hooglund 1973:229–245. See also Kielstra 1975:251.

5. The estimate is based on the tables of required labor per hectare throughout the various parts of the agricultural production cycle provided by Saedloo 1974.

6. Unfortunately, no quantitative data are available about the statement that labor is "wholly or mostly family labor."

7. See Hooglund 1975:120–122 for a number of examples. Also see MCRA 1974c:42, and other similar village studies by MCRA, and Azkia, et al., 1976:44. See also Antoun 1976:3–9.

8. For similar accounts, see Ashraf 1973:32–35; Alvandi and Rostami 1979:34.

9. See Shanin 1966:240–255 for a fuller discussion.

10. Similar trends are prevalent among small farmers elsewhere. A World Bank study of small farmers of India and Pakistan concluded: "Among the characteristics peculiar to small farmers are (i) a high proportion of land devoted to food crops; (ii) a low proportion of output marketed (a high proportion retained for home consumption); (iii) a more diverse crop portfolio; (iv) greater aversion to risk; (v) a greater scarcity of cash and capital resources; and (vi) more abundant family labor than other larger farms" (World Bank 1979:ii).

11. I am thankful to Minoo Alvandi for pointing out this category of self-consuming "farm producers."

12. There is, of course, a variation also according to proximity of villages to urban markets. All reports indicate that near urban markets even the very small farms allocate the bulk of their land to production for sale. In more isolated areas, on the other hand, there is a much higher degree of subsistence farming. See Azkia 1969:105; Ule 1973:114; MCRA 1975d:5; MCRA 1975e:48–49; MCRA 1976a:33–35; MCRA 1976b:26–34; Alvandi and Rostami 1979:36–37.

13. Aresvik also notes "Power-driven water pumps were few and far between before the mid-1950s, but by the end of the 1960s over 2,000 deep-well pumps were being imported each year" (Aresvik 1976:45). By 1973 a total of 9,351 deep wells and 31,180 semideep wells existed in Iran. The World Bank report by Price (1975:annex 2, p. 2) also gives relative figures, indicating declining irrigation by qanats. New over-ground canals and wells provided an increasing share of irrigation.

14. See also MCRA 1974c:8 and Salmanzadeh 1980:150.

15. See also MCRA 1977a, 1977b, n.d.(a), and n.d.(b). A medical doctor from the Caspian town of Babolsar wrote to the *Tehran Economist* (February 25, 1978): "I deal with workers who work daily from 7 A.M. to 3 P.M. in a factory. Then they go and work on their land, or try to find other employment to augment their income a little bit." Similar tendencies have been reported in other countries. See, for instance, World Bank 1979:123–128.

16. The fact that the largest two categories of holdings are not exempt from this problem of land fragmentation confirms my earlier suggestion that a considerable part of these holdings are not cultivated as single holdings either directly or through rentals to large capitalist farmers; rather, they are rented in small pieces to peasant households. See also Price 1975:13.

17. For similar reports, see Ashraf 1973:26–29; Hooglund 1975:168; and MCRA 1977a:1.

18. Samir Amin (1970:5–6) carries out detailed calculations for Senegal to show that if the area under cultivation cannot be increased sufficiently or alternative employment is not obtained, changing from traditional to mechanized agriculture reduces the peasant's net income. Kula (1976:41–43) quotes results of research that was carried out during 1937–1938 on 600 plots in twenty-one villages in India,

showing "that such plots yielded an average annual income of 88 rupees, if calculations are based on market prices and no account is taken of the cost of family labour, nor of interest on capital; if, however, we include in the calculations the cost of family labour on the basis of the prices paid at that time and in that region for wage-labourers and an interest of 3 percent on capital, the same plots turn out to be greatly deficient (an annual deficit of 90 rupees)." To apply criterion of capitalist enterprises to the workings of a peasant family producer, however, is patently absurd: "If, in order to launch a particular productive activity, A kilograms of raw material and B labour-days are needed, and if the "entrepreneur" has at his disposal A kilograms of raw material and B + X labour-days with no other possibilities for employing the excess labour, then the value of all labour that enters into the productive process must be regarded as equal to zero. In this sense one could say that the "peasant-entrepreneur" applies marginal theory correctly." This is why "Positive reaction to market incentives appears only when it becomes possible to use the available means of production in a variety of ways, and especially when the land becomes a capital investment like all the others and the labour used on the farm plot can be sold outside it, should it happen that calculations show the plot to be running at a loss." Otherwise, the economic behavior of a peasant family runs often in the opposite direction from a capitalist unit. For the classical treatment of these problems the work of Chayonov (1966) remains unique.

19. See also World Bank 1979:101–105.

20. For a classical treatment of these issues Kautsky (1970) remains unparalleled.

21. Agricultural wages in Iran are notoriously low. In the late 1960s, male agricultural wages were as low as 40 rials (55 cents) a day. For women it was half that much. By 1972 the Agricultural Sample Survey (table 145) showed a daily wage for male workers of 98 rials a day and 52 rials a day for female workers. Even in 1975, at the height of the construction boom, when the pages of the *Tehran Economist* were full of complaints about high agricultural wages, they did not exceed 250–300 rials per day for male workers and 150–200 rials per day for female workers. These workers were employed a maximum of three months per year.

22. One technocratic "expert" suggested at one time that the government should organize mass transfer of workers between hot and cold climates of the country during summer and winter seasons. See *Tehran Economist*, April 7, 1977.

23. A *Financial Times* report on agribusiness in Iran (October 21, 1976) made the following observation: "Finally all the projects have run into human problems created, perhaps inevitably, at the beginning when some 6,500 families were moved from the land to be developed. The idea, logical enough, was to clear the land of these people who had traditionally used it for grazing and cropping, move them into resettlement centers and then rely on them as the source of labor. Not only have they been reluctant to move, they have also been reluctant to work for others on land which historically they regarded as theirs.".

24. A World Bank report warned at the time that "more attention requires to be given to education and persuasion of the potential benefactors under this law in order that its objectives are understood and appreciated. There is no provision under the existing law for a promotion campaign in the development areas although this may be included in the by-laws. It is extremely important for the successful outcome of this legislation that emphasis is given to persuasion rather than coercion in its implementation" (Price 1975:19–20).

25. Iranian capitalists in agriculture allowed a 15–20 percent rate of profit in their calculations of costs of production. See, for instance, *Tehran Economist*, May 28, 1977; June 18, 1977; and July 14, 1977.

26. The data for table 34 and figure 2 are compiled from the pages of the weekly *Tehran Economist*, "Registry of New Companies," since I have not been able to gain access to the central registry of companies in Iran. The data are of necessity incomplete and inaccurate. First, not all company registrations are printed in the *Tehran Economist*. Second, not all companies register at similar stages of their operation. Some register months prior to actual operation, while others become registered companies years after. Third, what is recorded in the *Tehran Economist* as "registered capital" is not the total cost of projects, neither is it clearly defined. In certain instances it includes price of land. In other cases, it does not. Nonetheless, because the data cover a large number of firms over a six-year period, they tend to confirm aggregate tendencies in capital movement in agriculture also reflected in figures provided by the Central Bank reports.

27. All information about shareholders of companies are taken from the source discussed in note 26, above.

28. In discussing some of the problems faced by capitalism in agriculture, Marx concluded: "The moral of this story, which may also be deduced from other observations in agriculture, is that the capitalist system works against a rational agriculture, or that a rational agriculture is irreconcilable with the capitalist system — even though technical improvements in agriculture are promoted by capitalism. But under this system, agriculture needs either the hands of the self-employed small farmer or the control of associated producers" (quoted in Shanin 1966:250).

29. Plan Organization of Iran, Statistical Center, *Statistics of Iran's Foreign Trade* for 1970–1975 (Tehran).

30. The Near East itself fares rather badly compared with the rest of Asia. Figures for grain yields in 1970 were 1.7 tons per hectare for Asia as a whole, excluding Japan, which had a 6.7 tons per hectare yield, 1.3 tons per hectare for Africa, and 2.1 tons per hectare for Latin America. See McNamara 1981:248.

31. Qahreman (1982:151–154) also reviews the results of two regional studies in Kermanshah and Khuzistan. In the first case, yields are higher in smaller, less capital-intensive farms. In the second case the reverse is true.

32. This seems to have been a phenomenon of the 1970s. The only other figures available indicate that in 1972 only 32 percent of the households had radios, only 4 percent had gas cookers, 2 percent had tape recorders and 1.4 percent had refrigerators (Plan Organization of Iran, Statistical Center, *Household Budget Statistics — Rural Areas* for 1972 [Tehran]).

33. The spread of transistor radios in a country with a very high degree of rural illiteracy (56 percent for men and 83 percent for women in rural areas according to the 1976 census) is very important. Both the previous regime and the current one, therefore, insist on absolute control of radio and TV broadcasting.

34. See MCRA 1975e:66; 1976a:40; 1976b:10; 1976c:18.

CHAPTER 7

1. "The Paul Maris Reader," December 7, 1953, pp. 49, 50, Ford Foundation Archives, New York.

2. V. Webster Johnson, "Rural Credit in Iran," draft report, July 12, 1956, p. 4, box 9 (Iran—Rural Village Development A976 to 55-77), Agricultural Credit Seminar file, November 6–10, 1956, Ford Foundation Archives, New York.

3. See MCRA 1971:part 1. For production cooperatives, this list was to be preceded by the main aim of the co-op, "common exploitation of agricultural land, privately owned or rented." See also Ashraf and Safai 1977:34.

4. Bank loans have interest rates between 6 and 20 percent. Co-op loans have a flat 6 percent interest.

5. For earlier figures on the value of fertilizers sold through co-ops, see Ashraf and Safai 1977:39. The 1974–1976 figures constitute about 28 percent of total chemical fertilizer consumption.

6. See, for instance, MCRA 1975d:233–238.

7. See Aresvik 1976:107; Ashraf and Safai 1977:41.

8. Data are taken from SCFK 1973b.

9. Even this level of governmental control was disliked by the peasants. Similar problems existed in the farm corporations. See Hajebi et al. 1971:107.

CHAPTER 8

1. See, for example, the various writings of the Organization of Iranian Marxist-Leninists (later named the Union of Iranian Communists), in particular the early issues of their organ, *Communist. Setareh Sorkh* (Red Star), the organ of another split from the Tudeh party, put forward a similar line.

2. For a full discussion of all these points see, for example, Shanin 1966; Wolf 1969; Alavi 1973.

3. This situation is not peculiar to Iran, of course. As a result of the development of capitalism in many Third World countries over the past few decades, very similar tendencies have developed elsewhere. See, for instance, Cohen et al. 1979.

4. All the assertions and arguments that follow, unless otherwise specified, are confirmed in newspaper reports for the period 1979–1980. Reports for later periods are similar, though less frequent, more muted, and not as accurate, since the new regime progressively tightened its censorship over the press.

5. See also Ashraf 1982:27; Mahdavi 1982:69–70.

6. Rude's observations about Latin American peasant actions of an earlier period apply here only in a political sense. He states, "the peasants' response [in Latin America] to repression or to seizure of their lands was purely defensive and, as in 'pre-industrial' society elsewhere, they were committed to a restoration of the past. . . . Such an attitude—the desire to restore or maintain the past rather than to stake a claim for something new—persists until the present day" (Rude 1980:75). In the Iranian experience there was a mixture of demands "committed to a restoration of the past," as well as demands that staked "claims to something new.".

APPENDIX A

1. The details of payment procedures were worked out through a number of "administrative decrees," issued by the cabinet in the winter of 1962. These can be found in Ministry of Agriculture 1962:251–258. For an English summary of these decrees, see Platt 1970:54–57 and Zandjani 1973:78–85.

2. See Platt 1970:98 and Zandjani 1973:168.

APPENDIX B

1. Among the more recent sources see, for instance, Ramazani 1982:75–76 and Rubin 1980:109.

2. For concise coverage of the events of this period see Bakhash 1984:24–35. For statements of clerical leaders on these issues, see Davani n.d.:vol. 3, pp. 31–46 and 89–112.

3. Iranian television was, in fact, owned by a Baha'i at this time.

References

Abdel-Fadil, M. 1975. *Development, Income Distribution and Social Change in Rural Egypt (1952-1970). Cambridge.*

Abrahamian, E. 1982. *Iran: Between Two Revolutions.* Princeton.

Abrahamian, E., and Kazemi, F. 1978. "The Non-Revolutionary Peasantry of Iran," *Iranian Studies* 12:259-304.

ADBI (Agricultural Development Bank of Iran). 1978. *Study of the Corporations Exploiting Land Downstream Mohammad Reza Shah Pahlavi Dam* (in Persian). Tehran.

Agah, ed./pub. 1982. *Agrarian and Peasant Problems* (in Persian). Tehran.

Ahmadi, A. 1962. *Five Years Serving the Shah* (in Persian). Tehran.

Ajami, I. 1973. *Sheshdangi* (in Persian). Shiraz.

Ajami, I. 1976a. "Land Reform and Modernization of the Farming Structure in Iran." In Farmanfarmaian 1976.

_____ . 1976b. "Agrarian Reform, Modernization of Peasants and Agricultural Development in Iran." In Jacqz 1976.

_____ . 1978. *Summary of the Results of Land Reform in Five Provinces* (in Persian). Tehran.

_____ . 1981. "Reconstruction of Peasant Agriculture and Development of Commercial Units" (in Persian). *Arash* 5, no. 4:87-102.

Akhavi, S. 1980. *Religion and Politics in Contemporary Iran.* Albany.

Alavi, H. 1973. "Peasants and Revolution." In Gough and Sharma 1973.

_____ . 1975. "India and the Colonial Mode of Production." *Socialist Register,* London, pp. 160-197.

_____ . 1980. "India: Transition from Feudalism to Colonial Capitalism." *Journal of Contemporary Asia* 10, no. 4 (December): 359-398.

Alavi, H., and Shanin, T., eds. 1982. *Introduction to the Sociology of "Developing Societies."* New York.

Alexander, Y., and Nanes, A., eds. 1980. *The United States and Iran: A Documentary History.* Frederick, Md.

Alvandi, M. 1982. "On the Division of the Crop According to the Five Factors of Production" (in Persian). In Agah 1982.

Alvandi, M., and Rostami, T. 1979. *Report on Seasonal Migration of Villagers in the Isfahan Area* (in Persian). Isfahan.

Amin, S. 1970. *The Development Mechanisms of Groundnut Cultivation 1885-1970.* Dakar.

_____ . 1974. *Accumulation on a World Scale.* New York.

Antoun, R. 1976. "The Gentry of a Traditional Peasant Community Undergoing Rapid Technological Change: An Iranian Case Study." *Iranian Studies* 11, no. 1 (Winter) 2–21.

Antoun, R., and Harik, I., eds. 1972. *Rural Politics and Social Change in the Middle East*. Bloomington.

Aresvik, O. 1976. *The Agricultural Development of Iran*. New York.

Arrighi, G. 1973. "Labor Supplies in Historical Perspectives: A Study of the Proletarianization of the African Peasantry in Rhodesia." In Arrighi and Saul, 1973.

Arrighi, G., and Saul, J. S., eds. 1973. *Essays on the Political Economy of Africa*. New York.

Ashraf, A. 1970. "Historical Obstacles to the Development of a Bourgeoisie in Iran." In Cook 1970.

————. 1973. *The Social and Economic Characteristics of Production Systems in Iranian Agriculture* (in Persian). Tehran.

————. 1982. "Peasants, Land, and Revolution" (in Persian). In Agah 1982.

Ashraf, A., and Safai, M. 1977. *The Role of Rural Organization in Rural Development—The Case of Iran*. Tehran.

Azkia, M. 1969. *Dargazin Farming Corporation* (in Persian). Tehran.

Azkia, M.; Irvani, M.; Nik-kholq, A.; and Askari, N. 1976. *Report on Sistan and Khash* (in Persian). Tehran.

Bakhash, S. 1984. *The Reign of Ayatollahs*. New York.

Baldwin, G. B. 1967. *Planning and Development in Iran*. Baltimore.

Banani, A. 1961. *The Modernization of Iran: 1921–1941*. Stanford.

Baran, P. A. 1957. *The Political Economy of Growth*. New York.

Bauer, J. 1983. "Poor Women and Social Consciousness in Revolutionary Iran." In Nashat 1983.

Benedick, R. E. 1964. *Industrial Finance in Iran*. Boston.

Bennholdt-Thomsen, V. 1980a. "Investment in the Poor: Analysis of World Bank Policy." *Social Scientist* 8, no. 7:3–20.

————. 1980b. "Investment in the Poor." *Social Scientist* 8, no. 8:32–51.

Bernstein, H. 1977. "Notes on Capital and Peasantry." *Review of African Political Economy*. 10:60–73. Reprinted in Harriss 1982.

————. 1982. "Industrialization, Development, and Dependence." In Alavi and Shanin 1982.

Bharier, J. 1971. *Economic Development in Iran, 1900–1970*. London.

Bookers Agricultural and Technical Services, Ltd., and Hunting Technical Services Ltd. 1974. *National Cropping Plan: Inception Report*. Tehran.

Bowen-Jones, H. 1968. "Agriculture." In *The Cambridge History of Iran*, vol. 1. London.

Bradby, B. 1980. "The Destruction of Natural Economy." In Wolpe 1980.

Brandt Commission. 1980. *North-South: A Programme for Survival*. London.

Bundy, C. 1972. "The Emergence and Decline of a South African Peasantry." *African Affairs*, no. 71:369–388.

Byres, T. J. 1974. "Land Reform, Industrialization and the Marketed Surplus in India: An Essay on the Power of Rural Bias." In Lehman 1974.

Central Bank of Iran. 1973. *National Income of Iran: 1959–1971*. Tehran.

Chayanov, A. V. 1966. *The Theory of Peasant Economy*. Homewood, Ill.

Cohen, R.; Gutkind, P. C. W.; and Brazier, P., eds. 1979. *Peasants and Proletarians—the Struggle of Third World Workers*. London.

Davani, A. N. D. *Movement of the Iranian Clergy* (in Persian). 11 vol. N.p.

Denman, D. R. 1973. *The King's Vista*. London.

Dorner, P. 1972. *Land Reform and Economic Development*. Harmondsworth.

Eckstein, A. 1955. "Land Reform and Economic Development." *World Politics* 3:650–662.

Eckstein, S.; Gordon, D.; Horton, D.; and Carroll, T. 1978. *Land Reform in Latin America: Bolivia, Chile, Mexico, Peru, Venezuela*. Washington, D.C.

Elkan, W. 1973. *An Introduction to Development Economics*. Harmondsworth.

English, P. W. 1966. *City and Village in Iran*. Milwaukee.

Fallah, S. V. 1982. "Mechanization of Iranian Agriculture" (in Persian). In Agah 1982.

FAO (Food and Agricultural Organization). 1969. *Provisional Indicative World Plan for Agricultural Development*. Rome.

Farmanfarmaian, K., ed. 1976. *The Social Sciences and Problems of Development*. Princeton.

Foster-Carter, A. 1978. "The Modes of Production Controversy." *New Left Review*, no. 107:47–77.

Frankel, H. 1943. "Industrialization of Agricultural Countries and the Possibilities for a New International Division of Labour." *Economic Journal*, June–September, pp. 188–201.

George, S. 1976. *How the Other Half Dies*. Harmondsworth.

El-Ghonemy, M. R. 1966. *Report of the Development Center on Land Policy and Settlement for the Near East*. Rome.

Gilbar, G. 1978. "Persian Agriculture in the Late Qajar Period, 1860–1906: Some Economic and Social Aspects." *Asian and African Studies* 12, no. 3:312–365.

Gough, K. and Sharma, H. P., eds. 1973. *Imperialism and Revolution in South Asia*. New York.

Gregory, T. E. 1935. "Conclusions—An Economist's Comment." In Hubbard 1935.

Gupta, P. S. 1973. *The Problem of Employment and Unemployment*. ILO Mission Working Paper. Geneva.

Hadary, G. 1951. "The Agrarian Reform Problem in Iran." *Middle East Journal* 5, no. 2:181–196.

Hajebi, V.; Keshavarz, H.; and Safi-nejad, J. 1971. *Nivan Nar Farming Corporation* (in Persian). Tehran.

Halliday, F. 1979. *Iran: Dictatorship and Development*. Harmondsworth.

Harriss, J. 1980. *Contemporary Marxist Analysis of the Agrarian Question in India*. Working Paper no. 14, Madras Institute of Development Studies. Madras.

———. ed. 1982. *Rural Development: Theories of Peasant Economy and Agrarian Change*. London.

Hegland (Hooglund), M. 1980. "One Village in the Revolution." *MERIP Reports*, May, pp. 7–12.

———. 1982. "Religious Rituals and Political Struggle in an Iranian Village." *MERIP Reports*, January, pp. 10–17.

Hooglund, E. J. 1973. "The Khwushnishin Population of Iran." *Iranian Studies* 6, no. 4 (Autumn):229–245.

———. 1975. "The Effects of the Land Reform Program on Rural Iran: 1962–1972." Ph.D. dissertation, Baltimore.

———. 1980. "Rural Participation in the Revolution." *MERIP Reports*, May, pp 3–6.

——. 1982a. *Land and Revolution in Iran: 1960–1980.* Austin, Tex.
——. 1982b. "Rural Iran and the Clerics." *MERIP Reports,* March–April, pp. 23–26.
Hubbard, G. E. 1935. *Eastern Industrialization and Its Effect on the West.* London.
ILO (International Labour Office). 1973a. *Mechanization and Employment in Agriculture.* Geneva.
——. 1973b. *Employment and Income Policies for Iran.* Geneva.
Jacoby, E. 1971. *Man and Land.* London.
Jacqz, J. W., ed. 1976. *Iran: Past, Present, and Future.* New York.
Johnson, V. W. 1960. "Agriculture in the Economic Development of Iran." *Land Economics* 36, no. 4:313–321.
Johnston, B. F. 1970. "Agriculture and Structural Transformation in Developing Countries: A Survey of Research." *Journal of Economic Literature* 8:369–404.
Johnston, B. F., and Kilby, P. 1975. *Agriculture and Structural Transformation.* London.
Johnston, B. F., and Mellor, J. W. 1961. "The Role of Agriculture in Economic Development." *American Economic Review* 51, no. 4:566–593.
Kamangar, A., ed. 1974. *Land Reform, Rural Cooperatives, Etc.* (in Persian). Collection of Laws, Decrees, By-Laws, Etc., no. 7. Tehran.
Kaneda, H. 1973. *Agriculture.* ILO Mission Working Paper. Geneva.
Katouzian, M. A. H. 1978. "Oil Versus Agriculture: A Case of Dual Resource Depletion in Iran." *Journal of Peasant Studies* 5, no. 3 (April):347–369.
Kautsky, K. 1970. *La question agraire: Etude sur les tendences de l'agriculture moderne.* Paris. Originally published in German, 1899.
Kazemi, F. 1980. *Poverty and Revolution in Iran: The Migrant Poor, Urban Marginality, and Politics.* New York.
Kazemian, G. H. 1968. *Impact of U.S. Technical Aid on the Rural Development of Iran.* New York.
Keddie, N. R. 1960. "Historical Obstacles to Agrarian Change in Iran." *Claremont Oriental Studies,* no. 8.
——. 1972. "Stratification, Social Control, and Capitalism in Iranian Villages: Before and After Land Reform." In Antoun and Harik 1972.
——. 1980. *Iran: Religion, Politics, and Society.* London.
Khamsi, F. 1969. "Land Reform in Iran." *Monthly Review,* no. 21, July, pp. 20–28.
Khamsi, F. S. 1968. "The Development of Capitalism in Rural Iran." Master's Thesis, Columbia University.
Khatibi, N. 1972. "Land Reform in Iran and Its Role in Rural Development." In *Land Reform, Land Settlement, and Co-operation.* Rome.
Khosravi, K. 1976. *Sociology of Rural Iran* (in Persian). Tehran.
Kielstra, N. O. 1975. *Ecology and Community in Iran.* Amsterdam.
Kolagina, L. 1980. *Domination of Imperialism over Iran* (in Persian). Tehran.
Kristjanson, B. H. 1960. "The Agrarian Based Development of Iran." *Land Economics* 36, no. 1:1–13.
Kula, W. 1976. *An Economic Theory of the Feudal System.* London.
Ladejinsky, W. 1950. "Too Late to Save Asia." *Saturday Review of Literature,* July 22. Reprinted in Walinsky 1977:130–135.
——. 1964. "Land Reform." Paper presented at Conference on Productivity and Innovation in Agriculture in Underdeveloped Countries, Massachusetts Insti-

tute of Technology, Cambridge, Mass., June 29–August 7. Reprinted in Walinsky 1977:354–366.

Ladjevardi, H. 1985. *Labor Unions and Autocracy in Iran*. Syracuse.

Lambton, A. K. S. 1953. *Landlord and Peasant in Persia*. London.

———. 1969. *The Persian Land Reform 1962–1966*. London.

Laporte, R.; Petras, J.; and Rinehart, J. 1971. "The Concept of Agrarian Reform and Its Role in Development." *Comparative Studies in Society and History* 13, no. 4 (October): 473–485.

Lehman, D., ed. 1974. *Agrarian Reform and Agrarian Reformism*. London.

Lele, U. 1975. *The Design of Rural Development — Lessons from Africa*. Baltimore.

Lewis, W. A. 1954. *Economic Development with Unlimited Supplies of Labour*. *Manchester School of Economic and Social Studies* 22, no. 2, May.

Luxemburg, R. 1968. *The Accumulation of Capital*. New York.

McLachlan, K. S. 1968. "Land Reform in Iran." In *The Cambridge History of Iran*, vol. 1. London.

McNamara, R. S. 1981. *The McNamara Years at the World Bank*. Baltimore.

Mahdavi, H. 1982. "The Thirty-Year Transformation of a Village in Qazvin" (in Persian). In Agah 1982.

Mandel, E. 1975. *Late Capitalism*. London.

Marsden, K. 1973. "The Technological Change in Agriculture, Employment and Over-all Development Strategy." In ILO 1973a.

MCRA (Ministry of Cooperatives and Rural Affairs). 1968. *Study of Village of Husseinabad* (in Persian). Tehran.

———. 1971. *Sample Constitution for a Rural Cooperative Society* (in Persian). 3d ed. 1971.

———. 1972. *Study of Labor Force and Development Potentials in Sanandaj Rural Areas* (in Persian). Tehran.

———. 1974a. *Study of Labor Force and Non-Agricultural Activities in Hamadan Villages* (in Persian). Tehran.

———. 1974b. *Study of Labor Force and Development Potential of Non-Agricultural Activities in Rezaieh Villages* (in Persian). Tehran.

———. 1974c. *Study of Possibilities of Forming Collective Farm Groups* (in Persian). Tehran.

———. 1975a. *Study of Farm Corporations in Qir, Afraz, Kazerin, and Firouzabad after the First Period* (in Persian). Tehran.

———. 1975b. *Study of Development Potential of Non-Agricultural Activities in Six Rural Regions* (in Persian). Tehran.

———. 1975c. *Preliminary Study of Rural Production Cooperatives:Nasseri, Varleh, and Shahmaran* (in Persian). Tehran.

———. 1975d. *Study of Social and Economic Situation of Members of Rural Cooperative Societies in Kermanshahan* (in Persian). Tehran.

———. 1975e. *Study of Social and Economic Situation of Members of Rural Cooperative Societies in Kerman* (in Persian). Tehran.

———. 1976a. *Study of Social and Economic Situation of Members of Saqiz Area Rural Cooperative Societies* (in Persian). Tehran.

———. 1976b. *Study of Financial and Debt Situation of Peasant Members of Rural Cooperatives in Five Areas* (in Persian). Tehran.

———. 1976c. *Study of Financial and Debt Situation of Peasant Members of Rural Cooperatives in Three Areas* (in Persian). Tehran.

———. 1977a. *Study of Migration and Abandonment of Land by Peasants in Areas Covered by Rural Production Cooperatives: Gachsaran, Fahlian, Ouch Tappeh, Varleh, and Maroun* (in Persian). Tehran.

———. 1977b. *Study of Economy of Kashmar Villages* (in Persian). Tehran.

———. 1977c. *Study of Migration of Peasants in Hamadan Villages* (in Persian) Tehran.

———. 1977d. *MCRA Activities in Formation of Farm Corporations and Rural Production Cooperatives through March 20, 1977* (in Persian). Tehran.

———. N.d.(a). *Study of Labor Force and Development Potential of Ardabil Villages* (in Persian). Tehran.

———. N.d.(b). *Study of Labor Force and Development Potential of Lahijan Villages* (in Persian). Tehran.

Ministry of Agriculture. 1962. *Land Reform in Iran* (in Persian). Tehran.

———. 1963. *The Golden Leaf in the History of Iranian Agriculture and Peasantry* (in Persian). Tehran.

Moghadam, F. 1977. *A Study of Some Selected Villages in Iran.* Tehran.

Mohammadi, M. 1973. *On the Agrarian Question in Iran and Its Democratic Solution* (in Persian). n.p.

Mo'meni, B. 1980. *The Agrarian Question and Class War in Iran* (in Persian). Tehran.

Nashat, G., ed. 1983. *Women and Revolution in Iran.* Boulder, Col.

Niblock, T., ed. 1982. *Iraq: The Contemporary State.* London.

Nik-kholq, A. A. 1971. *A Socio-Economic Study of Samsekandeh Farm Corporation* (in Persian). Tehran.

No'mani, F. 1980. *Development of Feudalism in Iran* (in Persian). Tehran.

OAS (Office of Agricultural Statistics, Ministry of Interior). 1960. *National Census of Agriculture* (in Persian). Tehran.

OCI (Overseas Consultants, Inc.) 1949. *Report on the Seven-Year Development Plan for the Plan Organization of the Imperial Government of Iran.* New York.

Okazaki, S. 1968. *The Development of Large-Scale Farming in Iran: The Case of the Province of Gorgan.* Tokyo.

———. 1969. "Shirang-Sofla: The Economics of a North-east Iranian Village." *Developing Economics,* no. 7:261–283.

Pahlavi, M. R. 1961. *Thought at the Service of Peasants* (in Persian). Tehran.

———. 1962. *Collection of Speeches, Messages, and Interviews of His Majesty Mohammad Reza Shah Pahlavi* (in Persian). Tehran.

———. 1967. *The White Revolution* (in Persian). Tehran.

———. 1982. *Answer to History.* New York.

Petras, J., and Laporte, R. 1971. *Cultivating Revolution: The U.S. and Agrarian Reform in Latin America.* New York.

Plan Organization of Iran. 1956. *Second Seven-Year Development Plan of Iran, 1955/56–1961/62.* Tehran.

———. 1960. *Review of the Second Seven-Year Plan Program of Iran.* Tehran.

———. 1961. *Third Plan 1341–1346 [1962/63–1967/68].* Tehran.

———. 1975. *Preliminary Survey of Rural Cooperative Societies* (in Persian). Tehran.

Plan Organization of Iran, Statistical Center. 1968. *National Census of Population and Housing — 1966.* (in Persian). Tehran.

———. 1972. *Manpower Survey* (in Persian). Tehran.

———. 1973. *Results of the 1971 Agricultural Statistics* (in Persian). Tehran.

_____. 1976. *Results of Agricultural Census, Phase I, 1973* (in Persian). Tehran.

_____. 1977. *Results of Agricultural Census, Phase II, 1974* (in Persian). Tehran.

_____. 1981. *Results of National Population and Housing Census—1976* (in Persian). Tehran.

Platt, K. B. 1970. *Land Reform in Iran*. AID Spring Review. Washington, D.C.

Preobrazhenski, E. 1967. *The New Economics*. London.

Price, O. T. W. 1975. *Towards a Comprehensive Iranian Agricultural Policy*. Agricultural and Rural Development Advisory Mission of IBRD, Report no. 1. Tehran.

Qahreman, B. 1982. "Two Notes on Commercial Agriculture in Iran" (in Persian). In Agah 1982.

Ramazani, R. K. 1982. *The United States and Iran*. New York.

Ray, A. 1951. "The Problem of Economic Development in Backward Areas with Special Reference to Iran." Ph.D. dissertation, University of Michigan.

Rubin, B. 1980. *Paved with Good Intentions: The American Experience in Iran*. New York.

Rude, G. 1980. *Ideology and Popular Protest*. London.

Ruhani, S. 1977. *An Analysis of the Movement of Imam Khomeini* (in Persian). Qum.

Saedloo, H. 1974. *A Discussion of Agricultural Labor and How to Calculate It in Iranian Agriculture* (in Persian). Tehran.

_____. 1978. *Problems of Iranian Agriculture* (in Persian). Tehran.

_____. 1979. "Identity of Iranian Agriculture—I" (in Persian). *Ayandeh* 5, nos. 4–6 (Summer):210–223.

_____. 1980. "Identity of Iranian Agriculture—II" (in Persian). *Ayandeh* 5, nos. 10–12 (Winter):774–803.

Safi-nejad, J. 1966. *Talebabad* (in Persian). Tehran.

_____. 1974. *Boneh* (in Persian). Tehran.

Salmanzadeh, C. 1980. *Agricultural Change and Rural Society in Southern Iran*. Cambridge.

SCFK(Sazman-e Cherik-haye Fadaii Khalq). 1973a. *On Land Reform and Its Direct Impacts* (in Persian). N.p.

_____. 1973b. *On Farm Corporations* (in Persian). Rural Study Series, no. 3. N.p.

Shaji'i, Z. 1965. *Members of the National Consultative Assembly During Twenty-One Legislative Sessions* (in Persian). Tehran.

Shanin, T. 1966. "The Peasantry as a Political Factor." *Sociological Review* 14, no. 1:5–27. Reprinted in Shanin 1971.

_____. 1972. *The Awkward Class*. Oxford.

_____. 1980. "Defining Peasants: Conceptualizations and Deconceptualizations—Old and New in a Marxist Debate." *Peasant Studies* 8, no. 4:38–60.

Shanin, T., ed. 1971. *Peasants and Peasant Societies*. Harmondsworth.

SMKI (Sazman-e Mujahedin-e Khalq-e Iran). 1972. *The White Revolution and the Countryside* (in Persian). N.p.

Sodagar, M. 1979a. *Analysis of Land Reform* (in Persian). Tehran.

_____. 1979b. *Growth of Capitalist Relations in Iran* (in Persian). Tehran.

Szentes, T. 1976. *The Political Economy of Underdevelopment*. Budapest.

Theobald, R., and Jaward, S. 1982. "Problems of Rural Development in an Oil-Rich Economy: Iraq 1958–1975." In Niblock 1982.

Thompson, C. T. 1976. "Impetus for Change: The Transformation of Peasant Marketing in Mazandaran, Iran." In Farmanfarmaian 1976.

Tuma, E. H. 1965. *Twenty-Six Centuries of Agrarian Reform: A Comparative Analysis.* Los Angeles.

Ule, W. 1973. "Land Reform in Iran and the Development of Agricultural Shareholders' Companies." In Treydte and Ule 1973.

UN (United Nations). 1951a. *Land Reform: Defects of Agrarian Structure as Obstacles to Economic Development.* New York.

———. 1951b. *Measures for the Economic Development of Underdeveloped Countries.* New York.

United States. Congress. Senate Committee on Foreign Relations. 1980. Congress Joint Economic Committee, *Economic Consequences of the Revolution in Iran.* Washington, D.C.

USDA (US Department of Agriculture). 1970. *Economic Progress of Agriculture in Developing Nations: 1950–68.* Washington, D.C.

USDS (U.S. Department of State). 1949. *Point Four, Cooperative Program for Aid in the Development of the Economically Underdeveloped Areas.* Washington, D.C.

———. 1965. *American Foreign Policy 1961.* Washington, D.C.

———. 1976. *Foreign Relations of the United States, 1948,* vol. 5:*The Near East, South Asia, and Africa.* Washington, D.C.

———. 1977. *Foreign Relations of the United States, 1949,* vol. 6:*The Near East, South Asia, and Africa.* Washington, D.C.

———. 1978. *Foreign Relations of the United States, 1950,* vol. 5:*The Near East, South Asia, and Africa.* Washington, D.C.

USNSC (U.S. National Security Council). 1961a. "The Current Internal Political Situation in Iran." National Security Files, box 115, Iran—3/21/61–3/31/61 file. John F. Kennedy Presidential Library, Boston, Mass.

———. 1961b. "Position Paper on Iran." National Security Files, box 115, Iran—1/61–2/61 file. John F. Kennedy Presidential Library, Boston, Mass.

———. 1961c. "U.S. Political Policies in Iran." National Security Files, box 115, Iran—5/15/61 file. John F. Kennedy Presidential Library, Boston, Mass.

Vadi'i, K. 1973. *Introduction to Rural Sociology of Iran* (in Persian). Tehran.

Walinsky, L. J., ed. 1977. *Agrarian Reform as Unfinished Business—the Selected Papers of Wolf Ladejinsky.* London.

Warne, W. E. 1956. *Mission for Peace: Point Four in Iran.* Indianapolis.

Warren, B. 1980. *Imperialism: Pioneer of Capitalism.* London.

Warriner, D. 1955. *Land Reform and Economic Development.* Cairo.

West, Q. M. 1958. *Agricultural Development Programs of Iran, Iraq, and Sudan.* Washington, D.C.

Wilber, C. K. 1969. "The Role of Agriculture in Soviet Economic Development." *Land Economics* 45, no. 1 (February):87–96. Reprinted in Wilber 1973.

———, ed. 1973. *The Political Economy of Development and Underdevelopment.* New York.

Wolf, E. R. 1969. "On Peasant Rebellions." *International Social Science Journal* 21. Reprinted in Shanin 1971.

Wolpe, H., ed. 1980. *The Articulation of Modes of Production.* London.

World Bank. 1974. *The Economic Development of Iran.* Tehran.

———. 1975. *Land Reform.* Washington, D.C.

———. 1979. *Small Farmers and the Landless in South Asia.* Washington, D.C.

Zaldivar, R. 1974. "Agrarian Reform and Military Reformism in Peru." In Lehman 1974.

Zandjani, H. S. 1973. "Allocation of Resources under Agrarian Reform in Iran." Ph.D. dissertation, University of Cambridge.

Index

Abdel-Fadil, M., 214
ACB (Agricultural Cooperative Bank),
172, 176–77, 179, 204,
Accumulation, primitive. *See* Primitive
accumulation
Acheson, Dean, 64, 65, 66, 215
ADBI (Agricultural Development Bank
of Iran), 122, 147, 148, 149,
152–54, 175, 177, 180; as creditor
of capitalist agriculture, 170
Additional Articles. *See* Land Reform
Act of 1962, second stage of
ADFI (Agricultural Development Fund
of Iran), 175–76, 177
Adl, A. H., 72
Africa: colonialism in, 13, 212; grain
production of, 221; conversion of
"surplus" labor to non-farm work
force, 35
Agah (ed./publ.), 151
Agency for International Development.
See AID
"Agrarian reform," 28. *See also* Land
reform
Agribusiness(es), 122, 145, 149–55,
165, 220; failure of in Khuzistan,
151– 54; international, 151–54; pre-
empted by peasants, 201. *See also*
Agriculture, capitalist
Agricultural Bank of Iran, 204, 205
Agricultural Cooperative Bank. *See*
ACB
"Agricultural Credit and Rural
Cooperatives" (conf.), 82
Agricultural Development Bank of
Iran. *See* ADBI

Agricultural Development Fund of
Iran. *See* ADFI
Agricultural Development Poles,
145–46, 154, 168
Agriculture: capitalist, 141–55, 165,
221 (*see also* Agribusiness[es]); commercialization of, 114–64; critical
importance of, 82–84; economics
of, 143–44; foreign investment in,
151–55; in Iran and in U.S. compared, 84; mechanization of, 93,
100, 139–42, 170, 173, 201; nature
of product of, 13–14; small-scale
vs. large scale, 29–31; of Third
World, 23–32; "total package"
approach to, 28; workers in Iranian,
136–41 (*see also* Khoshneshins;
Nasaqdars; Sharecropping). *See also*
Farms; Landlords; Peasants, Iranian;
Sharecropping
Agriculture and Natural Resources,
Ministry of, 148
AID (Agency for International Devel-
opment), 67, 74, 78
Ajami, I., 99, 157, 159, 173
Ala, Hussein, 64, 215
Alam, Asadollah, 72, 206, 207, 216;
appointed Prime Minister, 79
Alavi, H., 16, 17
Alfalfa, 159
Alvandi, Minoo, 219
Amini, Ali, 76, 79, 91, 218; appointed
Prime Minister, 76, 78; resignation
of, 79
Amir Kabir, 207
Amlak. *See* Crown Lands Organization